THREE CORVETTES

A QUIET SUNNY AFTERNOON WATCH

[Page 29

NICHOLAS MONSARRAT
Lieut.-Commander, R.N.V.R.

THREE CORVETTES

COMPRISING

**H.M. CORVETTE
EAST COAST CORVETTE
CORVETTE COMMAND**

WITH 7 HALF-TONE PLATES

CASSELL AND CO LTD
London

CASSELL & CO LTD
37/38 St. Andrew's Hill, Queen Victoria Street
London, E.C.4

and at

Edinburgh, Melbourne, Sydney, New Zealand, Toronto,
New York, São Paulo, Buenos Aires, Karachi, Bombay,
Calcutta, Cape Town, S. Rhodesia, Accra, Paris and
Copenhagen.

First published	- -	*October* 1945
Second Edition	- -	*February* 1953
Third Edition	- -	*March* 1953
Fourth Edition	- -	*May* 1953
Fifth Edition	- -	*August* 1953
Sixth Edition	-	*September* 1953
Seventh Edition	-	*September* 1953

ACKNOWLEDGMENTS

The Author and publishers wish to express their indebtedness to the following for permission to reproduce the photographs in this book : Lieut.-Commander R. F. J. Maberley, R.N.V.R., for the frontispiece ; the *News Chronicle* for the plates facing pp. 88, 89, 120 ; the Admiralty Press Division, for the plate facing p. 121 ; Lieut.-Commander H. V. Cronyn, G.M., R.N.V.R., for those facing pp. 184, 185.

Set in 11 point Garamond type and
Printed in Great Britain by Wyman & Sons Ltd., London, Reading and Fakenham
953

CONTENTS

H.M. CORVETTE

EAST COAST CORVETTE

CORVETTE COMMAND

LIST OF ILLUSTRATIONS

FOREWORD

THIS collection of three short books—all originally
published during the war—covers time spent afloat
from 1940 to 1943. It is not a complete picture (nor
anything like it) of the whole of the Battle of the
Atlantic during that period; it is an account of one
man's naval service during three critical years of the
battle, when I had the luck to be serving in small ships
in this crucial theatre of war.

All these books started as "notes"—notes for a
future war novel. That was why I started keeping a
diary, early in 1940; that, and for the pleasure and
relief of writing, in the middle of bloody war, when I
was a watch-keeping officer in a corvette on Atlantic
escort, and the whole world seemed composed ex-
clusively of violence, fatigue, and worry.

The notes—though I didn't know this at the time—
were intended to be the basis of *The Cruel Sea*. But
The Cruel Sea turned out to be quite a different book,
and a long way ahead in any case—ten years, in fact,
though again I didn't know it at the time. Finally, I
had the notes published as a series of smaller books,
for a reason that impels many men to write and to
publish—I thought I was going to be killed.

Basically, it's an arrogant idea—that you have something to say, and must say it while you can. But the
Battle of the Atlantic was like that—death and fear at
sea, and then, in harbour, the wish to tell people about
it before you went out on convoy again. (It was a
battle we had to win, if we were to exist at all—and
that was something we *did* know at the time.) In
addition, we *all* thought we were going to be killed:
the war book that would shake the world seemed a
very long time ahead: perhaps too long for one's

current chances of survival. Meanwhile, here was a story.

Here is the story now—incomplete, disjointed, but first-hand. The three books are progressive, because by 1943 we had stopped losing the Battle of the Atlantic, and had started, very slowly and painfully, to win.

If you detect too much pride in this progression, or too much pleasure at having survived three years of watch-keeping at sea, or too much astonishment at attaining command, you may put it down to relief.

N. M.

1953.

H.M. CORVETTE

TWO-MINUTE ALIBI

THIS book is not a masterpiece: I have not had time to write one. It is a collection of notes, jotted down from time to time, of things seen and met with during two years of escort-duty in a corvette. It is sometimes depressing and crude: so is escorting convoys; it is not wholly serious, and there again it follows the job. It contains a lot of "I" because it concerns my ship: I was there at the time, and such coy evasions as "this correspondent" or "the present writer" or "one swears one felt one's sea-boots completely filled with water" seem a very zigzag course to steer.

Finally, owing to security reasons, it is less interesting than it might be. But that, of course, is one of the horrors of war, to be patiently borne by writer and reader alike.

N. M.

CHAPTER I

COMMISSIONING

OUR draft-chit had been endorsed, magnificently,
" Report on arrival to Admiral Superintending Con-
tract-built Ships," which conjured up a picture of a
penetrating eye and an acre of gold lace on either arm ;
but after a tour of a small shipyard which, noise for
size, must have rated one of the highest in the business,
we could not escape the conviction that our No. 1 suits
(of warranted superfine pilot cloth), our gloves, our
correctly slung respirators, our factory-fresh turn-out,
was a dangerous waste of elegance. For the place was
undeniably dirty, full of such hazards as girders, coils
of rusty wire, cranes taking swings at the passers-by,
red-hot rivets describing arcs through the air overhead,
and bunches of men aiming baulks of oily wood, like
battering-rams. Now and then there would be a dull
splash as a ship was launched—or so it seemed. To
preserve that elegance of ours we had continually to
draw ourselves aside, like old ladies scandalized in
Piccadilly ; and, unlike old ladies, often wonderfully
immune in the most dubious of situations, sooner or
later we were going to be soiled by contact with our
surroundings.

" There'll be no admirals in this joint," said M. to
me. " It's expecting too much altogether."

There seemed to be almost everything else : above
all, there was a stupefying row going on the whole
time, with everyone contributing according to his
means : most of it was riveting, but even small boys
with nothing else to do would be idly hammering on
sheets of iron as they talked. (I dare say they were
training for the more responsible jobs : I swear they

3

deserved them.) To make ourselves heard at all we had to shout; and it is foolish (and unhelpful) to shout, " What a horrible noise ! " so we mostly kept silent and looked for our quarry.

There was, as we had suspected, no admiral, but instead a helpful works-foreman who directed us to a hut labelled, dauntingly, " NAVAL OFFICERS KEEP OUT " ; and installed there we found an R.N.V.R. officer, with a red face and a square chin, dressed in a working suit which made us look and feel like the First and Second Dudes in a tastelessly lavish production. He had two stripes to our one, and was in fact the First Lieutenant. After we had announced ourselves he looked us over carefully, from a good many angles : it was difficult to tell which, if any, he liked. (We were both ex-amateur yachtsmen, granted commissions by an Admiralty Selection Board very likely persuaded to a sense of crucial emergency by Dunkirk.) After a bit the First Lieutenant said : " What can you do ? " and after we had told him he said : " Well, well." He was an Australian, accustomed to herds of dumb animals.

M. and I toured the ship together, as green as grass. Neither of us had seen a corvette before, though there were certainly enough of them about : indeed, it seemed as if, up and down the Clyde, anyone who had ever handled a hammer had set a pole up in his back garden and started building a corvette. Ours was afloat, almost finished, and jammed with workmen : the chief noise was supplied by some last-minute riveting going on on the after gun-platform, but there were several minor performers of note among the welders, caulkers, joiners, carpenters, and plain crash-and-bangers employed on board. We were an hour on our tour, mostly climbing over obstacles and avoiding paintwork, but examining every discoverable corner and going over the ground from bridge to magazine and fore-peak to tiller-flat : we liked the look of her, though she was as yet more

like an unfinished factory than a ship. Here and there
ratings were at work—the advance guard of the crew
drafted from barracks, mostly leading-hands testing out
their departments : in the W/T cabinet the Leading
Telegraphist, caught in a maze of different-coloured
wires, was having a cup of tea. M. said : " Getting
it all shipshape ? " and the Leading Tel. answered :
" No, sir."

Aft, the Torpedoman was arguing over the depth-
charge rails with a welder, a Clydeside dockyard-matey
with an accent like a roll of drums. This was my
department, and I listened, while M., who was taking
over Gunnery Officer, went forward to look at his
gun and presently came back nursing a bleeding hand.
It seemed he had closed the breech in a new and wrong
way.

When we returned to the hut the First Lieutenant
said : " Well, what do you think of corvettes ? " I said
I liked them : M., a reserved character, said it had all
been very interesting. The First Lieutenant said : " I've
been in trawlers up to this," and added : " Now you
can get busy correcting King's Regulations and Admiralty Instructions, Part One." The corrections lay
in a neat pile of printed booklets, not more than five
inches high. Alongside was a pen and two bottles of
ink.

Odd sight : Stoker Petty Officer making a sort of
doormat-bootscraper out of metal beer-bottle tops nailed
upside down on a board. He claimed it his own idea,
and no hardship to provide for.

We came to know K.R. and A.I., and those interminable corrections, and we came to know that hut,
our headquarters for ten days. Until we were formally
in commission it was the hub of everything : of checking
stores, of ammunitioning, of conferences with dockyard
officials, of the formidable amount of paper-work—

signals, correspondence, watch- and quarter-bills, chart folios—in which we were all soon involved. The crew arrived in driblets, more guns arrived by crane and alighted on their mountings like settling sea-gulls : the Chief Engine-Room Artificer arrived and was immediately involved in a technical blizzard over the suction-and-outlet system. The Captain arrived—no, he had been there all the time.

On the ship, progress could be measured by the decreasing amount of noise aboard ; soon we were able to enjoy as much as half an hour of tranquillity at a time. Carpets appeared in our cabins, the wardroom lost its carpenter's-shop look and became habitable : a man went round on a float painting in our pendant numbers, a key-board with not less than sixty bunches of keys made its appearance and was, inevitably, put in my charge. The coxs'n, a West-countryman of broad accent, broader beam, and humour broadest of all, emerged as a character, a directive force of outstanding value in handling the crew. (I liked some of his expressions. " He wears a green coat, sir," he once said of a rating very lively in the mess-decks and very slow at tackling a job of work ; and again, less elegantly, of one of the duller seamen : " He's wood from the —— up," and yet again : " He's very seldom up top "—signifying " He's bald.") Bit by bit, the ship's heart moved across from the hut and started beating in the ship itself.

Said the Captain, staring out of the window across the dock, to the First Lieutenant :

" Put the ship in commission at midday to-day."

It was only a matter of saluting while the spotless ensign was hoisted, sending a signalman to the mast-head with the commissioning pendant, and mounting an armed sentry on the jetty alongside ; but what a difference it seemed to make, that transfer from floating shell to one of His Majesty's ships of war in commission. We walked differently when we were aboard, we sat in the wardroom with a sense of formal proprietorship; we even came to resent the dock-workers crowding the decks and strolling about without care or caution. That was no way to treat the ship. . . . She was ours now: anyone else was there on sufferance, and no one else mattered.

When I signed the first wine-chit of the commission —" Two Plymouth gins "—I felt as if I were founding a dynasty. As time went by, this turned out to be true.

We broke more new ground that same day and night, initiating ourselves and the ship into the Navy's apt ceremonial. There was Colours at sunset—hoisting our own Preparative for the benefit of the two other corvettes in the dock-basin, saluting as the bosun's pipe shrilled, dividing the summer evening air, and the ensign came slowly down—all of it was new, and all moving for a score of reasons. And I made the ship's first Rounds the same night, tailing a small procession of the quartermaster, leading hand of the watch, and duty Petty Officer: through the mess-decks (crowded, silent, attentive), up on the fo'c'sle-head to look at the shore-wires, aft to the galley where some sort of tea-party was in progress (though not after I had left). All that, again, was new, and something one could enjoy for unanalysable reasons, somehow bound up with the compelling phrase " in a seaman-like manner ": to write in the Night Rounds book: " 21.00, Rounds Correct," and initial the entry was to stand warranty for an orderly and disciplined tribute to tradition.

" 06.15, Call Officer-of-the-Day.
   06.30, Hands fall in : Wash down."
This was the sting in the tail of the First Lieutenant's night orders; it stung me, and after a late session in the wardroom to celebrate commissioning, I could have

done without it. But duty (and a certain remembered glitter in the First Lieutenant's eye) got me turned out, hurriedly dressed, with such compromises as sea-boots for ordinary shoes and a scarf instead of a collar and tie, and put me on a cold, windswept upper-deck as the fall-in was piped, to stare at a muster of nineteen seamen who stared reproachfully back. Then the duty leading-hand reported the watches correct, the sweepers were told off and hoses rigged, and presently those rather bleak early morning noises, of bristles and squeegees and the gurgle of water in the scuppers and freeing-ports, made themselves heard.

The rating in charge of the hose brought to his job an energy and a scrupulous zeal not always appreciated by the upper-deck sweepers, whose sea-boots now and then took the full force of the attack and who were inclined to hurry the job and get below to the comparative holiday known as " squaring off mess-decks and flats." I dodged the main stream and went aft to the galley, where the Leading Cook was heating up a good quart of dripping-fat in a saucepan and the wardroom steward making a brew of tea, from which I claimed a hand-out. The Stoker Petty Officer of the morning watch came up the ladder, took six puffs at a cigarette, crushed it out against the depth-charge rails, and went below again, followed by the black cat which had already attached itself to the ship, with the obvious promise of more to come. Ashore, a trickle of workers was coming through the dock-gates, some of them making for our gangway where the sentry, counting aloud, was practising his own stylized version of " Present Arms." The cold haze which had overhung the dock-basin when I first came up was already beginning to disappear.

I waved to the Sub. on the neighbouring corvette, and he answered with a semaphore message of which I could only read the first word—" what." I repeated it back, and there, in frustrated confusion, the matter rested. . . . When, from forrard, I heard "Cooks to the Galley" being piped, I went below to shave and finish dressing, and make myself fit to see Colours hoisted at eight.

A second gigantic assortment of charts was delivered shortly before we sailed. At the top of the box was the "Arctic Pilot," and underneath a chart of the navigable parts of the Danube. Said the Leading Signalman, looking over my shoulder as I unpacked the consignment:

"Seems like we're going to get some variety, sir. I could just do with a slice of Old Vienna."

"Pipe 'Stations for leaving harbour' in five minutes," said the First Lieutenant to the quartermaster; and to me he added: "You take the after-part, and if you get a wire round the screw, God help you."

My foreboding that only with God's help would I avoid turning the screw into something like one of those old-fashioned frame-aerials was not borne out, probably because the leading-hand of the after-party was a leading-seaman of extreme competence, clearly accustomed to the code of whistle-blasts and mystical signs which came in a steady flow from the bridge. It was he who translated into action the first technical obscurity, "Single up to the breast and spring!"—i.e. let go all ropes except a single breast-rope and a single rope running from aft to a shore-bollard about amidships: without him I might have plunged about for hours and still guessed wrong. (Hitherto, in my experience, one had simply said "About time to cast off," and suited the action to the word, fending off the jetty with one's leg.) Judging from the uproar forrard, M. was having trouble with the windlass, which gave me time to reel some of the spare wire out of the way, before the next manœuvre.

We needed a tug at each end to get us out of the dock-basin and into the stream, and it took us some time to hook on to ours, the heaving-line being brand-new and the seaman in charge of it a painstaking worker who was not going to be flurried by a mistake or two. The deep silence from the bridge which attended our efforts made an effective commentary. . . . But presently the tow was secure, and we were out in the narrow tributary stream which ran into the Clyde— a stream lined with dockyard workers from our own and other yards, who had left their jobs to give us a cheer and a wave as we passed. It was their last moment, and our first : I wished I could go up on the bridge to get the full savour of it, but my job was aft, in case we had for any reason to cast off the tow. So down-stream we went, slowly and evenly, not yet in our own element or under our own power, but setting out on our journey none the less : a Clyde-built ship leaving the Clyde, with her builders watching her and wishing her God-speed.

I had time to watch my after-party at work, and to like the way they got down to it. About half the crew were Active Service—i.e. regulars, and the rest were "Hostilities Only" ratings, or as the cox's called them, with more humour than truth, "Hostile Ordinary Seamen." But whatever their background—and the H.O.'s ranged from van-boy to statistical accountant —they buckled to their new job with admirable keenness. I think that all of us, officers and men alike, felt the same about the ship : that she was something between a brand-new toy and a—well, almost a sacred charge, a unit whose reputation had to be made and whose laurels won. We had to work, from now on, to get going, to tune up, to perfect the fighting instrument that had been given us : she was a good ship, a grand ship—corvettes *are* attractive and workmanlike—but we had to deserve her, and that meant hard work. The Clyde had done its famous best for us : from now on the charge was ours.

There is a process known as " signing for the ship."

It is one of the higher mysteries, conducted behind drawn curtains, but roughly speaking it happens after full-power trials, the working of the windlass, and the firing of every gun and depth-charge thrower carried, and is a contest between the contractors, who say everything is marvellous, and the Captain, who has a list a mile long of defects and shortcomings he wants put right before he will finally take the ship over. As can be imagined, it may be a very tense occasion indeed.

But when it is concluded, as sometime it must be, all is love again, and double gins. And soon after, the first sailing-orders arrive; they are endorsed " SECRET," and begin : " Being in all respects ready for sea, H.M.S. *Flower* will proceed . . ."

CHAPTER II

WORKING-UP

I SHARED the morning watch (4 to 8) with the First Lieutenant on the passage to our base, after keeping the first watch (8 to midnight) as well. In these early days, we worked watch-and-watch about, until the two children (M. and I) could be trusted with weapons of war; later, of course, we were in three watches, of which I kept the Middle (midnight to 4 a.m.) for seventeen months. To be perfectly frank, this was not the hardship it may sound : in fact I preferred this arrangement, for the main reason that I was left alone unless (or until) all hell broke loose, and could run the watch as I liked, without interference and in peace : the Captain was turned in, in his sea-cabin, the First Lieutenant did not relieve me till four, and I was free of the odd assortment of visitors who were inclined to crowd the bridge at other times. (I *hate* being watched or supervised, when I am doing my best and making no mistakes.)

But all those personal problems and arrangements, of course, were still to come, on that first night at sea.

The log-entries when we took over at four o'clock read :

> " WIND : Direction 270, Force 2–3.
> WEATHER AND VISIBILITY : bc 7.
> SEA AND SWELL : 21.
> CORRECTED BAROMETRIC PRESSURE IN MILLIBARS :
> 1002."

all of which is the dull sea-language for a lovely night. We had passed an inward-bound convoy in the first watch, before the moon got up, being challenged out of complete blackness by a very wide-awake destroyer ; but now it was clearer, with a smudge of land just visible, and the ship progressed steadily, finding her easy speed, having nothing to deal with as regards weather, but behaving admirably under helm and promising a ready and able performance in the future. From the wing of the bridge I could distinguish the hard outline of the fo'c'sle-head, the sky cut by the mast and forestay, the line of foam at the bow : beyond was a brilliant spread of moonlit water, silver on black, and beyond that the ring of darkness, retreating before us, closing in astern. The " group-flashing " light we had picked up half an hour earlier was just coming abeam, and fine on the bow a cluster of lights low in the water marked a line of fishing-boats working the inshore tide. I reckoned we could just about pass them without altering course, though I didn't suppose I should have any say in the matter.

From the other wing of the bridge came the First Lieutenant's voice : " I'm going inside to log that light and have a smoke. Sing out if you see anything."

He disappeared inside the compass-house, and I had the ship and the watch to myself.

I moved across to the centre of the bridge, stirred to an odd exhilaration. Behind me a faint—a very faint

—glow from the screened binnacle showed the face of the Asdic rating, intent and serious : at my side the signalman of the watch was fiddling with his Aldis-lamp, and out on the bridge-sponsons the two look-outs stared ahead, the pointed capes of their duffle-coats in sharp outline against the sky. Centred thus, with fifty-odd men sleeping between decks, with the whole ship entrusted to me as a kind of intricate going concern, I felt tremendously responsible, and tremendously alert too. She was all mine : from this nerve-centre on the bridge—myself—could go out a pulse that would be felt from end to end of the ship : she would respond to it, and she would do what I told her, she would move at my word. Magic moment of authority ! Quite possessed by the idea, prompted to pure foolishness by this novelty of power, I bent to the voice-pipe.

"Port ten."

From below came the quartermaster's answering voice : "Port ten, sir." And then : "Ten of port wheel on, sir."

"Midships."

"Midships. . . . Wheel's amidships, sir."

"Steady."

"Steady. . . . Course South, eighty West, sir."

"Very good." I waited perhaps twenty seconds. "Starboard ten. Steer North, eighty-five West."

"Steer North, eighty-five West, sir."

The First Lieutenant made himself heard from behind the chart-table screen : "What's going on out there ? "

"We passed a floating log," I called back, feeling slightly silly. "It looked too big to hit."

A vague grumble indicated that the explanation passed muster. Only the starboard look-out, peering over the dodger at virgin sea, seemed to betray an injured incredulity. No logs, big or small, had got past *him*.

Up another voice-pipe came the Captain's voice. "Fore-bridge ! "

" Bridge, sir."

" Who's that ? "

" Monsarrat, sir."

" Where's the First Lieutenant ? "

" Just looking at the chart, sir."

" M'm . . . How far have we got ? "

I gave the last light abeam, and the time.

" M'm . . . See anything ? "

" The next light just looming, sir : the bearing's all right. Ship to port, going our way. Fishing-boats inshore."

" Quite a party." And then, surprisingly : " Feel all right up there ? "

" Yes, sir."

" Very good. Tell the bosun's-mate to call me at a quarter to eight."

" Aye, aye, sir." Below, the voice-pipe cover clicked shut, cutting me off. Of such small exchanges, lit with sudden humanity, is homage born.

It grew lighter. The best thing about the morning watch, this, the thing one looked forward to from four o'clock onwards, the thing I was to miss greatly in the middle watch later on : dawn coming up, ships in station, and all secure. . . . There is, at sea, a certain swift change from moonlight to dawnlight that is very easily recognizable ; at one moment, it seems, the water is silvery, glowing, with each breaking wave throwing off a small wash of phosphorescence, and then when next you look it has taken on a livid hue, a cold, dull grey which is the day's first signal. The ship's outlines fill in suddenly, and all the bridge-personnel becomes figures and faces instead of shadows—grey, tired faces, mostly, but welcome for their return to normality. Then up comes the sun, to complete the colour-process and dry off the damp shoulders of your duffle-coat ; and up comes tea, with the steward foraging for the cups and plates of the night's picnic ; and lastly up comes your relief, which is best of all.

You've earned your breakfast, and it's those lovely soused herrings again.

We arrived at our destination.

"What a grand place," said M. to me as soon as we were moored. "It's a pity we've got to work."

Work we did. Daily we exercised everything, with a wild sense of crisis. We abandoned ship, we repelled boarders, we got out the kedge-anchor (an intolerable operation, this) : we closed up action-stations against the stop-watch, we fought fires, we prepared to tow, we put an armed landing-party ashore amid a hurricane of cheers. There was even a suggestion, happily suppressed, that we should exercise the Confidential Books, throwing them overboard to see if they sank, in accordance with the regulations. . . . We fired guns, and signalled, and took soundings ; we demolished the target at gun-practice, but on the other hand we made a supreme hash of our first depth-charge drill, due to a fault in the electric buzzer-system. ("Really, sir, you don't know whether to laugh or cry," murmured the coxs'n to me, as we surveyed one thrower-crew awaiting the order to fire, and another arguing the toss as to whether two rings meant "Fire" or "Fall out.") But we learnt quickly during those weeks : almost before we knew it had happened, we emerged as a ship's company instead of a crowd of individuals, we took shape as a disciplined force with a routine, practised and practised again, for any and every eventuality. It was hard work, and we wasted no time, but we could see the results from day to day, and they were encouraging in every particular.

Our first defaulter.

"Halt ! Left turn ! Off caps ! Ordinary Seaman Jones, sir : one, was absent over leave two and a half hours, two, did return on board drunk, three, did create vandalism in the mess-decks."

" What—er—vandalism was this, coxs'n ? "

" Broke up a mess-stool, sir, and tried to light the stove with it."

" What have you got to say, Jones ? "

" Had a few drinks, sir."

" Is that all ? "

" Yes, sir."

" Serious offences, all these. And you made a nuisance of yourself, too, keeping a lot of people awake. First Lieutenant's report."

" First Lieutenant's report. On caps ! Right turn ! Quick march ! "

" Spoilt our record, coxs'n."

" Got to sometime, sir. Human nature."

Sunday morning brought us Divisions on the fo'c'sle, the only space large enough to accommodate the whole ship's company ; and a very smart turn-out it was, too, the two ranks facing in-board, the wind stirring the seamen's collars and ruffling our hair as we stood bare-headed for prayers. And afterwards came the Captain's Rounds, a most thorough progress through every part of the ship, which looked (on that occasion) like a millionaire's yacht—a millionaire with an inquisitive eye and a passion for spit-and-polish.

Later in the morning I attended " Up Spirits," though the sight of the rum going down, tot by tot, was tantalizing to a degree. And then " Pipe down " was sounded, and a true Sunday calm fell on the ship : we lay to our moorings in shelter and warm sun, and revelled in our hard-won peace.

Alas, to have one's afternoon nap interrupted by the ominous words : " Leading-Seaman Black, sir, reports the loss of a salt fish, and wishes to state a complaint."

This is going to be a long one.

We went out on exercises with a submarine, but all

that, save for one innocent oddment, must be shrouded in mystery. The oddment is this. To help an inexperienced ship, and to avoid waste of time, the submarine at first sometimes tows what are called "buffs"—mark-buoys at the end of a warp—when it is submerged; and it must be related that during my first Asdic attack the machinery failed, and I looked up (after a lengthy and profitless sweep all round the horizon) to see the buffs coming in at high speed and delivering a smashing attack on our starboard quarter. Said the Captain, as we scraped clear with a thin ripple to spare: "I don't think you've quite got the idea. This practise is for our benefit, not the submarine's. They're meant to be strictly neutral down there."

When we dropped a test depth-charge the explosion killed half a dozen guillemots which must have been diving nearby. The dead birds lay breast downwards on the water, with bowed heads and flat, outstretched wings: they seemed to be praying, or making an exaggerated satirical obeisance.

By way of a change, I swapped horses and had a day out in the submarine before we left.

All of it was interesting, and unexpected too. I thought I would be conscious of being under water, and possibly nervous—indeed, at the very beginning I had been mortally afraid of turning claustrophobic, and possibly disgracing myself; but at no time was it possible to realize that we *were* submerged. The occasional noise of the hunting corvettes, sounding oddly like goods trains, passing overhead, was the only indication that we were under water: otherwise (save for the cramped space) it was no different from being, say, in the forrard mess-deck of a corvette. And it was all amazingly quiet: there was no vibration and no engine noise, and orders were given almost in a whisper, instead of the wind-quelling shout we had to use on our own bridge. It had been rough on top before we dived, but down here there was a deep peace; nothing threatened, no one stirred save the two men at the hydroplane controls, their eyes on the depth-gauges, their hands fingering the wheel-spokes like harp-players reading an intricate score.

The minute wardroom, with everything neatly slipped into place, was no more than a passage-way from one end of the boat to the other; and the cramped space made for a recognizable comradeship between officers and men, of special value when one man's mistake might mean disaster for all of them. But one could not help being struck by the adroitness and the marked competence of everyone aboard: when the klaxon sounded for diving-stations nothing much seemed to happen, and yet, when one looked round the control-room, every lever and wheel and knob had been closed up by a crew which slipped into place like pieces of the same machinery.

Only when the order " Periscope depth ! " was given, preparatory to surfacing, was a slight sense of crisis to be observed: it was conceivable that a blunder might be made and one or other of the hunting craft would be in the way: one could feel a certain tenseness in each person—the Officer-of-the-Watch staring at his gauges, the crew with their hands ready on the Kingston-valve levers, the Captain (a young lieutenant) gripping the periscope training gear. Then the periscope broke the surface, and the Captain, suddenly relaxing, gave an order over his shoulder and climbed up to the conning-tower; and presently, touched by a breath of fresh air, I looked up, and there above us was a square of blue sky.

It is, perhaps, worth remarking that, with my eyes on the future, I noted that the view of the surrounding surface craft through the periscope was distressingly sharp and clear.

It was the energetic habit of the Senior Officer of the base to put out in a fast motor-launch directly after lunch, and, choosing his victim, approach at speed on the blind side of the ship, in the hope of catching the Officer-of-the-Day off his guard or the Captain literally napping. As he was almost a professional Angry Man, it is good to be able to relate that, thanks to luck and a series of reliable quartermasters, we were never caught out.

Our " passing-out " day at the end of our working-up period also went off without mishap, though there was one moment, when the order " Pressure on the fire-hoses ! " produced a trickle that would not have quelled a daisy, when the situation looked dynamic. But it passed : we were officially congratulated on the day's performance ; and the same evening a bunch of reports, on the ship and on each officer, made their appearance. They were rather like school-reports, and induced the same expectant nervousness.

The Captain came off best : then the First Lieutenant : then M. : then me. Some sort of coincidence, no doubt.

Off again, nearer the war and our job ; at anchor, awaiting sailing orders.

On a nearby shoal, with her mast and one funnel showing above water, there lay a sunk destroyer full of dead Frenchmen. Her story had been one of the brief horrors of the war : an explosion aboard had been followed by a fire, and the ship gradually became one vast incandescent torch. Now she lay there, a rusty, weed-washed charnel-house, marked by a green wreck-buoy ; and many times later, as we came up the river at dusk and drew nearer that green, winking eye, I would project my mind below the surface of the water, and try to picture the horror's details, and what it was our anchor saw as it shattered the still water and plunged below. Indeed, I could not help this imagining, which always persisted long after we had swung and settled to our anchor : the mast proclaimed an ugly angle in

the near-darkness, the green eye accused me—" You
are alive," it said : " we are dead, very dead—charred,
swollen, abandoned—and there are scores of us within
a few hundred feet of you." It was the other side of
the medal, frightful in its detail, final in its implication.
It was not the R.N.V.R. : it was our introduction to war.

I came aboard by the last liberty-boat after a spell
ashore, and went down to the wardroom, where M.
was correcting charts.

" Our orders have come," he said. " We're off to-
morrow morning."

" What are we getting ? " I asked. " Iceland ? Alex-
andria ? Or some nice soft job, defending a pier in
North Wales ? "

" None of those. Convoy escort, North Atlantic."

" Oh . . ." I picked up the wine chit-book. " What
are all these double gins ? "

He smiled. " Convoy escort, North Atlantic. And
winter coming on."

CHAPTER III

WORKING

A CORVETTE would roll on wet grass.

Our measure of rough weather is domestic, but reliable. Moderate sea, the lavatory-seat falls down when
it is tipped up ; rough sea, the radio-set tumbles off
its bracket in the wardroom.

Some trips are good, some not. There was one, in
calm weather, with an easy-going Gibraltar convoy, that
was a picnic, the kind of jaunt which costs a guinea a
day, with fancy-dress thrown in, in peace-time ; there
was another, that took us far North and West, that

was a long nightmare. For when, seven days out, we
turned round to go home, an easterly gale set in : we
went five hundred miles in the teeth of it before it
moderated—five hundred miles, and six days, of screaming wind and massed, tumbling water, of sleet and snow-
storms, of a sort of frozen malice in the weather which
refused us all progress. Nothing could keep it out :
helmets, mittens, duffle-coats, sea-boot stockings—all
were like so much tissue paper. " Cold ? " said the
signalman, as he pulled his hand away from the
morse-lamp and left a patch of skin on the handle :
" Cold ? I reckon this would freeze the ears off a brass
monkey."

There are cumulative miseries to be endured during
a really wet night on the bridge : icy water finds its
way everywhere—neck, wrists, trouser-legs, boots : one
stands out there like a sodden automaton, ducking
behind the rail as every other wave sends spray flying
over the compass-house, and then standing up to face,
with eyes that feel raw and salt-caked and streaming,
the wind and the rain and the treachery of the sea. Of
course, heavy weather need not always make life so
miserable : if corvettes are in no hurry, and can afford
to ease down and lie-to with their bows just off the
wind, they do very well—as far as that's concerned,
they are prime sea-boats ; but if they have to proceed
with any determination, they put their nose smack into
it every time. Twice we have had windows smashed
up on the bridge by seas which curled up and broke
right on top of them : surprise-packets we could have
done without. We're not complaining : just remarking
on the facts. . . .

Cheerful dialogue on being called for the middle
watch, rough weather :
 " Is it raining ? "
 " No, sir—just washing over."

Midnight means taking it all on again : mounting the ladder with an effort, watching for the square of sky (sometimes scarcely perceptible) which will tell you what the visibility is going to be like ; listening to see if it is still blowing as hard as when you were last on watch. It usually is.

Apart from the noise it produces, rolling has a maddening rhythm that is one of the minor tortures of rough weather. It never stops or misses a beat, it cannot be escaped anywhere. If you go through a doorway, it hits you hard : if you sit down, you fall over ; you get hurt, knocked about continuously, and it makes for extreme and childish anger. When you drink, the liquid rises towards you and slops over : at meals, the food spills off your plate, the cutlery will not stay in place. Things roll about, and bang, and slide away crazily : and then come back and *hurt* you again. The wind doesn't howl, it *screams* at you, and tears at your clothes, and throws you against things and drives your breath down your throat again. And off watch, below, there is no peace : only noise, furniture adrift, clothes and boots sculling about on the deck, a wet and dirty chaos. Even one's cabin can be a vicious cage, full of sly tricks and booby-traps : not a refuge at all, rather a more subtle danger-spot, catching you relaxed and unawares and too dead-tired to guard your balance. Sometimes, at the worst height of a gale, you may be hove-to in this sort of fury for days on end, and all the time you can't forget that you are no nearer shelter than you were twenty-four hours before : you are gaining nothing, simply holding your own : the normal rigours of the trip are still piled up, mountains high, in front of you.

A most unholy chaos can be caused on the upper deck when, in bad weather, things get adrift and are not immediately secured. We once had some heavy oil drums which broke away aft, and were washing about

with a tremendous noise, dragging all sorts of oddments
—planks, fenders, heaving-lines—in their train: to get
them under control again we had almost to stalk them,
dodging out of the way as they crashed to leeward,
gradually getting more and more ropes secured and
finally smothering them. And another time, a rough,
pitch-dark night, one of the boats which was swung
out rolled itself right under water, smashing the griping-
spar and jumping its releasing gear at one end: it hung
down by the after falls, its bows in the water at one
moment and then lifting and crashing against the ship's
side as we rolled. It looked, and sounded, nasty.

"Have a crack at securing that," said the Captain,
after watching it for a couple of minutes. "But don't
kill yourself. If it's no good, cut it adrift."

The right order. . . . It took an hour, and the six
toughest hands of the watch, but we got it inboard in
the end, not much the worse for wear, and securely
lashed in its chocks. I think I almost enjoyed that
struggle, floundering about on the boat-deck with the
seas washing over, leaning outboard at the end of a
life-line to try and get the falls hooked on again. It
was nearer the sea-going of the past, less official, less
organized, less war-like.

Discussion on the bridge, at the height of a gale, of
how we came to be drafted to corvettes.

Captain: "I was told it would be like luxury
motoring."

Self: "I was told I was damned lucky to get one."

Voice of Asdic rating: "I was detailed off, sir."

When the ship crosses the storm-centre, there comes a
sudden lull, and then the wind starts to blow from the
opposite direction, setting up a baffling sea. It seems to
come at you from all angles, rather like the meeting of
the tides in Pentland Firth at the top of Scotland:
shapeless humps of water are thrown together crazily.

and when the wave-tops break they are caught and blown back like a horse's mane, or a crest of white hair suddenly whipped up.

Running with a heavy following sea at night has its own hard-won loveliness. The long streaks of foam are lit eerily by the moonlight: the enormous pile-up of water which collects, hissing and roaring, under the bow, seems suddenly to explode into a broad phosphorescent smother which in a moment is left behind. Looking aft, one sees the stern cant up before a black wall of water: the water overtakes, slides underneath and past, and breaks at the bow, its attack spent. The ship yaws, the compass swings: from below comes the quarter-master's muttered curse as he braces his feet and hauls the wheel over to meet the next ponderous weight of sea.

Simile-spinning in the middle watch.

Northern lights—like giant streamers stirred by a sky-wide fan: like an amateur-operatic rendering of Don Giovanni's purgatory: like the fake flames of a pale electric fire. . . .

" Bosun's mate ! "

" Bosun's mate, sir."

" Get me a cup of tea and the note-book in my top drawer."

It is pleasant to notice the first patch of drying deck after a storm. It spreads. It means peace. But it covers, between decks, a chaos which until then there has been no chance to set to rights. In the mess-decks, water is everywhere: there are benches broken, things washing about on the deck, off-watch stokers trying to sleep and cursing the sweepers at work cleaning up. The wardroom is like an abandoned battle-field: arm-chairs have slipped their moorings and crashed the whole length of it, packed bookcases have burst open, and in the pantry all the steward's cunning has not prevented a formidable expense of crockery.

There's a respite now, anyway : hot meals again instead of tea and corned-beef sandwiches ; sleep without being tipped out of your bunk, a whole watch without once getting wet. The upper-deck Petty Officer gets to work squaring up, the seaman-gunner of the watch cleans the Lewis and Hotchkiss guns, the Leading Signalman checks over his rockets and flares, the Torpedoman greases the depth-charge releasing gear, examines all the primers, tests the electric circuits. Work comes as a relief, after the discomfort and the cramping inactivity of the past few days.

In the calm darkness, there sounds the beat of an unseen bird's wings, flailing the water as it evades the ship. We seem to be moving through a bath of phosphorescence ; our bow-wave can be seen, streaming away into the darkness on either side, and ships in company, even half a mile away, have a luminous line from stem to stern along their water-line.

When you are in convoy, station-keeping at night becomes an endurance test, a matter of staring without respite, concentrating on a little blurred image far ahead or abeam which may be the right ship—or a smudge on one's binoculars. If, in poor visibility, a zigzag is ordered, it has to be worked out on time instead of on distance, and becomes a sort of qualified guess-work : you run the outward course for so many minutes, until the convoy is right out of sight, and then you turn and run back till you meet them again ; the whole manœuvre is a recurrent act of faith.

There is tremendous difficulty, sometimes, in hanging on for hours to a ship which seems to fade devilishly to nothing if you relax for a moment ; but the difficulty gradually lessens and is at last forgotten, if you are lucky, in the joys of the morning watch, with the light coming up and showing the convoy still there, still in formation, still ploughing on, and one day nearer delivery. And there is a certain satisfaction, too, in rounding up stragglers, shepherding them, grading your signals between " Can you squeeze a few more revs ? " and a forthright " Keep better station in future."

But on the whole the compensations of watch-keeping at night are few, and tremendously realized : the comfort of a small, wavering stern-light, of a big ship easily seen and recognized : of a duffle coat : of a cup of near-solid cocoa half-way through the watch. They are the things you count on and cling to, the things that seem to be on your side against the enemy You grow, almost, to love them.

A ship may be so blurred by darkness and rain that its outline, even close to, is no more than a dubious smudge in the gloom ; and that is what you have to hold on to for four long hours, under orders to remain at an exact bearing and distance from it. And all that time the weather can best be summed up in the coxs'n's phrase : " Dark, sir ? You couldn't see a new sixpence on a sweep's ——."

There is something completely satisfying in the attention, the loving care even, that one can give to a watch, especially at night : keeping an all-round, all-time lookout, keeping mathematical station and a fast, wide-angle zig-zag, doing your very best for four hours and handing over the watch as if it were a neat and shipshape package.

Sometimes, even when there is nothing doing, the Captain comes up in the middle watch ; saying nothing at first, noticing everything, and then perhaps settling down to talk, with relays of tea at intervals to sweeten the session. (Some watches, indeed, are so boring that a cup of tea is an event, a banging door a relief from flat monotony.) The coxs'n also is an occasional visitor, usually introducing himself with a bar of chocolate or some home-made titbit from the Petty Officers' mess ; perhaps to season his advice, discreetly and often very indirectly tendered.

In default of visitors or emergencies, one talks to the duty signalman—a different one every night. The talk ranges widely, most of it concerned with the future, some of it (as is natural at 3 a.m.) highly pessimistic. I remember one such discussion, of what it would be like after the war, where we would live and what job we would go for. The signalman favoured a country pub, with just enough custom to keep things going. . . . But the talk had, as usual, a nostalgic air about it—it was dependent on so many things, so many chances of fortune, so many hazards : it might even stand or fall by something that was going to happen in the next five minutes. . . . Even to use the phrase "after the war" took for granted the twin unmentionable doubts, of victory and of personal survival.

Strain and tiredness at sea induce a sort of hypnosis : you seem to be moving in a bad dream, pursued not by terrors but by an intolerable routine. You come off watch at midnight, soaked, twitching, your eyes raw with the wind and with staring at shadows ; you brew a cup of tea in the wardroom pantry and strip off the top layer of sodden clothes ; you do, say, an hour's intricate cyphering, and thereafter snatch a few hours' sleep between wet blankets, with the inflated life-belt in your ribs reminding you all the time that things happen quickly ; and then, every night for seventeen nights on end, you're woken up at ten to four by the bosun's mate, and you stare at the deck-head and think : My God, I *can't* go up there again in the dark and filthy rain, and stand another four hours of it. But you can, of course : it becomes automatic in the end. And besides, there are people watching you.

But when you are working in three watches, and have
eight hours off at a time, there is luxury in coming off
watch : the luxury of relaxing, smoking, putting on
bedroom slippers, turning on the electric heater and
feeling your face thawing and losing its stiffness ; all
with no sense of hurry. It can be comforting below :
one *can* forget all the menaces outside. So far I have
been lucky in having had only one acute attack of nerves
—lying down, strained, alert, unable to sleep, just
waiting for it : waiting for those shouts, that rush of
water, that iron clang . . . . But that was in the middle of
a rough party, when another escort-vessel had been sunk,
and I don't imagine I was alone. I hope not, anyway.

There is a steady deterioration of food during a trip :
we have five days or so of comparative comfort, and then
beans set in, and corned beef, and tinned sausages, and
biscuits ominously labelled with the name of a firm which,
in peace-time, was famous among dog-lovers the world
over.

" Steward, is this bread fresh ? "
" No, sir—reconstructed."

Satisfaction, after a ten days' outward battle, of once
more giving helm-orders with " East " in them.

As with convoys, so with watches : they can be
specially good as well as specially bad. The first landfall of the return journey makes one of the best—it is
comforting to meet the friendship of coast-lights again,
to be (as they say) under the Fighter Umbrella, to be
on the map and an ascertainable spot on it too, instead
of staring eternally at stars and the last ship of the wing
column and anonymous unidentifiable water. Besides,
the watch goes quickly : there are lights to be picked
up and checked, bearings to be taken, little sums in Four-
Points and Running Fixes to be added up : possibly the

convoy alters its formation, and there is some chivvying
to be done : one is at work as a sailor instead of as a
pair of bored eyes. And above all, it means that there will
not be many more watches ; another day of it, thirty-six
hours perhaps, and one will be tied up to something
solid and enjoying sleep without a miserly limit to it.

Near land, the porpoises and the sea-gulls play round
the ship, giving us the first welcome. The sea-gulls have
a trick of skimming round the bows close to the water,
ready to plane upwards if there is a second player coming
the other way. Human beings need four sets of traffic
lights, and slavish obedience thereto, to do this in safety.

Now and then there comes a quiet sunny afternoon
watch, with the Captain and all other officers turned in
below, with nothing for me to do but take one Meridian
Altitude sight and see that the quartermaster keeps his
course, with the signalman washing out an ensign in
a bucket of suds. And sometimes it is a prelude to a
whole row of luxuries within a few hours : tying up to
the oiler and ringing off engines : the silence and peace
which descends on the ship when the mail comes over
the side and is distributed : the first night in port, the
first drink, first undressing, first sleep.

At our usual base there is one small dock, nicknamed
" The Garage," that has become Corvette Headquarters.
At the end of a convoy it is crammed with ships ; and
this recurrent association, and the chance of exchanging
visits, is remarkably pleasant, particularly at the end
of a trip which may have been rough in one way or
another. The various visiting captains usually fore-
gather in the C.O.'s cabin : down in the wardroom
some moderate junketing sets in ; it is good to relax,
and tell competitive lies about the one that got away.

Of course, this lotus-eating doesn't last for ever : the
mail will have brought enough paper-work to last a

dozen good men a fortnight. Reports, as long as your arm, are called for if a ship has as much as had a queer look from a porpoise ; and internal peace in the dock is very likely shattered by a snooty blast from the Senior Officer about jetty-sentries, or about the Guard Corvette being responsible for cleaning up the very nasty rubbish-dump left by the preceding escort-group. But while quiet reigns, it is just what we want. We're possibly going out again in a matter of hours, anyway.

Snow in the navigation-lights going down river : driving past the bridge, glowing green or red for an instant and then disappearing.

More satisfying to the lover of nature than to the Navigating Officer.

Rounding up a big convoy and getting it into shape, particularly in bad weather, can be hard work, and doubly so if you are canteen-boat—i.e. the junior cor-vette, detailed for the odd jobs.

There has come to be, among merchant ships, a very high standard of convoy discipline, and the greater part of the " forming up " can safely be left to them ; but even so there are always plenty of oddments to attend to. You may be sent up and down the lines counting heads : you may be detailed to close one of the ships and give him last-minute instructions on the loud-hailer—and he is invariably a foreigner with neither English nor megaphone : you may be sent to chivvy an outlying straggler ; and all the time you are getting a steady trickle of signals from the Senior Officer—" Tell the fourth tanker to fly his pendants "—" Find out where that little one is straying to "—" Has So-and-so dropped his pilot ? "—" So-and-so reports steering defect : close investigate." Sometimes, from the upper deck of a bigger ship, you see a long line of khaki or Air Force blue, faces staring down, hands waving, and you know you've got something even more worth escorting than usual.

Incensed by some free-style manœuvring on the part
of his charges, the Commodore hoisted the signal for
" Manœuvre badly executed " : the hoist was repeated
(no doubt with full hearts) by all the other ships in
convoy, with the exception of half a dozen confirmed
stragglers and wanderers in the rear, whose hoists were
incorrect and signalled instead " Manœuvre well executed." . . . I should like to think they did it on
purpose.

The last sight of land impresses the mind as much
as the first landfall of the homeward journey.

The convoy is now in shape, the escorts correctly
stationed : each ship knows its proper position, its
opposite number, the amount of room it has to play
with ; all we now have to do, every ship in company,
is to stay in station, make no smoke, keep on going,
turn the right corners, and make our number prettily
on arrival. . . . We're on the job once more, and it's
a job we know (and I suppose) like ; and when one
looks about and sees the faint line of land, our last
contact with the normal world, slipping away on the
quarter, and the convoy proceeding as an orderly unit
on a journey wherein it must make its own tracks and
meet such emergencies as come its way, one is aware
of the moment as a memorable and significant one.

By now there is probably no ship in company that
does not know of these emergencies at first hand, and
will acquit itself in seamanlike fashion if any of them
arise ; but for good or ill we are on our way, for the nth
time challenging the sea and the malice of the enemy :
the convoy to make the journey against all hazards, and
we to see that it does not fail for want of a show of teeth.
When land fades astern the party is on once again, the
ring is formed.

There is a certain comradely pleasure in meeting an
aircraft on long-range reconnaissance. A wide-awake
look-out picks it up, the signalman of the watch challenges

and is answered; and then it flies past, sometimes quite close, giving little dips of its wings and flirts of its tail; the pilot waves, and you wave back, and you think: "My God, I wouldn't care to be so far out in an aeroplane," and he is probably thinking: "My God, I wouldn't care to be down there in that sea." The sense of being on the job together is a very strong one. Some of them are well worth looking at, too, especially the Catalinas, extraordinarily graceful in flight, and the squared-off business like Whitleys.

Usually they are most energetic, going away into corners to look at suspicious waves and then scampering back to report. And, of course, as a means of keeping submarines out of harm's way below the surface they have, time and again, proved themselves invaluable.

Cross-talk:
Destroyer : " Can't you keep up ? "
Corvette : " We have been investigating astern."
Destroyer : " Well done."

A big convoy at sea, well closed up and keeping good station, has an immense air of purpose : seen as a whole, it is a fine and rewarding spectacle. Lines of ships— big ships, loaded deep : ships crammed with deck-cargo, ships with aeroplanes all over their upper-works, like peeled almonds stuck in a pudding ; bluff, good-looking tankers (a modern tanker is probably the best-kept and best-looking ship of all)—they make up a whole fleet, an Armada which no onslaught of the enemy can scatter. Round them the corvettes and destroyers play, almost in droves : a ring hard to crack, harder still to pierce. One can only feel proud to be one of the company to be trusted with a watch and a ship when there is so much at stake, and when such grim efficiency is the rule.

Some of the destroyers in company may have famous names, many of the corvettes a string of successes to their credit. Often we know some of the customers, too : there may be ships in the convoy that we have escorted half a dozen times before, old friends that have survived many a rough party and are still coming up for more. Sometimes they recognize us, and send individual greetings. We like that. But it is the convoy as a whole that takes the eye and the imagination. Making its steady and determined way, having limitless reserves of power and nerve to call on, it is, somehow, such a good thing to belong to.

Christmas at sea brings no holly, no turkey : only the snow is seasonable, only the lovely Christmas surprise may still make its appearance. " I've sent a hand aft to read the Yule log," said M. to me as I came up on the bridge at midnight, " and I've been saving that joke since ten o'clock. A happy Christmas to you ! "

In the morning, a festive signal from the Commodore : " Happy Christmas. Keep well closed up." In the afternoon, a long-range Santa Claus, showering seasonable gifts rather wide of the mark, with no one's name on them this time. In the evening, a rising sea which filled our stockings for us. Never mind : one day nearer home.

After checking depth-charges :
" Next time we drop one of these it may not kill a submarine—it may not even explode—but by God ! we'll have its right number."

One incredibly dreary slow convoy, which sometimes seemed to be no more than drifting in with the Gulf Stream, was redeemed and indeed glorified by the fact that the Commodore had had a difference of opinion with the leading ship of the nearest column, and the two of them spent their time enlivening the watch and each other by exchanging cracks, of which, " Pay more attention to station-keeping," and, "Your signal is wrongly hoisted and meaningless," were the least objectionable. "What's the hoist?" I would ask the signalman, as an effervescent burst of bunting fluttered up, covering all halliards and overflowing to the triatic stay. "Another alter-course?"

The signalman, examining a little-used part of the code-book, shook his head.

"No, sir—they're just chewing each other's ears off again. Something about 'discharge of offensive waste matter.'"

Satisfactory sight: two convoys, outward and inward bound, meeting within half a mile of each other, nearly half-way across the Atlantic. Naval navigation!

The first time we met an American escort-group at sea, and took over their convoy from them, was an occasion which should have been dramatic, and was of course nothing of the sort. There *was* a small exchange of international courtesies, including (from them): "Hope the convoy itself will be American one of these days," which we thought handsome of them, as well as accurately prophetic; but there the hands-across-the-sea stuff began and ended. (I'm not sure what I had been expecting: something heroic in the "March of Time" style, possibly.) But it was good to see the Stars and Stripes again, for the first time in this war, and to know that a potent ally was, officially or not, ranged on our side at last. I had latterly been meeting a certain number of Americans ashore, mostly ferry-pilots resting between transatlantic trips delivering bombers—men, out-spokenly partisan, who had certainly known their own mind and translated it into action: doubly welcome were their sea-going counterparts, blessed by authority and free to wear their uniforms.

Ordeal for an officer-of-the-watch: corvettes and

destroyers (of unequal speed, turning-circle, and general manœuvrability) hurrying to a rendezvous in line abreast : set speed, zigzag an exact number of degrees every few minutes, and damn your eyes (with the widest publicity) if you get out of station.

In any case the rendezvous is very likely an impossible one : 300 miles at 15 knots in half a gale, on the off-chance of finding twenty ships that have been hove-to for three days in a position depending on a week-old estimate : with visibility less than two miles, and about six hours of daylight to play with. No wonder the senior officers of escort-groups are men of half-humorous despair.

For a convoy to heave-to in bad weather, especially if it has to turn to face a following gale, endless care is needed, and a good slice of luck as well. There may be sixty ships or more, close together and with unequal and sometimes very large turning-circles, swinging round 180 degrees into the wind, and many of them may have been yawing wildly for the past hour. Getting round is a slow operation—for the smaller ships dangerously so ; and when it is accomplished there is usually a good deal of trimming up to be done before the convoy is in shape again.

In the night they separate for safety's sake, perhaps clinging to one consort, one pin-point stern-light in a howling wilderness, shouldering the waves, shaking themselves free of water when they ship a heavy one, their screws turning just enough to keep steerage-way. On watch in a corvette, it is a matter of patience and a damned good look-out ; for there is usually some smart Alec who decides that he's had enough of it, and squares away before the gale and comes roaring down-wind at fourteen knots, leaving it to the other bloke to get out of the way.

When daylight comes, if the weather has moderated, we look hopefully round, sight one ship and then a couple more, dash backwards and forwards persuading them to form up; and then, with, say, six tankers and a couple of merchant packets in company, comes the job of guessing the night's drift, roughing out some sort of D.R. position and laying a course for the next rendezvous or landfall. If you sight other ships on the way, you coax them into the party; sometimes it is a case of two corvettes, each with a miniature convoy in tow, trying to attract custom by bluffing about the sights they haven't taken or by specious promises of joining the main body in two hours at the outside. . . . And, of course, you pray all the time for improving weather and a sight of the sun, which will put an end to guess-work and prevent the whole issue running ashore at either Namsos or Ostend.

Terrific calculations take place as soon as we make our first landfall, calculations as intricate and as dependent on fortune as any Delphic prophecy.

The stake is a high one—the saving of a tide. If the main diverted portion causes no delay when it breaks off: if the convoy can increase speed by at least half a knot: if we are not landed with the X, Y, or Z portions, bound for different ports: if we can find the Outer Buoy quickly and part company there instead of escorting all the way home (usually the canteen-boat's job): if we can then break the port speed-limit without attracting the attention of an examination vessel: if there is no fog in the approaches: if we can get up river in an hour and a quarter and oil in two and a half—then we'll just get through the dock-gates with ten minutes to spare and gain a whole night ashore.

Signal from air-escort over convoy:
"Fancy escorting a bloody Irishman."

Destroyers sometimes lose the convoy. Then, having been unseen for three days, they dash up when the convoy is just going up river and start signalling all round the horizon. In the end, you come to think that they have been there the whole time without any unaccountable gaps.

Perhaps they even deceive themselves.

Once, when we were nearing home, we had a signal that mines had been laid in the approach-channel, and that ships were to anchor until the fairway was clear. Escort vessels congregated while sweeping was going on, seemingly impatient, but when the port was declared open there was no sort of competition to be first down the line. A great deal of cumbersome manœuvring took place, and such signals as " Please pass ahead of me "— " I am not oiling now—go ahead "—" My speed reduced to three knots—will go up last " passed to and fro like smooth drawing-room courtesies. . . . Finally a large, baleful destroyer signalled to the junior corvette : " Proceed up river forthwith," and the rest of us fell gracefully into line. Dinner with the Borgias was served.

There is satisfaction in delivering a big convoy : a long line of laden ships that have been in company for thousands of miles, now moving slowly up river at the end of their journey, is one of the finest sights that the war can offer. No wonder one watches them with pride and a certain proprietary pleasure as well ; they have been a responsibility for many days and nights, and now the responsibility is discharged. Even if there are gaps they are not big ones ; they have been closed and forgotten in the routine triumph of the majority.

That's why we like our job, I suppose : it shows results. We are proud of those results and of a lot of other things besides. And why not ? We *are* proud of our ship, of the way she can take it and the tough answers she can hand out in return : we think she's a good outfit to belong to. We are proud of our crack guns'-crews, and of our immensely resourceful signalmen. (I myself am proud of my depth-charge section :

the last time it was in action it tossed the things overboard like chicken-feed and, in rough weather, broke its own *harbour* record for firing and reloading.)

We are proud of the scores of convoys we have escorted; proud of being a good ship's company. We have to be: the job calls for nothing less. We have seamen aboard who can meet any emergency and deal with it; and the Captain is the best seaman of all. We are proud of that, too.

We like reading about ourselves in the newspapers: we enjoy what one might call their highly coloured under-statements. We are the smallest ships that operate regularly in the North Atlantic in winter: we have to keep going in appalling weather, weather that must really be seen to be believed. After a long and rough trip, when everything in the mess-deck—bedding, lockers, spare gear—has been wet through for days, and cooking anything but tea has been out of the question, we may have to oil, store, and go out again all in a matter of hours. We may be closed up at action-stations for days on end: certainly we are often never out of our clothes for a fortnight or more at a stretch.

Why not be proud? Destroyers are all right, of course; but corvettes are the tough babies, and we're in corvettes.

For a variety of reasons the job is very much easier in summer: the weather is kind, the sun a blessing, the nights short and (up North) barely dark. With only three hours or so to develop their attack, submarines can by day be kept below the surface by our aircraft and made unable to catch the convoy up in the short time when surface progress is feasible for them. But against this, longer daylight gives the bombers far more chance: sometimes darkness is only the short respite between two attacks.

It is a harsh fate (or a harsh Admiral) which sends

corvettes, not equipped with refrigerators or more than
a limited supply of fresh meat and vegetables, on the
south-bound run in summer—fifteen days or more of
blinding heat, solaced by tinned beans and beautiful
corned beef. Coming on top of Arctic weather all
winter, it did seem that they were doing their worst
for us. And how quickly summer was over : two
Gibraltar runs and a boiler-clean, and we were back to
the merry North Atlantic, and a particularly murderous
party in vile weather to kick off with.

CHAPTER IV

INTERLUDES

GOING down to Gibraltar, in midsummer.

The sea became calmer than ever, the sky a deeper
blue, the sun a hot caress ; the barometer scaled un-
believable heights, and stayed there. Daily the sextant-
angle at the meridian showed a more tropical figure.
We passed whales and basking sharks, and once a turtle,
padding manfully westward. M. swore to having seen
flying-fish in his watch : a warm breeze, imaginatively
spiced with oranges, blew from the south-east, and odd
rigs were seen about the ship—bare legs, singlets,
sandals, shameful tattooings. . . . Even the fact that,
after ten days at sea, meals now consisted (in tropical
heat) of tinned sausages and beans and smoking hot
potatoes in their jackets, and that there was no lime-
juice or fruit of any kind, could not spoil the attraction
of that southward journey.

It was the genuine summer begun at last, the relief
and compensation we had all been waiting for throughout months of winter hardship ; no wonder there were
sing-songs and the drone of a mouth-organ in the dog-
watches, no wonder there were naked stokers laid out

like half-cooked bullocks on the after-deck, no wonder that, in the canvas bath rigged in the port waist, a noisy road-house gaiety was soon under way. This was what we had all been earning ever since the black onset of last October.

And what a landfall was granted us to finish up with —Spain on the port hand and Africa on the starboard: Cape Trafalgar and Cape Spartel, with a glow in the sky ahead marking the lit waterfront of Tangier. My watch ended with Tangier abeam, but I stayed on while it grew lighter, and Tarifa came into view and an extra-ordinary smell of burnt grass came out of Africa, and dawn broke and the Rock showed at last, and the failing lighthouse off Europa Point winked twice and then gave in to the sun.

The harbour was full of heavy stuff; the Rock, close to, was as impressive as I had expected, and always suggesting more than it revealed—stones that were something else, scrub that surely hid weapons, sunlight over all: a bristling fortress decked out as scenery. Gibraltar becomes a sort of Boom Town at night, the narrow streets crammed with Forces in white or khaki shorts. Standing, as I did, at a balcony window with a tallish glass of Tio Pepe sherry, one looks down on Main Street chockful of people, a parading stream eddying out at the corners and overflowing into shops and bars. The latter, luring customers with music and chorus-singing, do a roaring trade; and in the oddly-named shops everyone buys silk stockings and cosmetics and perfumes of considerable fame and rarity and suspicious abundance.

Travel, for the lazy or romantic, is by gharry, a species of crazy open four-wheel cab, very light and springy, which dash about like operatic chariots. There is (or was) no black-out: women are rare, and wary.

On our first night ashore we attended rather a good

party given by some Merchant Navy survivors who
seemed to think they owed us a drink or two. We met
them in the Grand, all togged up in Gibraltar suits
and rainbow shirts, and we had an uproarious polyglot
session, with Swedes, Dutch, Belgians, and Danes
bobbing up continuously to drink our healths and
(presumably) return formal thanks to us. But we felt
we needed none of that: theirs had been the ordeal
and theirs the brave endurance.

Thoughts after a shopping expedition.
One cannot help being conscious of a certain futility
in convoying, sometimes at great risk and loss of life,
shiploads of goods to Gibraltar in order to buy them in
the shops there and bring them back by corvette. Rough
trips apart, I think this was one of the reasons why we
came to dislike what some of us called " The Gibraltar
Packet " and others " The Silk-Stocking Run."

We were lying almost in the shadow of *Ark Royal*:
rather an uncomfortable neighbour to have, the target-
ship of two angry Air Forces. It must be odd to be in
a " hunted " ship like that, always being shadowed,
always ripe for an attack; knowing that whatever port
you put into you're sure to be traced before very long,
knowing also that the inhabitants are probably saying:
" Nice to see them, but I wish they'd move on somewhere else. . . ."

One of the best things about our stay at Gibraltar
was wearing tropical kit—white shirt and shorts, white
stockings and shoes, and white cap-cover: an extraordinarily cool rig which made one feel fresh and clean
immediately one put it on. Forgotten were duffle-coats,
sea-boot stockings, thick oiled-wool sweaters: this, at
last, was the luxury life we had been born to. . . .
We used to work in the morning, not very hard—
since our mails had not caught us up there was

hardly any official business: "Pipe down" would be sounded after lunch, "Liberty-men to clean" at four, and after that there was nothing to do but enjoy ourselves.

Usually we would bathe at Rosia Bay, swimming out into the Mediterranean as if it were once more an *haute monde* playground; and then, in the cool of the evening, we would walk down into the town, and there shop lazily, and sip sherry at the Embassy Bar or the Bristol, and dine *à l'espagnol* off onion soup and rice-with-trimmings and smooth Algerian wine: the kind of dinner that goes on and on. . . . It was out-of-the-war, of course, and almost traitorously escapist: too much of it would have made us feel guilty and destroyed its savour; but as a severely-rationed interlude we felt that we could take all that came our way.

We were lucky not to come in for a bloody job which fell to another corvette—taking another ship's dead to sea and burying them.

What with the hot weather and the fact that most of them had spent two days in an oil tank (where an explosion had blown them), the corpses were already nearly liquid; but they were yanked out, identified, sewn up in blankets and wheeled across to the corvette —oozy packets trundled by men with handkerchiefs tied over the nose and mouth. . . . There they lay all night, leaking a vile and sickening fluid into the scuppers sprayed at intervals, watched by a quartermaster (what a job for a young rating!), and on the following night they were buried; and for a week afterwards a stink hung about that ship that no effort or antidote could get rid of.

That must have been an odd burial: pitch darkness, the chaplain shining a torch on his prayer-book, the pipes shrilling as thirty-eight bodies went down the chute one by one, making their successive quick trails of phosphorescence. But if the opportunity offered on another occasion, I should still be willing to take the description at second hand.

We were in collision, in thick fog, with a Portuguese trawler on one of our homeward trips; very little was damaged besides the port boat and a section of bow-plating, but while it lasted the encounter was impressive.

Fog tests the judgment very highly indeed, particularly in convoy, where the way in which a nearby ship can fade away as if washed over with dirty chalk, makes station-keeping half guess-work and half a sort of direction-finding by ear. All the senses are alert. You stand on the bridge, sniffing cold, vaporous air, listening to and trying to tabulate the various fog-horns, staring at the blank wall ahead. With the engines at " Slow " and the oily sea making no noise against the bows, the silence is extraordinary. Deceptive also : fog blankets the sound in some directions, magnifies it in others. The look-out or the signalman will sing out " Whistle on the starboard beam ! " when you have just classified the sound as coming from dead astern, if not slightly to port. . . . Either may be right : it's not a question of good hearing or even of practice ; it is luck. The signalman may have heard the sound directly, you may have heard it reflected off a layer or a bank of colder air. You cannot know for certain : all that *is* certain is that you must make up your mind, and then act— decisively, unhesitatingly—one way or another.

But in this case confusions of sound did not enter into it : the trawler, lit but silent, came to us at right angles on the port bow. If she had not hit us she would have hit one of the ships in convoy. We sighted her lights about a minute before the collision ; she was moving far too fast, and there came the instant realiza-tion (*felt* rather than calculated) that we could not miss each other. Having given all possible orders (" One short blast "—" Hard a-starboard "—" Full astern "— " Sound mess-deck alarm bell "—" Close watertight doors ") we could only stand on the bridge and wait for it. There was a sound of air going into life jackets at high pressure. . . . The lights, suddenly very near and menacing, seemed to throw themselves at us ; there was one startled shout from the bridge of the trawler and then the crash.

Not a sharp crash but a long drawn-out grinding. Due to our quick turn to starboard we had closed on a converging course, our port bow to his starboard one, instead of a right-angle cut which might well have sunk one or other of us. The two ships closed, surging against each other, parted momentarily, and then closed again : expensive smashing noises came from up forrard, and below me the port boat, splintered and stove-in, was forced over its griping spar and fell inboard. We could see the trawler clearly now, in the few moments before she sheered off : a big, heavily-built ship with high spoon bows and one man on the bridge staring up at us as if roughly awakened from a deep dream. Perhaps such was the case. Then we drifted apart and the trawler faded out once more till only her lights could be seen.

Sent below by the Captain to see what the damage was, I forced my way through a throng of half-asleep and rather reproachful ratings, and went into the mess-decks. It was odd, and disconcerting, to see light through the bow-plating, but the main damage seemed to be well above the water-line, the forepeak being still quite dry and in fact remaining so for the rest of the trip. (Rough weather, of course, would have made it quite a different matter, but we were lucky in that respect.) I attended to one casualty, a surprised steward who had been thrown out of his cot and had cracked a rib, and then went up to the bridge to report.

Up on the bridge also was a Leading Stoker, a reputed linguist, who had been summoned to address the trawler through the loud-hailer. The exchange was a short one, and inconclusive at that. He called out : " Barco !

Habla Inglese ? " and the answer came back : " Portuguese ship ! You damn' fool ! " And that was really all. She claimed no damage, we were fit to proceed, and there was a convoy to attend to ; so after we had prised her name and number out of her (a long and disjointed business, sounding rather like a badly translated play) we rang " Slow ahead " and got back on our course. It might have been very much worse, and thoughts of leave while the ship was under repair certainly sweetened the rest of the watch.

The upper-works of an odd ship showed themselves above the horizon.

" Close me ! " signalled the senior corvette decisively. " I'm going to investigate."

We wound up to something near our maximum speed, we turned to starboard and laid a course for the stranger. Within a quarter of an hour it was revealed as not one ship but rather a lot ; battleships, cruisers, a big ring of destroyers, escorting aircraft droning overhead. . . . After a surprised moment : " Resume previous course," signalled the senior corvette : " Formation is friendly." As we turned to port again we signalled back : " What price glory ? "

We had an engine breakdown one morning, when we were by ourselves and on our way to a rendezvous. A knock developed, slight at first and then growing and growing till it seemed to fill the whole ship. Before long it was obvious that we would have to stop engines and investigate : never a popular necessity in the Western Approaches. . . . The repairs took us about six hours, and during all that time we lay motionless, our seaboats swung out, the perfect target for air or underwater attack. We had, of course, wirelessed our position, but a feeling of tension filled the whole ship—it was a very clear day and one looked round the immense circle of wide, flat sea and thought : somewhere in that circle there may be, at this very moment, a submarine looking at us through its periscope and shaping up for an attack. Perhaps more than one submarine ; perhaps a clutch of half a dozen. . . . Said M. to me, reflectively : " In the old days there used to be an order, ' Down funnel, up sail ! ' I wish we could give it now."

I remember going down to the engine-room to see if I could hurry things up at all, finding a ring of engine-room ratings, Stoker Petty Officers, and the Chief gathered round the offending crankshaft, and withdrawing again without saying anything. Anxiety was excusable, but it was obvious that they were doing their utmost without any chivvying from the bridge.

When we got going again you could almost hear the ship sigh with relief. A straight scrap we don't mind : we do mind being at the wrong end of a target-practice.

The next time it happened to us we were in company, which made things a lot easier, and we could also manage slow speed without tearing things to bits. But as we had the prospect of at least ten days at sea, and the damage might easily become worse, we made a signal to the senior corvette, telling her the tale and requesting permission to return to harbour for adjustments or repairs. The reply came back : " Approved. Do you require an escort ? " to which we answered : " Would prefer it if possible."

From the other corvettes through whom the exchange had been passed came an instant twitter of signals, full of resource and inventiveness. " Am prepared to escort *Flower* to base," was the generous offer of one. " My A/S gear unsatisfactory, suggest I return with *Flower*," said a second, in whom eagerness had induced some rather muddled thinking. " Would be glad of chance to refuel," was a third optimistic suggestion which would not stand even superficial scrutiny. . . . But it was the Senior Officer himself who made the great sacrifice.

"Follow me," he signalled: "returning to harbour in company. What is your maximum safe speed?"

Coming alongside a French-manned oiler.
I went aft in pitch darkness, trying to think of the exact French equivalent of "Take that forespring forrard and make it fast."

After strife. We sailed into the inlet in the dusk of early evening, and into a different world. There was a little village opposite our anchorage, with an unromantic name; but what a village! There were lights in its streets, there were windows uncurtained—or curtained in friendly yellows and blues and reds such as we had not seen for months; there were buses with unscreened lamps and yellow bicycle lights, and a bonfire or two. Dusk here was not the beginning of total gloom or the onset of danger, but the signal for lighting the hearth and the way, for the comfortable exchanges of neighbour and neighbour.

From the bridge we stared at it in astonishment, for it was violently against the law and it invited the contemporary horrors; and then we realized. It was not a defiant village, it was the other half of the world, the world free from fear and preserving its sanity: it was Ireland, Ireland still evading the toils; it was peace. . . . And often during the evening we could come up from below to look at it, staring in contemplative wonder at this strangest of all sights—dear normality; and in some degree or other we all thought: "Christ, this war! If only we lived across there. . . ." The international aspect was (to me) obscure; for here we were at anchor, one of His Majesty's ships of war in commission which had somehow escaped hateful reality and come upon a haven. Was it a licensed haven, or was it the blind eye? And how little it mattered! Dear village, dear cottages lighted and unafraid, dear unharmed corner of a scarcely remembered world.

In the morning the international aspect became (again, to me) even more obscure; for we signalled to the Irish side and presently took off an Irish pilot. He was small, diffident, and efficient; and when I inquired how it was that Irish pilots were allowed to pilot British men-of-war, he made the entirely reasonable comment: "Now why should you be sending up the river for a Six-Counties' man when there's a good Irish pilot waiting for you on the doorstep itself?"

The channel was, at times, extremely narrow. Said the Captain, standing by my side, unexpectedly: "You've only got to give 'hard a-starboard' and we could all be interned for the duration."

Conversation-piece in Northern Ireland.
"Go ashore and get me a paper."
"Any special one, sir?"
"Yes, get me the *Independent*."
"The *Independent*, sir?"
"Yes, there's sure to be an *Independent*."
There was.

Northern Ireland was another place where we slackened off, in a rather special way. For some reason our stay there developed into a faintly mad-house session, the effect of Ireland on a normally hard-working and routine-ridden ship's company being to induce a sort of fairy-like unreality; in fact, we all became Irish, and made the most of it.

Odd, unexplained people came aboard, and ate their lunches on the upper deck; disreputable children wandered about at will, hazarding their teeth on ship's biscuit. A feud developed with the corvette alongside: the rival quartermasters faced each other across the gangway, muttering threats and fingering their side-arms. It was nothing for respectable petty officers, returning from liberty via the other ship's fo'c'sle, to report to the Officer-of-the-Day in some such formula as, "Returning on board, sir, with fender and heaving-line." We went for a bicycle ride past the Eire customs (a signpost by the roadside, deserted after office hours), and returned, laden with eggs, butter, and strawberries, and impelled by Guinness to a breakneck speed. Couponless, I was able to buy some silk stockings by initiating a whip-round among the shop-girls, who each contributed one coupon and a brilliant smile. The Captain, drinking in a pub on the dock-side, found himself joined by his four officers one after the other. I counted them as they arrived, and presently realized that there was no one left on board. (It was attributed to lack of liaison, excused, and very shortly forgotten.) And among many other manifestations of the Irish spirit, there was a second case of creating vandalism in the mess-decks.

On our last night I went ashore with H., our recently joined junior officer, a jovial ex-barrister of spacious build. I recall two things about that night. The first was seeing a huge church, almost a cathedral, with a lighted porch beckoning us across the street. On an impulse I said : " Let's light a candle to the holy saints above " (that was how one talked in Ireland), and we tiptoed in, silent, slightly awe-struck, chockful of milk-stout and religious feeling. Inside the porch the first thing we saw was a blue notice, " YOU MAY TELEPHONE FROM HERE," and the second a placard : " TOWN HALL A.R.P. STATION. FEMALE DECONTAMINATION CASES, FIRST ON THE RIGHT." The other thing I remember was asking at the hotel if drinks were procurable after hours, and being cheerily answered : " Sure they are, sir—there's a Naval Base upstairs." There was, too—almost a floating one.

A boiler-clean seems to render the ship, and the duty-officer, quite derelict.

With the boilers blown down, the whole ship is very cold : she is lit by unreliable shore-lighting which has a habit of packing up when you need it most ; she has a general air of disuse not lessened by most of her innards being spread out over the engine-room casing. All officers except yourself are on leave. You sit and sit (and drink and drink) and nibble at the enormous amount of paper-work before you: other corvette officers in the same position come over to grouse in company, friendly destroyer-blokes come aboard to borrow stationery and stay to commiserate; it is like a Chekhov play pushed sideways into the dock. And when, as sometimes happens, repairs take a long time; when you miss your group, when weeks elapse and there is still no sign of going to sea; then a positive rotting-away atmosphere seems to set in. Friends come back from long and hard trips, and make pointed remarks about depot ships; some one chalks H.M.S. *Wallflower* in a prominent position opposite the gangway; you find yourself looking round the wardroom and thinking; we can't move now—imagine the break with tradition. . . . And soon, in any case, there will not be enough oil left to go and get some more.

There are shore-blokes who come aboard when you are trying to work and expect a mid-morning gin as an inalienable right. There are shore-blokes who, having got that gin, lean comfortably back and enlarge on the theme: "I *wish* I could get to sea instead of being stuck ashore." Some, wistful ones, really mean it; others patently do not. H. and I developed a rather amusing game with people we thought were shooting a line in this respect. We would let them run on, telling us the sad tale of their frustration, and we would then profess ourselves willing, *and able*, to get them sea-going jobs any time they wanted them. "My uncle, the Admiral, can easily fix it for you," H. would say, with a great air of patronage. "What job would you like? Minesweeping at Sierra Leone?" There would be half-hearted agreement and a pinned-on smile, and then, rather late in the day, the bad news that the speaker, after all, had a tendency to catarrh which unfortunately precluded war-like activity. Otherwise, of course . . .

You get sick of them in the end; you cannot help contrasting natural wire-pullers who get themselves snug jobs with natural co-operators who take whatever job is given them and get on with it. To the gin you pour out for them is added a fairly stiff measure of contempt.

And there is the other kind : the inshore hero, who sits at the end of the bar. He has one of those tiddley little yachts which breeze up and down the river bullying merchant-men and sending us silly signals like, " You have given the wrong recognition letters," or, " You are approaching a prohibited anchorage," or, " You have a fender hanging over the stern." He gets command-money, hard-lying money, and a reputation for coolness and courage. He is invariably in great form in the bar, as brave as a lion : explaining what is wrong with our convoy-screening system, using two tumblers and an ash-tray and gestures of unflinching defiance.

Later on, when we had run through despair and dull resignation, we became much more light-hearted about paper-work; doing our best with it, certainly, but refusing to be worried by accumulations which we could not avoid. Back from a ripe convoy, you can't exactly give a broadside of enthusiasm to preparing a memorandum on the advantages experienced from using wrapped bread : particularly when you are fresh (hardly the right word) from ten days' hacking at ship's biscuit. . . . To delve at random into the " Pending " file, to pick out some likely-looking morsel, blow the dust off, and deal concisely with it—surely that's the most the paymaster branch can expect.

There are " strong " characters among the crew who wear you down by doing things they shouldn't and always having to be told about it. One day you forget to tell them, or you get tired and think : " Oh, hell, it'll all be the same in a hundred years," and there you are : a precedent is established, and they have won yet another round. There are others who make vaguely insubordinate remarks just within hearing : they are trying it on, and unless checked will make a habit of it and get out of control ; but how can you check a man for saying, " I wouldn't pick a Jerry out of the water, orders or no orders." Surely it would be better to wait till the occasion arises, and then take the appropriate strong action. . . .

Alternatively, how difficult it is to tick off a good bloke, well-behaved and efficient, who suddenly goes wrong—or who, perhaps from carelessness, develops some habit you do not like. For by his good behaviour he had, almost, earned a privileged position, or at least the right to a certain latitude ; you respect each other, and there is an undercurrent of friendship : is it worth spoiling this for something basically unimportant, some petty toe-the line regulation ? In a way, you yourself should make some effort and sacrifice towards the smooth working of the ship ; and this acceptance of individual foibles may be part of that effort.

One finds difficulty also in ticking off someone like a Chief Engine-Room Artificer, old enough to be your father and at least an individualist.

Numbered among the crew are unknown humorists whom you only learn about accidentally, when you happen to go forrard in the dog-watches ; there you find an able-seaman, whom you had set down as slow and none too bright, giving a mouth-organ recital or an exhibition dance to his enthralled mess-mates, or a cross-talk act good enough for the music halls, if quite unsuitable thereto. To be rated as humorists also, in a different tradition, were the two superior ordinary seamen, recommended for commissions, who put in a brief, enchanted period in our lower deck. Of them it is related that, on first coming aboard, they strode into the stokers' mess-deck and asked cheerily: "Are there any other Cambridge chaps here?" I have had no reliable account of the stokers' reaction.

They came to fit in better than that later on, though there was one whose habit it was, when on look-out duty, to report anything of interest with the words, "I say, sir, rather suspicious object over there!" (His best effort was: "I say, sir—water-spout!" It was a lighthouse.)

It is perhaps worth touching on the problem (not applicable in this case) of what to do with a really useless rating of this sort—i.e. a "gent" who simply does not satisfy naval standards of seamanship. Sooner or later you have to send in a report on him—an honest report which decides his future sphere of usefulness. To keep him in the ship as an A.B. is to keep so much dead wood: the status of officer might just enable him to pull his weight. But is promotion to be on these lines? Should good manners and lack of a localized accent draw the attention and give a man such a pull? Surely it should be the best *sailors* who are advanced to commissions, rather than men of gentle birth, about whose naval future one is in despair.

In my capacity as Senior Medical Officer (acting, unpaid), I once had occasion to send a chit to Naval Sick Quarters, to accompany "So-and-so, Stoker First Class, who is believed to be suffering from the complaint commonly known as crabs." The answer came back in due course, signed by a Surgeon-Lieutenant, R.N.V.R.: "I confirm your diagnosis, and add that your stoker is also suffering from the complaint commonly known as the Itch (scabies). For your future reference, crabs, by the way, are called 'Pediculosis Pubis,' or Little Pattering Feet on the Private Parts."

I should like to meet that man.

A Commander visited the ship, to give us pleasure

and the once-over; with a comet-tail of officers he toured us very thoroughly, asking innumerable questions (dear me, we thought, what an inquisitive man) : for some reason he picked on H. as the weakest link in the chain, and what a good guess that turned out to be.

"What's your job?" he asked H., as soon as he got aboard.

"Barrister, sir," answered H. cheerfully, glad to be on safe ground. "I'd been in practice about five years when——"

"I meant your job in the ship," interrupted the Commander, looking rather old-fashioned at him.

"Signal Officer, sir."

"Ah . . . How many ten-inch projectors do you carry?" he asked, when we were up on the signal bridge.

H., confusing projector (a morse lamp) with projectile, and being none too certain about either, replied :

"I'm not sure, sir. And I'm afraid the Gunnery Officer is on leave."

The Commander got out of this *impasse* by ignoring it : I suppose he thought he had been misheard, or perhaps he had already decided that H. was rather simple. We moved on, a silent, thoughtful party.

A little later on a sound of Morse coming in at high speed was heard from the W/T cabinet.

"Can you read that?" asked the Commander, rounding on H. suddenly.

"No, sir."

"Pity. You could intercept the German broadcasts."

The picture of H., a slow mover, intercepting German broadcasts in Morse was too much for me. I turned away, and gave my attention to some nearby paint-work. H., visibly weakening, but still rashly eager to clear his yard-arm, tried to put the reasonable citizen's view-point.

"I'm afraid it's rather too fast for me, sir."

" I thought you said you were the Signal Officer,"
said the Commander, as if he could not believe his ears.

" Well—*faute de mieux*, sir."

" What ? "

" *Faute de mieux*, sir."

" Oh . . ." A keen glance, suspicious of insolence.
" *Faute de mal*, I should think you mean."

The French may have been vulnerable, but the
thought was clear.

Our former leading-steward, when rebuked (which
was often), had the habit of going into the pantry and
saying in a loud, carrying voice to the assistant-steward :
" Steward, you've *let me down !* I told you to get tea
and now the officers are *waiting !* "

Lighting up the boiler, the young stoker explained
the process for my benefit as he went along.

He turned a few knobs, seemingly at random, and
then took up a sort of long-handled pair of tongs with
a piece of cotton-waste at the end. This he dipped in
a can of oil, and lit with a match : then he opened a
small door under the boiler, and thrust it within. There
was a subdued roar, and then a glow through half a
dozen small windows. He turned two more knobs, and
then began to watch, carefully, a pressure-gauge above
his head.

He looked very young, to be allowed to play about
with machinery like that.

Sunday morning : returning from short leave, driving
into the port after a bad blitz.

Outside the town, a lovely sunny day ; but ahead
there were billows of black smoke, and soon the air
was fouled by smuts, charred paper drifting on the
wind,[1] an over-all reek of destruction. As we made our

[1] During the morning a rating brought aboard a half-burned page
from a Statute-Book which he had picked up seven miles outside
the town.

way the air grew darker and darker, shutting out the sun, the sky, the corners ahead : each street we traversed, by a dozen diversions, bumping over hoses, scuttering through broken glass and ruined woodwork, passing groups of intent rescue-workers or silent onlookers, showed a more appalling destruction. Tall houses lay in the street, flames showed through empty windows and gaping rents, shops and buildings sprawled over the roadways. The night must have been a fearful one.

When progress became impossible before the smoky chaos at the top of the main street, I tapped the taxi-driver on the shoulder and called out : " That'll do—I'll walk the rest." By force of habit he gave the correct traffic-signal and drew into the kerb—directly underneath a blazing building whose roof had already crashed through three flights. . . . Across the street it was the same, and farther on the same, and all the way to the ship the same : what was not still burning lay in red-hot piles of brick and wood ; what was not torn to pieces was blasted into a vile disorder. Even to the casual observer it was a frightful scene—the mounting furnaces, the thick, smoke-filled air, the huge spaces laid waste ; to a man born in that town it was heart-breaking.

We waited on board that same evening as the hands crawled round the clock towards another night, another testing-time, another ordeal. Hoses were rigged, sand-buckets filled and placed, wires run out to the opposite side of the dock in case the tall building alongside should take fire : the duty-watch were given their instructions and warned to stand by : but all these precautions seemed to be off-set, rendered foolish even, by the opposing facts—the ship lay in the heart of the docks, and within a hundred yards two uncontrollable fires raged, unsubdued from the previous night, pointing beacons across the whole night sky. The day died, the fires showed stronger ; at midnight the expected syrens went again.

It wasn't one of the worst raids; but it sufficed, it passed muster. We had a number of incendiary bombs on the fo'c'sle and on the warehouses alongside: some near-misses which fell in the dock made a disconcerting whistling sound. But the barrage, which had obviously been added to, was one of the most formidable things I had ever listened to; and at intervals the night-fighter boys tried their hand, the bursts of machine-gun fire being applauded by the crew. Then dawn, and a respite, and hot whisky all round.

We went down river at dusk, and anchored at the entrance, and from there watched the last heavy raid on the port. Occasionally a turning aircraft roared overhead, shaping up for another run over the target; but all one's attention was for the noise and the amazing display ashore—star-shells, flares, tracer from ships, the pin-point flicker of the barrage, the crash of bombs, sickening one.

Said the young Newfoundland rating at my side, slowly: "I didn't reckon for this sort of war. There's women and children there."

To be north-bound again, on one of the last fair-weather days of the year, came as a relief after the dusty havoc of our spell ashore.

It was a lovely day, of bright and warming sunshine, and we had the morning to waste. So we listered: doing turning-trials in a smother of wake, altering course to look at pieces of drift-wood: flying home-made kites for machine-gun practice, firing off all the guns at once at an imaginary aeroplane which was brought down in spectral flames; sinking a mine by rifle-fire, dropping an adroit test-depth-charge and collecting the harvest of fish.

Second winter: rough weather again; but now we

C

know all about it, now we've learned the drill, the routine of personal caution.

Hang on to something always: give no chances, secure everything movable, including the arm-chairs in the wardroom, clear your desk and wedge your books in the bookcase. When you are eating, watch with constant care the food and drink, which at any moment will dart for your lap. When you turn in, have your back against the bulkhead and crook your knees so that your thighs lie athwartships: this may keep you in place. But above all, if you don't want to be hurt, hang on to something, even if you're only taking a couple of steps: even if you are leaning against the bridge-rails having five minutes inoffensive think-of-home.

Second winter, second year in corvettes. Yes, it's all the same now: the job is standardized; survivors are even wounded in the same way, and all corpses are alike.

There *was* one change, however, and a marked one: it grew out of the sharpening crisis in our corner of the war, the quickening *tempo* of the Atlantic fight.

For things woke up, with the intensification of the "Battle of the Atlantic" that began in the turn of 1940-41; things came to the boil, and every phase of convoy-escort acquired a sharper edge to it. More danger for convoys, harder work for us; and more ships were sunk, though it wasn't a one-way affair by a long chalk—we drew more blood in the process, as the records will one day show. But this intensification brought with it a curious change in our outlook: it was, briefly, that we came to dislike everything that made sea-going easy and pleasant. To get convoys through, we wanted cover, and cover meant, in the last analysis, dirty weather.

It was odd to look forward, on setting out, to the chance of a gale—anyone who really wants the North Atlantic to do its worst in winter should be qualifying for a lunatic asylum—but that was what it amounted to. Before, all the emphasis of convoy work had been on navigation and station-keeping, and we had cursed the dark, moonless nights, the rain and mist, the lumpy seas that multiplied our difficulties ; now we hated the moon, and wanted only a black night and a bit of flying scud to draw the curtains round us. It made it infinitely harder to hang on to the convoy, it turned zigzagging into tip-and-run in the dark, but it was harder still for the submarines to trail us, and that weighed more than all the hardship and the intolerable strain that bad weather brings.

Oddest, and in a way saddest, of all, was the fact that we tended to develop the same feeling about going off watch : it used to be so welcome, that tired descent, but now it meant not much more than going below the water-line and entering a possible trap. And to feel this about leaving the wet bridge and putting off the burden was another nut-house qualification which would, in any other circumstances, have been conclusive. . . . But above all, it was sad : it meant that we were being cheated, daily and nightly, of our just reward and recompense.

I'm not sure that I can truthfully talk of " we " where all this is concerned : the others may not have felt it so strongly, or, indeed, at all. Better, perhaps, to say that one watch-keeping officer in corvettes came to prefer the fresh air, and the fresher the better.

CHAPTER V

ACTIONS: SURVIVORS

WHEN " Anti-craft stations " was sounded I put my tin hat on, and climbed up through the dusk to the after gun-turret : under a clear, frosty sky the gun's-crew

stood silent, watching, waiting, possibly nervous. I
said something or other, and they laughed, and relaxed : five young men, steel-helmeted and closely
wrapped against the cold, the white tops of their sea-
boot stockings standing out in the gloom : five young
men listening for sound above the ordinary disregarded
sound of the ship and the sea, staring at the stars across
which the mast swung a slow arc. To be together,
and to see the stocky gun-barrel cocked up at the sky
like a jauntily raised thumb, was to be reassured. . . .
And then, head on one side, I heard the sound we were
waiting for : far away on the other wing of the convoy
a single line of tracer fled upwards ; and without an
order being given the crew closed up round their gun,
the safety-catch clicked, and the layer slapped the breech
with his mittened hand and said : " Come on, Rosie,
win me a medal."

The brilliant fireworks of a dusk air attack : the
bomber flies very low above the columns, pursued and
harried by cross-fire from machine-gun tracer, by the
quick pom-pom flashes, by the burst of flame as the
destroyers' bigger guns go into action. Sometimes you
may see a line of tracer bullets describing a complete
semicircle, like a glowing fan opening and shutting, as
a plane flies low over a ship.

Satisfactory (in default of bringing it down) was the
sight of the day-bomber flying round and round the
convoy in gradually widening circles, kept at bay and
finally defeated by the escort's long-range guns, each
ship turning to bark at it, like a bad-tempered farm-
dog, as the plane entered its sector.

A huge column of water is thrown up after a near-
miss : it rises grey and white, edged with foam, higher
than the ship and hiding it completely, so that for all
we know it may have been hit. But when the turmoil

subsides, there is the ship still ploughing on : and you look at it and think : " I bet that brought 'em up on deck with their braces dangling. . . ."

Sometimes a single bomb falls, very wide of the mark, and that is all—the ugly incident is closed : it's odd to think that a bomber may have flown a thousand miles to drop that one bomb 10,000 feet through the clouds a mile and a half from the nearest ship, after which it turns round and heads for home again. . . . But that doesn't seem to alter the score, as far as Goebbels is concerned. I remember one occasion when, after a profitless and none too intrepid attack on the convoy by two Junkers 88's, no damage of any sort being done, we tuned in to Haw-Haw the same evening. " This morning," said that snarling voice, " aircraft of our gallant Luftwaffe attacked an important convoy 500 miles south-west of the Scilly Isles. Two ships were sunk, one of 5,000 and the other 2,000 tons, both having their whole sides ripped off ; and others were damaged." Query : is this Goebbels's own make-up, or is it based on the actual report of the aircraft concerned ? If it's the aircraft, how mutually embarrassing it must be for their crews, all of whom know it to be a pack of lies. And if it's Goebbels, how foolish the airmen must feel, to be given false credit : and how mistrustful of their own propaganda.

But now and then it is *they* who have the luck. After a quiet and unscathed journey of some 2,300 miles and fifteen days, it is depressing to lose a ship on your own front door-step, to some bloody little aircraft returning from a raid with one spare bomb.

When, in convoy, the sun goes down and the order " Darken ship ! " is piped, one has a feeling that the dividing line is being crossed, from the comparative tranquillity of daylight to the hazard and the startling crudity of things that go bump in the night. It's a sort of private signal that the party is once more on, a moment which has come to mean a great deal on board, and it is attended with care—deadlights are dropped and screwed home, screens rigged at the mess-deck entrances, the shutters of the bridge and the wheel-house put in place and secured. Then the duty petty officer makes his rounds—meticulous rounds, the most important made either at sea or in harbour; and when he comes up to the bridge and reports the ship darkened, one thinks : well, the convoy may be for it—we may be for it ourselves—but at least we're giving no chances and leaving no ends hanging out.

Among the minor trials of the middle watch are the porpoises which, with relish and great agility, play submarines at night—i.e. come darting at the ship's side at right angles, and then pass underneath with a swirl of phosphorescence. You get used to these April Fool torpedoes after a bit, and almost feel like joining in the fun yourself, but the first few times you find yourself ducking. . . .

There develops, unavoidably, a certain tension aboard as we approach the U-boat danger zone : we know that at any moment, from now on, we may be involved in some action which will test nerve and skill to the utmost : the feeling affects the whole ship, and it is almost a relief when the first explosion is heard and the first flare goes up, and you think : " Oh, well this is it. . . ."

But the tension for us is really nothing compared with what it must be for ships in convoy, and the amount of self-discipline and nerve needed to remain in station after another ship has been torpedoed. We at least have the relief—and possibly the safety—of action : we can crack on a few revs, fling ourselves about a bit, strike back formidably if the opportunity arises ; but they have to wallow along as if nothing had happened—same course and station, same inadequate speed, same helpless target.

Imagine being on the bridge of a tanker, loaded deep with benzine that a spark might send sky-high, and seeing the ship alongside struck by a torpedo, or another torpedo slipping past your stern, *and doing nothing at all about it*. Imagine being a stoker, working half-naked many feet below the water-line, hearing the crack of explosions, knowing exactly what they mean, and staying down there on the job—shovelling coal or turning wheels, concentrating, making no mistakes, disregarding what you *know* may be only a few yards away and pointing straight at you.

No amount of publicity, no colourful write-ups, no guff about " the little silver badge," above all no medals, can do honour to men like these. Buy them a drink ashore, if you like ; but don't attempt an *adequate* recompense. You won't get in the target area.

Going aft to my depth-charges, when " Action stations " is sounded, is now a routine which somehow never loses its significance or fails in its effect ; and the start of the routine has itself become almost a ritual.

Time, possibly, one a.m. (Good old middle watch : it gets all the knocks there are.)

" Captain, sir ! "

" What is it ? "

" Second ship, starboard wing column, torpedoed, sir. They're firing star-shell the other side."

" Very good. Sound off ' Action-stations.' I'll be up in a second."

When I am relieved of the watch I make my way down the ladder and across the boat-deck : below me in the waist there is a clumping of sea-boots as the thrower-crews run aft to close up and clear away for action. There's time to look round as I cross the deck in darkness, ducking under the funnel-guy which I cannot see but which comes two steps after the last boiler-room grating, and always the view—or lack of it—is the same : black water, now seeming very much closer, the silhouette of a nearby ship, the glow from a flare : perhaps, already, the flickering lights low down on the water which mean lowered boats and rafts. Then the coxs'n passes me, on his way forrard to take over the wheel ; and I say (as always) : " A fine night, 'swain," and he says : " Let's drop a few for luck this time, sir "—another ritual which marks the occasion as an authentic one.

Leaning against the rail by the ensign-staff, I can see below me the thrower-crews standing by waiting for their orders ; farther aft there is a group of spare numbers—off-watch stokers and communications-ratings—ready to bear a hand in reloading. Farthest aft of all, I can just make out the Seaman-Torpedoman bending over his depth-charge rails : as soon as he sees me silhouetted above him he calls out : " All ready, sir," in a voice half formal, half eager. I happen to know that he very much likes dropping depth-charges. . . .

Probably there is a murmur of voices, some of them angrily blasphemous—we all realize what those lights on the water mean, from long practice we can translate them accurately into loss of life, disablement, mutilation. Standing ready in the darkness, we hope for luck, and action.

Strange people come to the surface when " Action-stations " is sounded—stokers I had no idea were on board, rare faces that never otherwise see the light of day.

The first thing you notice when a ship has gone down is a hateful smell of oil on the water. (We grew to loathe that smell : as well as a ship sunk, it meant survivors drenched with fuel oil, coughing it up, poisoned by it.) But there is always an amazing amount of stuff left on the surface—crates, planks, baulks of wood, coal-dust, doors, rope-ends, odd bits of clothing—a restless smear of debris, looking like a wrecked jumble-sale, on which the searchlight plays. Here and there lights may be flickering: too often they are not the ship's boats you are hoping for, but empty rafts with automatic calcium-flares attached to them, burning uselessly, mute witnesses to disaster.

As soon as you come upon the scene you feel you must search it all thoroughly; you feel you must prowl round and miss nothing: you also *know* that you are not the only prowler, that even as you circle a raft or wait for a laden boat to come alongside, someone in the dark outer ring may be taking a sight of you, preparing as you loiter to run a fish and teach you the same lesson. Perhaps among the wreckage a white face or a raised arm appears: can you afford to wait, are they worth the risk of salvage, or will one more chance, one more effort of mercy, forfeit your ship? Already she is sufficiently in hazard: how much margin is there still left?

In semi-darkness, we passed a dead man floating up right, supported by his life-jacket. We shouted at him, but he stared back in silence. To cover up, a stoker called out: "So you won't talk, eh?" and there was a tiny laugh, a whisper of mirth drowned in pity.

Uncannily, some high, jabbering voices came out of the darkness: the engine-room telegraph rang "Slow," and then "Stop," and presently we saw ahead of us a bobbing black spot—one of the ship's boats we were looking for. We hailed it from the bridge, and were answered by a torrent of Chinese: I thought, "God, this is going to be difficult . . ." The wailing of high voices continued, almost operatic in its pattern—a slice of "Aida," cut thin and slipped into a 20-foot boat in mid-Atlantic; and then, breaking through them like a soloist with a will of his own, a strong Welsh voice sang out: "Shut up, the whole damn' lot of you."

The boat came alongside, a Welsh second-officer at
the helm : someone in it started flashing a torch carelessly, and was stopped by a crisp order through a
megaphone from the bridge. We took off twenty-two
Chinese firemen—" They must have sunk a laundry,"
said H. to me as we counted them coming over
the side—and then the boat, with revolver bullets
through her planking and buoyancy tanks, was set
adrift, though not before a certain number of
rescuers' perquisites—oars, blocks, shackles, a spare
water-breaker—had been prudently salvaged and borne
aboard.

They had that round score of Chinese sleeping in the
mess-decks for the rest of the trip. Said a signalman
to me one morning, reflectively : " It's funny to wake
up, sir, and see all those new faces."

Valuable time is taken up in lowering a boat and
bringing it in again, but it is often the quickest way of
picking up men in the water, who may be too exhausted
to climb aboard and too slippery with oil to be pulled
up. I was once in charge of a boat which was sent
away on this job, one dark night when a fairly high sea
was running ; and I remember the extraordinary difficulty we had in getting inboard men who had been
in the water for nearly four hours, who were almost
paralyzed with cold, and whose clothes (and in some
cases their naked bodies) were so saturated with fuel-
oil that it was like trying to land enormous greasy fish
with one's bare hands. A short, steep swell, that seemed
to lift us up and flick us about like a chip of wood,
didn't make things any easier.

This particular lot were lucky in having life-jackets
with lights attached to them : otherwise we would never
have seen them from the bridge in the first place. (These
lights—they are small naked bulbs clipped to the life-
jacket and connected to a battery in the breast-pocket—
have been the salvation of countless men, and the lack

of them must have been the death of countless more: a man in the water at night is almost impossible to see, and his voice, even in still weather, is lost in engine and water noises.) I forget how many we collected— about thirteen, I think, including a man so badly injured that it seemed hardly worth while giving him the extra agony of being handled. . . . When we got alongside again we bundled them over the side, the boat surging with every wave so that sometimes they could step straight aboard and sometimes could not even reach the foot of the ladder: the slightly nightmare quality of the occasion was heightened by the pitch darkness, the injured man's groans, and the thunderous noise of the chain ladder against the ship's side.

Soon there remained only the bad casualty to be dealt with. " Send a stretcher down for this one," I called up to the ship, and when it was passed we strapped him in, handling him as gently as the tossing boat allowed: he seemed unconscious at the end. Then a sling was rigged, and they started to heave in. But as he swung in mid-air the boat rose to a huge wave and lurched against the ship's side—or where it would have been if the stretcher had not been in the way. I felt that blow in my own guts. The man screamed once, sharply: I called out to the bow-oar: " Hold her off, for Christ's sake," and to the men on the tackle: " Heave away all you know—get him clear." It was, of course, too late, and I was glad it was dark: I didn't want to catch anyone's eye just then.

But the moment could be wiped out in action.

" Coxs'n ! "

" Yes, sir ? "

" How many hands up there ? "

" Cleared lower deck, sir."

" Very good. . . . Pass the falls." And to the hands with me in the boat: " Hook on ! "

" Hook on, sir."

" Haul taut singly ! . . . Hoist away ! "

That was that : the best we could do.

We once had a Negro survivor who would not strip, or let himself be warmed, or drink anything : all he wanted to do—all he *would* do—was to curl up in a ball with his head between his legs, and be left to himself. We covered him up with a blanket (which he immediately drew over his head) and let him lie. Said the coxs'n, looking down at him : " It's his religion, sir "—which for some reason seemed a completely fitting explanation.

Another Negro was brought aboard dead : he was well-formed, stark naked, and already stiffening as he was hauled over the side. I put my hand out to feel his heart : the skin I touched was cold, but very smooth and well-muscled. " Waste of time, sir ? " said the sick-berth attendant, giving his voice a slight note of question. " Waste of time," I repeated : " cover him up, and let's get on with the others."

The body, lashed to the rail, made a dark smudge in the port waist all night, stirring when the ship rolled ; now and then a patter of spray touched the sewn-up blanket. The cook, leaving his galley to bring the wardroom breakfast forrard, eyed it, retraced his steps, and came forrard by the starboard alley-way. . . . At ten o'clock, to the survivors' captain, three lascar seamen, and a small muster of hands, I read the burial service ; and then at a signal to the bridge the telegraph rang, the engines paused for a moment, and the neat weighted package went over the side.

Survivors in the mess-decks, filling every available space : asleep on the deck, on benches, against bulkheads : sitting at tables with their heads between their hands, talking, shivering, wolfing food, staring at nothing. Some of them half-naked, wrapped in blankets

and makeshift shoes: some with pathetic little card-
board suit-cases, hugged close: puzzled black faces,
pinched yellow ones, tired bleary white masks that
still muster a grin. Men half-dead, men cocky as be-
damned: men suffering from exposure, frost-bite, oil-
fuel poisoning, cuts, gashes, broken limbs: men hanging
to life by a wet thread. The bravest man I have yet
met was a survivor, a Yorkshire seaman with a broken
thigh and a fearful gash across his face. As I paused
in strapping up his leg, wondering whether he could
stand any more of it, he said: "Go on—I've a bit
saved up yet"; and when I was unskilfully stitching
his wound: "Now then, lad, none of your hem-stitching
—I'm not as particular as all that." I can't remember
any men who were *not* brave and patient in suffering,
but he holds the record, so far.

Going forrard to attend to casualties was sometimes
like stepping into a nightmare; but it was lit here and
there by glimpses of the sheer nobility of man, such as
could only beget confidence and pride.

Survivors in the wardroom, eating us out of house
and home: their bare feet on the carpet, their odd
scraps of uniform, their wet life-jackets which they do
not discard—all these are stock properties in our theatre
of war. They have a habit of dozing off in awkward
attitudes, but they look up, and smile, when one of
us comes off watch and puts his head inside the room.
Often they yarn to us about their previous escapes, or
produce photographs of their homes and families and
hand them round: once, rather sadly, a Belgian captain
talked of Leopold, and what his surrender had meant
to Belgian merchant seamen then at sea. It was this
captain who made us a formal speech of thanks, self-
conscious but manifestly sincere, on the last night of
the trip, when we had drinks all round in the wardroom and they toasted their rescuers.

People seize on odd things when the order " Abandon

ship ! " is given.   One third-officer had left behind his
note-case, containing all his papers and four months'
pay, but had pocketed a large shoe-horn, quite un-
consciously.

When I am ashore, and hear (as I have done) one
man telling another that he can get as much petrol
as he wants, by licensing all four of his cars and only
using one of them : when I see photographs of thousands of cars at a race-meeting for which a special fast
train-service is run : when I read a letter to a newspaper
complaining that the writer has had difficulty in obtaining extra petrol for the grouse-shooting season : when
I hear of *any* instance of more than the bare essential
minimum of petrol being used, this is what I think of.

A torpedoed tanker ablaze at sea, with all its accom-
panying horrors.

That's your extra ten gallons of petrol, sir and madam :
that's last week's little wangle with the garage on the
corner.   You might remember what you're burning,
now and then : its *real* basic coupon is a corpse-strewn
Atlantic.

It cannot be denied that the loss of another corvette
had its effect on our behaviour when next we ran into
trouble : there was certainly a return of that reluctance
to go below which I have mentioned before.   Many
of the crew slept on the upper deck or the gun-platform ;
some of the officers dossed down on the bridge, and
even failed to complain when they were relieved late.
We took home two of her survivors, signalmen, and
bloody thoughtful they looked the whole time.   In
fact it was an odd, faintly unpleasant, and almost affecting reminder of their ordeal and our own hazard, to
come upon them at night, as I did when I came off
watch : usually they would both be standing outside
the wheel-house, sleepless, strained, silent, and (I suppose) remembering.   I once tried to talk to one of

them on my way down, and found it impossible. Staring at the water, he was out of small-talk altogether.

Notes on a Naval survivor, Lieutenant R.

R. was in the wheel-house, with a sub-lieutenant who was drowned. He told me that his ship, turning under half-helm, was hit on the port side, level with the boiler-room : there was a big explosion, the ship gave a tremendous lurch to starboard, right on to her beam-ends, and broke in half ; both ends then started to sink, bows and stern upwards. R. climbed up till he was standing on the engine-room telegraph and when he was already under water, succeeded in opening the wheel-house door which was by that time above his head. He held his breath and shot to the surface.

There was a lot of oil about, but not much wreckage : he found a cordite-case to hang on to, and a seaman with him got astride a mine-sweeping float. They were then picked up by us. Others saved included all the bridge-personnel, a look-out who was in the A.A. bandstand, and another look-out in the crow's-nest, who waited until the mast touched the water and then swam out. A large number of the crew were in the port waist, just over the explosion, and must have been killed by it. Very few were below.

Note.—R., who had swallowed a lot of oil, came aboard suffering from what I thought was oil-fuel poisoning. He was walking about normally (though of course feeling a bit under the weather) for at least twelve hours, but when a doctor from a destroyer came aboard to take over my three worst casualties, R. complained that he was feeling ill and was put to bed. Though he got rid of most of the oil, he became worse : the doctor diagnosed a ruptured kidney or some internal hæmorrhage, and we proceeded home at full speed.

He was in my cabin, and I spent a good deal of time with him : he asked perpetually : "How long before we get in ? Can't we go any faster ? How far is it now?" and it was clear that he was simply fading out in a way very distressing to watch. He was conscious when taken ashore, but died in hospital the same night.

When he had survived so much, and had been actually walking about after his rescue, it was sad to hear that he had died after all.

We cruised slowly round the raft, looking at it through our binoculars. It seemed lifeless, and completely derelict: a tattered piece of cloth stuck up on a pole—the first thing to catch the look-out's attention—was all that stirred in a picture utterly forlorn.

I counted, as best I could, the untidy jumble of forms that lay round the pole in the centre. "Seven, I think, sir. None of them moving."

"We'll go alongside."

When the raft was hooked on I jumped down and began turning them over, though as soon as I had touched the first one's arm I knew that it was hopeless. We were too late by many days and nights. . . . But there was something in their attitudes, not of strain but of longed-for abandon, which seemed to say that these men had not, after a time, fought against death. That was the only thing on the credit side: that whatever tortures they had experienced, they had also experienced release, and been able to realize it.

Another time, unrelieved by any compensations. Half a gale blowing, the sea very rough, and a raft with three survivors clinging to it: we got a line across and took two of them off, and then the line snubbed and parted. Coming as close as we could, we threw another which fell right across the raft, but the man made no effort to secure it and it was swept into the sea again. "What's the matter with him?" I asked: "we can't do anything unless he wakes up and takes a hand himself." "He's awake, all right," answered one of the rescued men, "but he can't move. Broken arm and leg. He told us to go first. He's the mate."

We tried to get alongside, but it wasn't possible in that sea ; and swimming was out of the question, though there was no lack of volunteers. In the end we had to leave him. . . . As we drew away, he waved to us : not a summons, but a sort of half salute. Then he lay down again.

Ships don't always sink, no matter how big a fish they have stopped. We once brought home a torpedoed tanker with a hole like Elijah's cave in her side, into which the sea washed like surf into a bay. But she was well-built, and her bulkheads held : they held, in fact, for four hundred miles at three knots. On such a journey as this, you learn what patience is, and nervousness too.

It is rumoured that German submarines keep one of their torpedo-tubes packed with assorted " wreckage " —clothing, woodwork, etc.—and when attacked discharge this in the hope of foiling the pursuit. But unless they keep a Jew or a Pole there as well, ready for discharge at the same time, I reckon our sister corvette sank that submarine. The " human remains," collected and brought home in their refrigerator, were pronounced authentic.

CHAPTER VI

ONE TO THEM

SHORT Account of a Seven-Day Party.

First Day. A couple of long-range reconnaissance planes showed up about midday, but as usual they would not come within range : instead they flew round and round the convoy making sure of our course and speed, and left us about four—having no doubt prepared a reliable and detailed report, and having incidentally kept us at action-stations the whole afternoon. Some of the destroyers tried shots at them now and then, but it was hardly serious shooting. There was an alarm that night, probably a false one : I don't think the U-boats had picked us up previously, and it takes a little time to collect the pack after it has been put on the scent.

Second Day. Aircraft came over fairly early, high-level bombers : they kept us on our toes, but didn't get nearer than a near miss. Nor did we. There was also a couple of Focke-Wulfs playing round most of the day : routine shadowing, well out of range, but damned annoying all the time. There are thought to be " 4 or 5 " U-boats in the vicinity. Weather rather too good to be pleasant.

Third Day. Bombed by two Junkers 88's (?—too high to be certain) in the morning : they got rather close to one errant straggler who, having resisted all previous pleading, then and there caught up and resumed his station. A U-boat attack developed at night, and some ships were sunk : we were closed up at action-stations from ten o'clock till six-thirty in the morning, counter-attacking one contact without visible result but managing to collect some survivors. Not known how many submarines were involved : must have been two at least, judging by the conflicting reports of torpedo-tracks sighted.

Fourth Day. Unable to relax after the eventful night, as aircraft came over again on reconnaissance ; but the good weather was starting to break and by nightfall it was blowing quite hard—the middle watch was, in fact, the thickest and blackest we've ever had. Coming as it did just at the right time, we bore it with a certain fortitude; and when daylight came again without any incident developing, we congratulated ourselves on having shaken the submarines off. Sometimes it happens like that.

Fifth Day. Those congratulations were too soon. We heard aircraft overhead, above cloud-level, during the morning, and in the afternoon watch the weather cleared and they picked us up once more. One had a feeling of impotent rage against spotting aircraft which can with so little trouble put the submarines on the scent again. The convoy has fooled them, by good luck or bad weather, so that they're hunting far off the course and hourly getting farther; and then along comes a reconnaissance plane and brings them back again in half a day.

Nothing developed that night, but it was certain that they would be back before long.

Sixth Day. Bombing during the morning, shadowing most of the day; during the afternoon a couple of really grand destroyers joined the escort-group, settling down astern like Rolls-Royces ticking over. We had an idea that we would be needing them.

A quiet night, notwithstanding; one or two scares, but maybe we gave a few back.

Seventh Day. Routine shadowing most of the day, keeping us on the alert all the time; but the real climax came, as usual, at night.

It started fairly early, too: the first attack came at ten o'clock. We heard two explosions, and rockets went up: after carrying out the sweep ordered by the Senior Officer we saw lights on the water and altered course towards them.

Soon we came upon the usual muck drifting about —oil, dust, pieces of wood, corpses, clothing: then we heard voices shouting out of the darkness, and saw a cluster of men swimming : they were singing " Roll out the barrel " in chorus. We laughed when we heard that, and a rating in the waist called out : " Good lads ! We're coming ! " and the men in the water shouted back : " Three cheers for the Navy ! " I think most of us aft thought it should be " Three cheers for the Merchant Navy." We lowered a boat and collected all we could find : some of them, wounded and swimming in oil up to three hours, were already survivors from another ship, torpedoed four days before and rescued by the ship which had now itself gone down. One of them, clinging to a life-buoy, had been calling out : " Hurry up ! I can't hold on much longer," as we approached, and then, over and over again in a gasping voice : " Christ, I'm done ! Christ, I'm done ! " When he saw us drawing away again, not knowing that we had lowered a boat, he started screaming : " Don't go away ! You bloody cowards, don't go away ! "

We collected about thirty all told, picked up our boat again, and set a course for the convoy. I was working for nearly two hours in the mess-decks, attending to casualties (two internal, two badly gashed in the head, five minor cuts, and some needing treatment for shock) : half-way through, H. came forward and gave me a glass of whisky, which I needed. At about two o'clock, when I was on the bridge again standing my watch, two more ships were hit : from one of them flames shot into the air, and soon she was ablaze from end to end. Once more we went through the evolutions ordered, and once more dropped back to see if we could help the rescue ships.

The burning oil on the water now covered about a square half-mile, an immense wall of flame topped by a huge smoke-pall drifting away to leeward, which lit the sea for miles around. We closed this, looking for survivors which the others might have missed. If you want to know what tension is, or wish to gauge a captain's responsibility at such a moment, try stopping engines when silhouetted against solid flame, with an unknown number of submarines prowling round. We could see other corvettes, intent on the same job as ourselves, crossing and recrossing, black against red and yellow, and we could not help thinking : "That's the sort of target *we're* making. . . ." But we finished it at last, and quitted the effective back-cloth and started off again ; and then ahead of us we saw another explosion and flames going up in the air, and then sudden darkness. Someone said, aptly but unnecessarily : "That was a quick one," and almost immediately we got a signal to say that it had been one of the escorts, torpedoed and sunk.

I can recall the sense of shock which that signal brought to the bridge. Of course other ships had been sunk, but this was an escort vessel, one of our group, manned by fellow-sailors doing the same job as us and supposedly strong enough to be immune. . . . The blended feeling of rage and depression lasted till dawn —dawn, when another ship, a straggler far away from any effective cover, was shelled by a U-boat and had to be abandoned.

This was the last casualty, and it rounded off, with originality, an eventful night and (as it turned out) an eventful seven days.

I think we were all a little mad by the time we got in. We'd been at action-stations for virtually a week on end, missing hours of sleep, eating on the bridge or the upper deck, standing-to in the cold and wet and darkness. We'd had the aircraft plaguing us continually and the U-boats hunting, striking, losing, hunting, and striking again : we'd watched ships—too many ships— go down, and heard of our friends being killed and seen men drowning and had to leave them to it : we'd grown sick of destruction, light-headed with tiredness and strain. And above all we'd felt ineffective ; even though we knew that other escorts had struck back with notable effect there'd probably been nine submarines round us, and you can't do miracles—they had simply played hide-and-seek with the convoy, and a ripe game it was. . . . By the end, we'd had enough of it ; though if it had gone on I suppose we would have done the same.

In fact, I *know* we would. That's the main thing about a convoy : it doesn't retreat, or re-form on a new line or execute a strategic withdrawal to previously prepared positions. It sails on : having no choice and, in the last analysis, wishing none.

CHAPTER VII

ONE TO US

UNEXPECTEDLY, the U-boat surfaced about two miles ahead of us.

I don't know why she came up : perhaps we had kept her down too long, or she thought she'd try her luck at a shooting-match, or she may even not have heard us ; but we didn't waste time with speculations just then. Our first shot fell short, our second was dead in line but over, and our third ploughed the water just where she had crash-dived again. We dropped a pattern of depth-charges for luck on her estimated diving-position and then began a proper sweep.

We picked her up almost immediately, and ran in again and dropped another pattern ; this brought up some oil. Out on a wide turn and in again ; once more the charges went over the side, and once more, after a pause, there came that series of splitting crashes from below which told us they had well and truly earned their keep. Another run, and another still ; the afterpart was a scene of vast activity—firing, reloading, priming, setting : then the awaited signal from the bridge, and down went the charges and presently the surface of the sea jumped and boiled, and the Torpedoman rubbed his hands and called out happily : " Next for shaving ! "

More oil, and big air bubbles : we had the measure of him now. . . . I spoke on the bridge voice-pipe to H., who said we were doing well and ordered another rather special pattern. " I'm not sure I can manage that," I told him : " I'll have to give you the nearest size to it." Momentarily the Chief popped his head out of the engine-room companionway. " Isn't he sunk yet, sir ? " he asked. " We're getting properly shaken up down here." One more run, one more series of thunderous cracks—and then the sea, spouting and boiling, threw up what we were waiting for : oil in a spreading stain, bits of wreckage, woodwork, clothing, scraps of humanity. . . . Contact failed after that, and though we waited till dusk, nothing else worth collecting made its appearance. We had enough, in any case.

It was a dog's death, but how triumphant we felt— a triumph clinched, later that night, by a signal of congratulation from the Commander-in-Chief. And in the morning came another moment—perhaps the real moment—of the sweetness of success. We found the convoy, from which we had been detached nearly twenty-four hours before ; and as soon as we were in sight the Senior Officer signalled : " Well met and well done. Steam down the centre of the convoy : they want to give you a big hand." And so it was. When we came level with the head of the convoy the Commodore hoisted " Congratulations." It was repeated by every ship, and as we steamed down the ranks each ship waved and cheered. It made up for much of the preceding winter. . . . The last ship of all, a puzzled Greek, still had his answering pendant at the dip[1] as we passed—" Bunting-tosser's asleep," said our own signalman, outraged by the occurrence ; but we took the will for the deed. Even congratulations at the dip contributed to the sum total.

---

[1] Signifying " Signal-flags seen but not yet understood."

We'd worked a long time for that signal : steamed thousands of miles, been bored for days and weeks on end, spent scores of nights at the alert in wet and freezing darkness, sent and received thousands of signals. Over three hundred middle watches had gone to it, weeks of eye-strain, filthy weather in plenty, and God knows now many blasts from Senior Officer, from Captain (D), from Flag Officer-in-Charge, from the heart of Whitehall. . . . Only one more submarine, when it came to notching the stick ; but it settled a longer score than that, for us.

Another corvette in the same group had some U-boat prisoners aboard, whom she used to exercise every day on the upper deck. H. and I examined them one morning through our binoculars as we passed close by. They looked a scruffy lot, and most of them did not move about at all but stood in the waist, staring out at the convoy which was an exceptionally large one. Many of them, we could see, were frowning.

" Surly bastards ! " grumbled H. to me, as we watched them. " They're damned lucky to be alive."

" No, they don't look surly to me," I answered him. I indicated the convoy, forging ahead to England, as compact and as strong as ever. " I think they're surprised. In fact, probably they can hardly believe their eyes."

EAST COAST CORVETTE

FOREWORD

THIS is my second book on corvettes : as things are,
it is unlikely to be the last ; indeed, in my mind's eye
I can already visualize *Twenty Years in Corvettes* bursting
upon an exhausted public somewhere around 1960.
Once more it is only a collection of notes, set down at
odd moments ; there had been no time for anything
more elaborate, and no real inclination either. Making
notes on a ship and a crew at work is, in a way, part of
the job of sailoring : making a " story " out of them
is an entirely different one.

Time, as I say, has been severely rationed : truth is
not only stranger but shorter than fiction ; I have
therefore stuck to truth's bare outlines, sacrificing a
spy-plot and a love interest to the more fashionable
austerity. Readers who hanker after the Romance
of the Sea, in any form, must read between the lines.

N. M.

CHAPTER I

CHANGING OVER

THE expected signal was waiting for me when we got in, after another fourteen days' flurry in the North Atlantic ; and something in the Leading Signalman's eye as he handed it to me made me ask :

" What's the big news ? "

" Your draft-chit, sir."

I read it with extreme satisfaction ; it was far better than I had hoped for. " Lieutenant Monsarrat appointed to H.M.S. *Dipper* as First Lieutenant on relief joining."

" You're lucky," said M. when I passed it over to him " They're damned good ships—like small destroyers : twin-screw, all the refinements. Of course, they don't stay afloat for very long."

" Why not ? "

" They're on the East Coast—at least, some of them are—and you know what that means : Hitler's front doorstep. A bomb every five seconds. E-boats for tea, mines in your soup. Have a big gin."

" It'll be a change from this side."

" It certainly will. Like hail after rain."

But I refused to be daunted. It was a change that I wanted, above all things : a corvette in the Western Approaches is fine for a year, a trial for eighteen months, and a matter of staying-power thereafter ; I wouldn't mind coming back to it in the end, but at the moment I wanted something different from the interminable fourteen-day runs, the foul weather, the startling crudity of the past two years. It wasn't that I felt I'd earned it—you don't *earn* anything in war-time except the privilege of a tougher assignment ; it was just that I was ready to welcome the second course of a meal which had so far been all wind and gristle, piled rather high on the plate.

And, as readers of earlier pages may guess, I wanted the job of First Lieutenant. Two years as dogs-body, seeing only the blunt end of the ship, the second choice of leave, the drum-sticks of the chicken, give you a healthy ambition for higher things.

Leaving a ship is usually sad, no matter how good a job you are going to, and this one was no exception.

I had served nearly two years in her, joining ten days before she commissioned, up in the Clyde : her crew had been virtually unchanged throughout that time : together we had endured the Atlantic at its worst, the malice of the enemy, the few triumphs that had been our share of the Atlantic battle. There were men on board whom I would trust with my life, no matter how critical or violent the circumstances : the wardroom had a history of good parties, fierce poker sessions, talk that had often spanned an entire middle watch in harbour. The ship had been my home throughout a memorable slice of my life : she had taught me nearly all I knew of the Navy ; she and her crew were a happy and success-ful entity of which I had long been part. To leave her now, even for a job I had been looking forward to so much, was hard.

But certainly there was a lot to do before I was clear : books to be handed back, loan-clothing to be turned in, stores to be accounted for or smoothly explained away, correspondence to be gone into with my relief. He was (as is always the case) a cautious man, a man much slower to sign for things than I had been myself (I fully expect to receive, after the war, a huge bill for paint, soap, and soda consumed by the upper-deck depart-ment) : he wanted to see everything, to feel it over carefully for snags or flaws, and only then—slowly and reluctantly—could he be brought to admit its actual existence and sign for it on the dotted line. The trouble I had, for example, in persuading him that the wardroom sugar-bowl was a Bowl, Sugar, Pattern 615E, and not (as he maintained) a Basin, Slop, Pattern 921, was really past belief.

There was also the difficulty of getting the other officers to sign the audit of the Contingency Fund, which was another thing I had to get rid of. I had expected a certain caution in this respect, and I was ready to meet all reasonable queries; but it did not seem to me that the lengthy rearguard action they fought over it was a suitable tribute to our two years as messmates.

If I had not been confronted by the stuff itself, I would never have believed it possible that so much assorted junk could have been collected in one small cabin, and remained unnoticed until the time came to pack. It seemed as if I had never thrown a single thing away during the whole time I had been on board. I had originally joined the ship with two suitcases: I left it with four of them, plus a naval kitbag, a wooden chest, and my seaboots done up in brown paper. The total freight, assembled on deck by an awed quartermaster, excited suspicions which were freely voiced by everyone from the Captain downwards.

The Petty Officers gathered in the wardroom: the beer was sent round: the Coxswain cleared his throat and began: " I'd just like to say, sir . . ."

Farewell speeches look silly on paper, but they are moving under such circumstances as these. All the men round me had shared the excitement and the boredom and the testing-times of the past two years: they had proved themselves loyal, dependable in crisis, good to be alongside when things were happening. Now I was moving on, breaking up a pattern on which I had come to rely: my new ship might be of the same quality—it was odds that she *would* be—but I was leaving behind me a known company of friends, a guaranteed circle, and the fine feel of comradeship in action.

That was why, when the Coxswain, holding his glass of beer like a hymn-book in church, cleared his throat and began a hesitating and audibly-prompted speech, it was a moment of feeling and tension. But presently, the formalities done with, we were able to relax: the beer went round again as quick as a lasso, and there were jokes—about bad weather and rolling, about our U-boat, about the book I was supposed to be writing on corvettes. ("I hope you'll keep me out of it, sir," said one Stoker Petty Officer: "My old woman thinks this is a Boom Defence Vessel.") There was speculation as to what it would be like on the East Coast—speculation not wholly concerned with raising my spirits. Above all, there was, for me, a feeling that this was a good send-off, the right sort of ending to my stay in the ship: an ending clinched, a little later on, by a return visit to the Petty Officers' Mess, where their traditional generosity with farewell tots of rum went far towards wafting me over the gangway and along the dock-side in a state of unconcerned bliss.

The dock, when I left it, was full of destroyers and corvettes of our own and other escort-groups: some just in from sea, with upper decks still wet and the hands still in duffle-coats, others standing by ready to go out on the tide. Their masts and signal halyards made a patterned forest against the sky: there were ships with strong reputations, ships with odd or spectacular characters on board, ships with individual foibles which we had learned to respect. It was curious to think that a large part of the Battle of the Atlantic was fought from this small corner: that if you wiped out this dock and what it had done since the war started, the answer might be a starving Britain.

There is no boasting or self-satisfaction in that last sentence—one single corvette is less than a cog in the works. But she isn't a spanner in them either, and in saying farewell to that dock and all it stood for, one could draw pride and pleasure from having been a working part of it during the burden and heat of the day. It was going to be something to tell one's grandchildren about, if one could catch them in a listening mood.

A slow (and even stately) departure was offset by a quick-fire arrival. When I got to my new base, and reported, I was met by a positive whirlwind of information and instruction which swept me out into the roadway again almost before I had time to salute.

"Your ship's lying out in the stream," I was told, "and she's sailing in about ten minutes' time. You'll just make it if you start now. You'll probably have to leave your gear ashore, unless it's all ready for collection. Better get moving straight away : I'll have a signal sent for a boat, if they haven't hoisted it already. Down the road, first right, and then ask for the pontoon. Her pendant-numbers are ——, in case you have to scrounge a lift from someone else. Good-bye and good luck."

I had travelled all night, and I climbed aboard, with a couple of minutes to spare, feeling like the tail-end of a hurricane. Said the retiring First Lieutenant, who met me on the quarter-deck :

"We were betting on whether you'd make it before we sailed. That's about the only sort of excitement we get on this coast, these days."

CHAPTER 11

THE SHIP AND THE JOB

EXTRACT from the Captain's Standing Orders :

"The First Lieutenant is the Executive Officer, responsible to me for the cleanliness and efficiency of the ship, and the discipline and welfare of the ship's company.

"He is to maintain the ship's armament in an efficient working condition, paying particular regard to the instant readiness of the anti-aircraft armament both at sea and in harbour.

"Authority to award punishment is delegated to him

under the appropriate article of King's Regulations and Admiralty Instructions.

"In addition to his duties as First Lieutenant, he is Divisional Officer for seamen, responsible for their training : Anti-Submarine Control Officer : Sports Officer : President of the Canteen Committee : President of the Wardroom Mess.

"He should always remember that he may be required to assume command of the ship at a moment's notice, and should therefore acquaint himself as far as possible with the problems involved."

It looked like being a full day. . . . But what a grand ship she was, to have the run of. Listed in *Jane's* as a "patrol vessel" reclassified since the outbreak of war as a corvette, she was really, in looks and performance, a small destroyer, with all sorts of additions and refinements that put my last ship right back into the trawler class, by comparison. She had been built in the spacious days of peace-time, when things like aluminium and well-picked wood and non-austerity furniture were still available : she had twin-screws, big mess-decks, a ward-room on the upper deck, and a bridge far better designed than *Flower's* cramped cat-walk. She was elegant, she was fast. In personnel, too, she was much better off, with a Warrant Gunner and Warrant Engineer, and Chief Petty Officers in all departments instead of Petty Officers : together they made up a strong team of experts never likely to be caught off the top line. . . . Finally she had an R.N. captain, later to command a Fleet destroyer and exhibiting already the humanity and the absolute competence appropriate to that job.

The Naval Base from which we operated was small and self-contained, a sort of feudal village, graded in rank and consequence, where everyone knew everyone else ; and, like other villages, it had its odd characters, its oldest inhabitants, its scandal-mongers, and its essential unity and comradeship. There were people who had been stationed there since the war started, who had

WE ARE THE SMALLEST SHIPS

[*Page* 38

" . . . IF QUITE UNSUITABLE THERETO "

[Page 52

grown old and mellow in such jobs as the stamping of
passes and the prevention of waste; a walk along the
quay might bring you greetings from a dozen such old
stagers, always robustly cheerful, always glad to see a
new face or recognize an old one. It gave the changing
struggle at sea a homely background, a matey nucleus
round which the rough war revolved.

But it led, sometimes, to an outlook which might with
justice be described as restricted. I well remember once
visiting an officer, of the worthiest character but not
renowned for his energy of application, and finding his
whole office in a turmoil. Reference books littered the
desk, papers were scattered on the floor, a filing-cabinet,
half-rifled was in drunken disorder.

" Good heavens ! " I said, startled. " You're pretty
busy this morning."

" Busy ? " He exploded, banging his fist on an open
volume in front of him. " Busy ? I'm *furious !* By
God, I'll have the skin off their backs for this ! "

" What's gone wrong ? "

" Everything ! It's criminal ! They've spelt my name
wrong in the new Debrett ! "

On another occasion, when I was talking to one of
the secretaries whose department had recently changed
its senior officer :

" It doesn't make much difference to you, does it ? "
I asked. " I mean, won't he just carry on where the
other one left off ? "

He shook his head with great emphasis. " Oh, no !
Nothing like that at all. In fact, there've been some
big changes already." He pointed. " That desk-lamp
is new. *And both those book-cases.*"

But these were odd backwaters and eccentricities, by
no means the general rule. The place was justly renowned as being one of the best Naval Bases in Great
Britain; it had about it, both ashore and afloat, an air
of unruffled solidity and comradeship which is the only
sure foundation for successful sea warfare.

D

Back to the ship again, now the absorbing centre of my interest.

She had been on this section of the coast from the very beginning, escorting those coastal convoys which, every day of every week since September, 1939, have carried the life-blood of Britain to and from its heart : two and a half years, that was, of up-and-down and down-and-up, with an occasional patrol or a bit of mine-laying as a picnic treat. It had been, and still was, a lively assignment : this was the quick-trigger corner of the war, where things happened without warning—there were enemy air-bases within a long biscuit-toss, there were nests of E-boats lying in wait, there were sneak mine-layers who could set a deadly snare under cover of darkness, and then slide back un-observed. Danger seemed to go in cycles—a quick flare-up of activity, a period of calm, another stroke of luck or skill which sent ships on either side to the bottom, an armed truce again. . . . It was very different from what I had been used to, in the past : the Atlantic had been a matter of long drudgery and sustained tension, this was a lively three-round affair with the chance of a surprise knock-out any and every minute.

Of course (as was speedily pointed out to me when I mentioned an odd scrap or two in the Western Ap-proaches, adding a pinch of salt and thirty-per-cent. colouring matter to everything), things weren't what they *had* been on this coast, not by a long chalk. . . . That seemed to be the current watchword, at the time I joined the ship : things were quiet enough now, but you should have been here a year ago.

" Of course, there's absolutely nothing doing *now*," remarked the Captain one evening, when we had been talking of the after-Dunkirk days, and the extreme burden laid on the Navy and the Air Force at that time. " Any-thing could happen *then*, from hell to breakfast, but now. . . ." He waved his hand negligently. " A few E-boats. Aircraft now and then—torpedo-bombers :

they seem to have given up dive-bombing. Mines, occasionally. Things like that."

" Otherwise nothing ? "

" Damn all. But they have a Wrens' dance every fortnight or so, if you're looking for action."

I found I had enough to do, however, without seeking action in any quarter.

The First Lieutenant, as the saying goes, is married to the ship ; and it is not a marriage which can be left to take care of itself or which flourishes on neglect. First, the ship has to be kept clean. *Dipper* was, when I took her over, by far the cleanest ship in the flotilla, and my ambition to keep her like that meant a constant struggle with a variety of enemies. Lying out in the stream at a buoy gave plenty of opportunity for painting the ship's side : it also gave plenty of opportunity to liberty- and provision-boats which, ringed round with oil-stained motor-tyres (long overdue for the salvage dump) and the filthiest fenders imaginable, seldom left one in doubt that they had been alongside and had taken a clinging departure. One such chance visitor, expertly handled, could undo a whole morning's work with the greatest ease in a couple of minutes.

Another, minor, hostile element was the quayside dogs and cats which, unless watched, would multiply aboard as permanent residents. They had to be kept severely rationed ; and luckily I was backed up in this by the Chief Bosun's Mate, who had (or professed to have) his own sinister method of dealing with the menace.

Once, when I saw him eyeing a small rat-like mongrel that had crept aboard and was being given half a seaman's dinner (by a generous stoker) :

" Will you make arrangements to get rid of that one ? " I said. " You can hardly classify it as a dog, and we've got our full quota already."

" If we can take it to sea to-night we'll be all right, sir," he answered. Then, lowering his voice, he added, " Those little ones sink lovely."

My insistence on cleanliness of paintwork also brought me into occasional conflict with the Gunner, whose ambition was to have everything in his department " working "—i.e. covered by a generous film of grease and oil. This latter state naturally included the ratings in the Gunner's Party, men only too inclined to make their mark in every compartment they visited. Here, too, the age-old argument—whether you can legitimately take hands off cleaning guns and set them to stowing potatoes in the vegetable locker—was waged unceasingly. But it was, of course, a matter of adjustment, and we gradually worked out an effective compromise.

In any case the ship had to be efficient as well as clean : things had to work as well as to shine, guns had to impress both the ear and the eye. I don't think I was ever really caught out over this, though there was one occasion when the ship's bell, never ordinarily used but polished and repolished as a brilliant ornament for the quarter-deck, was found to be minus its clapper five seconds before a church service attended by a very senior (and fairly devout) officer. It was run to earth just in time, and a glad peal announced the fact ; but the search for it was a splendid illustration of the phrase : " No stone was left unturned."

Coming up harbour and securing to a buoy is a good example of a First Lieutenant's routine which must go like clockwork if it is to be effective : it entails some preparation beforehand, attention to detail, and, at the end, a busy quarter of an hour during which a lot of ground is covered.

By the time the ship passes the harbour entrance the bridle by which she will be secured must be shackled on and made ready, together with the various wires and heaving-lines : the hands must be piped into their No. 3 rig if the weather allows, the duty boats' crews warned, the postman rounded up and held in readiness for his " pony-express " dash ashore. The hands are then piped to " Stations for entering Harbour," and the Coxswain

takes the wheel; and then the whaler and the motor-
boat are both manned and turned out, the Gunner
supervising, while I have a quick look round the anchorage to see which ships are in harbour—they all have
to be piped as we pass them or (if they are junior)
answered when they pipe us.

In the whaler is the postman, and any hands who may
be required to land in a hurry—ratings taking examina-
tions ashore, for instance; and in the motor-boat is the
buoy-jumper, the athletic hand who, wearing a life-jacket
and his third-best suit, balances on the buoy and waits to
hook on the picking-up rope when we come up to him.

All this time we are passing destroyers at their moorings, and I am moving from side to side of the bridge
seeing that they are correctly piped. Then, at a certain
point on our way up harbour, I sing out " Lower to the
water-line ! " and both boats go down evenly till their
keels are about a foot above the water: this state of suspended animation lasts till we are about a hundred yards
from our buoy. Thereafter we produce a final flourish
of pipes for the Senior Officer's ship, and then, right
opposite him so that he can see the full beauty of the
manœuvre, I give the order " Slip ! " and both boats hit
the water an almighty smack as they are freed. The
whaler curves away towards the shore, the motor-boat
heads for our mooring-buoy, the First Lieutenant gives
a deep sigh of relief and goes down on to the fo'c'sle.

There, all is ready for the last part of the exercise;
and by now, ahead of us, the buoy-jumper is waiting,
doing his usual acrobatics as the buoy spins round.
We come up very slowly, stemming the tide a foot at
a time, while I signal the direction and distance off to
the bridge: a heaving-line is thrown, the buoy-jumper
catches it and hauls down the picking-up rope, and makes
the clip-hook fast to the ring on the buoy. I sing out:
" Hooked on, sir ! " and we heave away on the windlass till the bows of the ship overhang the buoy itself;
and then the bridle is lowered—a length of cable with

a mooring shackle at the end—and is in turn secured to the ring. "Shackle on, sir!" tells the bridge that their troubles are over, and there we are—we can with safety ring off engines, rig the ladder, and lay aft for the first cup of tea of the day, and the mail from home.

In good weather, of course, it's as easy as it sounds—it can all be done in slow time, and the Captain can lay the ship with its nose dead on the buoy, like a well-trained dog bringing back a rabbit; but if there's a sea to flick the buoy about, and a cross-wind to take the ship's head off, it becomes a ticklish operation. Buoy-jumpers, by standing orders, always wear life-jackets, and they often need them—I have seen a destroyer, in a high wind, drift sideways right *over* the buoy, with the buoy-jumper going down slowly like a scuttled ship and then coming up the other side, as good as new but not nearly as enthusiastic.

As the quartermaster who was watching with me said, that sort of thing isn't what you volunteer for.

When I took over, the ship had a ready-made routine which she had been following for two and a half years: a very different matter from commissioning a ship as First Lieutenant and inventing the whole thing yourself, from scratch. It simplified my work enormously, though of course it still left day-to-day jobs and problems which had to be adequately dealt with. She was strictly run, and consequently happy; and my task of applying and main-taining discipline on board—of "tempering harshness with severity", as the Captain put it one day—did not call for the constant nagging that is sometimes necessary.

Of course there were defaulters—leave-breakers, losers of property by negligence, ratings who (in the Coxswain's magic phrase) "tried to poke bravado at their superiors"; but they were never a daily routine, and only on very rare occasions did the full force of the First Lieutenant's Gestapo have to function.

Notwithstanding what I believe was a widespread

view to the contrary on board, I was not disappointed by this lack of opportunity.

Apart from special emergencies and exercises, a typical morning's work in harbour might be stretched to cover the following :

Seeing hands fall in at 07.45, and detailing work for the day ;

Scouring the upper decks for odd corners that may need a washdown or a lick of paint ;

Arranging a football match, and picking the team ;

Inventing (with the help of the Chief Bosun's Mate) a new kind of life-saving line, and having a couple of experimental ones made up ;

Entertaining the guests who creep aboard with various excuses, and remain there without any ;

Seeing requestmen and defaulters ;

Presiding at a meeting of the Canteen Committee ;

Demonstrating a new fire-fighting appliance to all hands, with real flames and no expense spared ;

Inspecting a side of beef which the ship's butcher maintains has got " right outside my jurisprudence, sir ";

Making out and signing various demands for stores, lost-by-accident forms, travel warrants, monthly and quarterly returns, watch and duty bills, clothing lists, and other oddments ;

Nipping ashore to the Pay Office to battle for somebody's rights ;

Having a conference with the Engineer on our forthcoming defect list ;

Duplicate all this during the afternoon, add the piping of passing ships, the arranging of boats for working parties and officers, a couple of air-raid warnings, and a possible shift of berth just when painting-stages have been rigged all round the ship's side, and it may explain the confidence with which First Lieutenants maintain that their allowance of one and sixpence a day is well earned.

Now and again, to wake us up, we have General Drill

—the Captain's delight, the First Lieutenant's nightmare : it consists of a morning given over to exercising any and every department of the ship, simultaneously or in series, to the accompaniment of any kind of diversion or crisis the Captain can devise.

It starts with the Captain coming out on to the quarterdeck rather too soon after breakfast, drawing on his gloves, and saying with a strange relish :

" All right, Number One, let's make a start with something straightforward. Port Watch of seamen lower both anchors to the water-line, and heave them in by hand : rig the sounding boom at the same time and take a sounding. Starboard Watch of seamen rig a dan-buoy ready for dropping, and get out hawsers ready to tow aft. Stokers shore up the lower mess-deck; pull the main fuse there, and have the Torpedo Party fix up emergency lighting. Signalmen dismantle the main aerial and rig a temporary one—one that works, too. First Aid Party remove injured man from the bridge by stretcher, and get him below. Now let me see. . . . Ah, yes——" as an afterthought, " Pipe 'Fire in the steering-compartment ! ' using smoke-helmets, have the stokers' gun's-crew man the gun and clear it away for action, send away the motor-boat to pick up survivors, and give the emergency gas-alarm in five minutes' time. Right—get going. Midshipman ! "

" Sir ? "

" Get a note-book and a stop-watch. We'll time all this, and see what the record is."

That is, perhaps, enough about the actual job : enough to indicate its scope and variety, and above all its interest. But it leaves out the most vital part of all. Though there was no moment of the day that did not bring its problem, there was, equally, no moment, from the very beginning, when I was not immensely proud of having been given the appointment. The ship buttressed that pride : to be her First Lieutenant was to have won a worthy accolade : and reporting the ship's company present and correct to the Captain at Sunday Divisions, I felt once again the sense of power and the access of confidence which had been mine when I stood my first watch alone at sea, back in my old ship.

There was humility in this sense of power; but there was all the pride in the world, too.

We could hardly have had a better wardroom—in its comradeship and joint enthusiasm, and also in its variety.

First the Captain—R.N., almost the naval officer of fiction : correct, resourceful, unfoolable, his handling of the ship a perpetual delight to watch. It was my first close-up of the Royal Navy at work, and I sometimes felt as if I were back at the kindergarten stage, assimilating knowledge in open-mouthed admiration.

Then myself—R.N.V.R., of course. "I like a few amateurs about the place," said the Captain once. "It reminds you that there is an outside world, after all. . . ." As long as that was all it reminded him of, I felt I could be satisfied.

The Pilot was R.N.R.—a professional seaman with the customary formidable skill in navigation. He had a sixth sense as to the ship's whereabouts, at any hour of the day or night, which I for one found most comforting : it seemed as if he only had to come up on deck, look round once, sniff the air, and then point to a dot on the chart, for everything to fall into line.

Back to the R.N. again with the Warrant Engineer —a typical " Chief," right on top of his job, full of technicalities and gadgets. He once, with the aid of a thermometer and a saucer of water, conducted what he called a " cosiness test " in the wardroom. The fire was banked up : all doors and ports were shut fast : after twenty minutes, he reported, ninety per cent cosiness was achieved. . . . No one present was inclined to quarrel with the report.

And lastly the Gunner—another " regular," and our oldest inhabitant. He could hardly have known more

about his complicated job, or been keener on passing
on what he knew ; he had been all through the last
war and was as much-travelled as most naval officers of
his length of service—India, China, the Mediterranean,
the Near East. He was very good company : full of
stories, and small oddments which he volunteered on
the spur of the moment. (" Do you know how to
time the five-second interval for a twenty-one gun Royal
Salute ? " he would ask suddenly. " You walk backwards and forwards across the foc'sle, saying to yourself : ' If I wasn't a Gunner I wouldn't be here—Fire
ONE : If I wasn't a Gunner I wouldn't be here—
Fire TWO : If I wasn't a Gunner . . .'.")

That was the total, for the greater part of my time
in the ship : though later on we had an eighteen-year-
old Midshipman to complete the pack, to do all the
odd jobs, and (personally) to remind me that I was
once young and sprightly, and the terror of the dance-
floor.

As I said at the beginning, we could not have had a
better wardroom. It kept us all perpetually enlivened,
and was the strongest possible background for what
proved an exacting job.

CHAPTER III

WORKING

GOING to sea really starts with this entry in my Night
Orders of the previous night :

" Ship is under sailing orders from 09.00.
    All ratings proceeding ashore to be reported to me.
    Mail will close on board at 10.30
    11.00. Secure for sea.
    11.45 (approx.). Slip."

The entry sets in train a whole routine, well-tried and absolutely foolproof, which will send us down river with no ends, human or otherwise, hanging out.

It means testing the steering-geer, the engine-room telegraphs, the revolution-counter, and all the electrical circuits controlled from the bridge. It means trying out all the noises we can make—sirens, bells, alarm-gongs, buzzers. It means taking off the bridle, and substituting a slip-rope, which releases us from the buoy in a second or two : it means keeping a check on all ratings going ashore, landing and collecting the last mail, closing all scuttles and watertight doors, taking in the ladder and the quarter-boom, stowing loose deck-gear, and finally hoisting the motor-boat.

It means, five minutes before sailing time, piping the hands to their stations, and special sea-duty men to the bridge, and then going up there to find the following assembly awaiting the fall of the flag : the Coxswain at the wheel, two quartermasters manning the telegraphs, four signalmen, a bridge messenger, and the Navigating Officer. It means looking down on the fo'c'sle, and seeing there the fo'c'sle-party, not yet fallen in, clearing up wires and fenders or just waiting about : the Chief Bosun's Mate with a hammer in his hand, ready to knock off the slip ; and the immaculate Midshipman standing in the eyes of the ship, ready for anything and very likely to get it.

The Captain comes up on the bridge, takes a quick look round, judging the tide, the strength of the wind, the position of other ships in the vicinity. We hoist " Request permission to proceed," and when it is answered by the Senior Officer of the flotilla the signal " Obey Telegraphs " goes down to the engine-room. Then comes the final order : " Slip ! " : there is a single hammer-stroke, a pause, and then the answer : " All gone, all clear forrard ! " As we move clear of the buoy I sing out : " Fo'c'sle-party, fall in ! " ; and then I cross over to the wing of the bridge, to take a final look round, to control the piping of other ships, and to make sure that our exit is, in every way, a good one.

Since it is done in the full glare of publicity, surrounded by a ring of hungry destroyers only awaiting the chance to give us a pair of pendants,[1] it *has* to be good.

Properly speaking, my station is on the bridge until we have cleared harbour; but when the hands have been piped to Defence Stations, and we are past the main anchorage, I usually take a walk round the upper deck and then go below to change into sea-going rig.

My new and beautiful suit makes this a pleasure. . . . It is only a glorified pair of overalls—but how glorified: lined with kapok throughout, neatly zip-fastened, water proof, wind-proof, very warm, and guaranteed to keep me and two other men (not obligatory) afloat for half a day in case of necessity. A pair of sheepskin-lined flying-boots rounds it off below, and keeps me firmly anchored to the deck in the strongest wind.

Attached to the suit is a safety-lamp of the plug-in type, also for use in the water; and in the pockets I carry a flask, a ration of chocolate, my identity card, money, cheque-book, keys, Post Office bank book, and Savings' Certificates. . . . All I have to do, if torpedoed, is to swim ashore and buy a cottage.

At one point, which need not be specified, on our outward journey, we pass a lightship. She dips her ensign, of course, as we go by, and we return the salute; but we usually embroider the ceremony on the loud-hailer if we have time. A plain " Good morning " is answered by a wave: comments on the morning's news or the course of the war call forth come philosophic rejoinder; to the remark " Did they lay any mines

---

[1] A ship's pendants, hoisted at the dip, signify: " You have done something wrong and have not yet corrected it."

round here last night?" they once answered: "We'll know in a minute. You're the first ship out."

Seeing her anchored there, month in and month out, prompts the usual speculations as to what the other chap's job is really like. Since war broke out this lightship's crew have seen thousands of ships go past; some of them to engage the enemy and catch the headlines later, others on their way to be sunk. But as this fleeting contact, on our passage out and in, is the only one we have with them, we never know if this idea of the changes and chances of mortal life strikes a bell.

Before taking up our station in the convoy-escort, we usually close up to the leading destroyer and receive written orders from her, using the line-throwing rifle to make the necessary contact.

This is, of course, fundamentally a weapon of peace, but it has its possibilities. The " bullet " which it fires is a metal rod with the line attached to one end of it; and given a calm day and a leading-seaman who knows his job, it is often possible to hit some quite senior officer with the missile. I know of no finer tonic at the start of a convoy than to send a gold-peaked cap spinning down into the drink, secure in the knowledge that it has all been done in the strict course of duty.

When we've got our orders we take up our appointed station on the screen. Sometimes we go about it easily, just drifting into place, sometimes we make an evolution out of it—going astern between the columns, for instance, and then darting out between a couple of close-spaced ships, turning in a flurry of foam, and settling down as if butter wouldn't melt in our turbines. It makes it interesting for us; and (as hoarse voices on megaphones indicate) it makes it interesting for the convoy too.

Most of the ships are old friends: some of them I've seen in earlier days, making the long Atlantic trip, others have been scuttling up and down Hitler's doorstep since war broke out. They are sometimes of peculiar shape and design, drawn right from the bottom of the bag to meet the emergency of war, and they often have pretty odd names; but ever since, on a rough party, we escorted a ship with the really extraordinary name of *Jolly Nights*, I have ceased to be surprised by these. . . . They are mostly heavily laden, and we hope that their cargoes are worth while. " Looks like a benzine tanker," said the Gunner once, of a big ship in company. " But you never know—it's probably two thousand tons of Woolton Pie." But whatever the filling, on this tricky and varied coast they need, and get, the most faithful shepherding during the time they are under our charge.

Over on the other side navigation was naturally all deep-water stuff—sight-taking, waiting for a glimpse of the sun or a favourite star, broad estimates of the course made good, and lashings of arithmetic. Here, close inshore, there is no occasion for using a sextant, and no room for guesswork either : to the ordinary hazards of coastal navigation the war has added its own refinement.

We have at our disposal a narrow swept channel, cared for by the mine-sweepers, provisionally fool-proof : it is marked by buoys at certain intervals, buoys which must be carefully checked as we pass them—if you lose count, and fail to turn a corner, you may find yourself taking soundings with the keel. In rough weather, at night, it is correspondingly difficult to count the flashes correctly ; the buoys bob up and down and are hidden by wave-tops, and if you miss one set of flashes and take " Three-every-ten " for " Three-every-twenty," the mistake may be a crucial one and you may finish up on the putty or (more probably) in a minefield.

Those are the first hazards—the long shoals, the mined aresa, the mines which may have been dropped long ago and lain dormant ever since ; and there are others.

It is a wreck-strewn coast: the green wreck-buoys wink all round you at night, the masts and spars of many ships stick out above the water close to the channel—ships mined or torpedoed or bombed or burnt out, ships driven ashore by stress of weather: all pointing the same moral of carelessness or inaccuracy or bad luck. They have to be carefully avoided; a cross-current will often start to sweep you towards one, and when you try to edge away from it the convoy on your beam bears down on you, leaving you no room to manœuvre, squeezing you between a ship too big to hit and a wreck too shallow to miss. At night, agonized cries go up on the loud-hailer as the green lights loom nearer. . . . I once heard a destroyer on the opposite side of the convoy sing out: " If you don't give me a bit more room, this wreck-buoy is going to refer to me as well." That is what it feels like—an inexorable weight pushing you to disaster, and not giving a damn about the outcome.

Sometimes, if the pressure becomes intolerable, you can slip between two ships and get inside the convoy; but at night this needs very careful judgment, and there isn't always enough room. And if the manœuvre fails, it leaves you with an awful lot of explaining to do.

Thought-provoking remark by deep-sea diver, encountered ashore:

" There's a funny thing about that wreck. It's got a skeleton with its head and shoulders half-way out of one of the port-holes."

The mine-sweepers are always with us, and God bless them for it.

Wherever you go on this coast, there is sure to be one somewhere within view: ranging in size from a tough-looking Fleet sweeper to a glorified drifter trailing a hank of grass rope aft. What a job it must be ! Perhaps someone, after the war, will compute the number of man-hours spent on mine-sweeping : on plugging up and down the same bit of channel or stretch of coast—line, navigating with painstaking accuracy, never skimping or cutting corners, running risks all the time, going first down the line every day as groundbait, to keep the sea-lanes open ; a job combining extreme danger with the most intolerable boredom.

Meet them ashore, and you won't be specially impressed : R.N.R. skippers, most of them foremost at the bar and red-hot at darts, but certainly not smart-looking nor particularly quiet. But see them on the job—going out in clumps in the early morning, scraping past the buoys so as to leave no bit of the channel unswept—and you'll know why such men were invented.

Now and again, at sea, you hear a " WHOOMF ! " You look round, and there is a small surprised ship scuttling away from a patch of boiling foam. That is a sweeper, having touched one off. . . . We once saw one of them almost overwhelmed by a gigantic explosion close astern of it : a huge column of water shot into the air, hiding the ship from us. When she emerged we called her up (feeling rather shaken ourselves) and said, a trifle patronizingly : " That was a big one." Her reply : " What was ? " put us in our place exactly.

But mostly it is boredom, and boredom again. Mine-sweeping crews have a song, exceptionally unquotable, which starts :

> " Sweeping, sweeping, sweeping :
> Always bloody well sweeping ! "

It goes to a well-known hymn-tune, and they sing it on the job. I can't say I'm very much surprised by the fact. If I had their life, I should do more than sing about it. I should scream.

The weather conditions we meet are what you would expect on this coast : cold winds, the perpetual likelihood of fog, short steep seas when it comes on to blow, an absolute cracker in the way of a gale now and then, and a sluicing tide nearly all the time. In rough weather, of course, you feel the lack of sea-room more than ever : if things get too bad out in the Atlantic you can always heave-to and drift gently for as long as you like, but here half an hour off your course might mean shipwreck. Nor can you afford bad steering or careless handling, when ships are so close together and the margin of safety on both sides is so narrow. To coastal convoys, rough weather is a challenge which must be met by ceaseless vigilance and attention to detail, at a time when physically and mentally you may be near exhaustion.

Dipper didn't roll half as badly as my old ship, but she was far less robust. You felt, all the time, that she would smash up if driven too hard : that she balanced her good looks by a certain frailty. Women may do this attractively : ships never.

Scene : A violent storm at sea.

Enter a signalman, bearing a weather report from the Admiralty reading " Sea slight, visibility good, wind fresh, moderating : further outlook, settled."

Signalman : " How do they work these things out, sir ? "

Self : " They've got all sorts of instruments and things."

Signalman : " Don't they ever look out of the window ? "

Having the Midshipman on watch with me is a real refinement, turning watch-keeping into a luxury operation. He does all the odd jobs which I find irksome— keeping the log up to date, noting the distance run each hour, checking the buoys, changing the charts as we go along. It leaves me free to survey the bridge like an eagle, to make the big decisions and the broad strokes of policy. . . . It is also pleasant to have company, particularly at night, when a companion who is prepared to make either strong cocoa or refined conversation, according to the mood, is a real asset.

His cocoa is very strong, and his conversation is improving gradually.

Sometimes, when the weather is suitable and nothing at all is happening, or likely to, I hand over the watch to the Midshipman and take the wheel from the quartermaster. I happen to enjoy steering the ship, but I seem to be in a minority here, judging from the spectators' faces. The Midshipman, with a worried look, keeps glancing from the compass to me, and back again : then he takes a quick look round the nearest ships, and then once more bends over the compass, with a " Can-we-survive ? " expression enough to disconcert the most able helmsman.

The quartermaster is different. He stands stolidly by, watching the steering-compass, saying nothing : occasionally he sucks his teeth or draws in his breath sharply. Sometimes his fingers twitch. That is all. Discipline is a wonderful thing.

Fog always seems to be lying in wait for us on this coast, no matter what the time of the year ; and sometimes, when the visibility gets too bad, the convoy has to anchor in a body and wait for things to improve.

The signal " Anchor instantly " is given by whatever means is most practicable ; and the manœuvre goes all right as long as everyone plays fair and acts on it straight away. But the degree of emergency implied tends to be given a very free interpretation : some ships are inclined to wait for the sound of the other fellow's cable rattling out before coming to a stop themselves, and others, even more mistrustful, haul out of line altogether to try and find a clear space away from the convoy. As that space usually contains an escort, the latter manœuvre is not popular.

When the fog clears away, all is laid bare : the majority of the convoy will be lying in their proper places with haloes round them, but here and there a lone ship. which has wandered off into a corner, now stands convicted of disobedience. She will have a whole range of excuses for this, varying from " Didn't receive the signal " to " Must have dragged anchor in the tideway," and you won't get any joy at all if you try to make something of it.

The first time we were bombed in fog was an occasion not difficult to recall in detail.

It was early in the morning, and visibility was, at the most, fifty yards : the convoy was going very slowly, nose to tail like cattle at dusk, with the possibility of having to anchor until the fog lifted ; and all our attention was being given to navigation and to trying to sort out the different sirens, which seemed to be coming at us from all round the compass.

We felt our way along, sniffing the woolly blanket which enveloped the ship, hating every moment of that muffled progress : the puzzling sirens, the drifts of fog swirling past the bridge, the rawness of the air—all added to the feeling of helplessness which fog at sea brings. We had quite enough to think about, without any complications ; and when one of the look-outs cocked his head sharply and sang out : " Sound of aircraft overhead, sir ! " we found ourselves beginning to take a Job-like view of the situation.

The noise, quickly confirmed, grew louder : the aircraft seemed to be circling round just above our heads ; and there, a glimpse of blue sky among the curling wisps of vapour indicated that there was perfect visibility a little higher up. It was obvious that the fog was lowlying, not much more than a sea-level blanket, and that though we had not yet sighed the aircraft, its pilot could probably see the mast of every ship in the convoy sticking out above the fog-bank, and could choose his target at leisure.

It is really extraordinary how naked you feel at such a moment—as if you were sleeping with your feet out of the window on a freezing night. The guns' crews, piped to Action Stations, looked up hopefully, but they might have been peering through frosted glass at a bird outside, for all the good it did. Then, while they were still peering, things began to happen. The noise was suddenly very near : through a gap overhead I had a second's glimpse of the aircraft peeling off for its dive, another of it half-way down, and then a view, startlingly clear, of four bombs leaving the rack and starting towards us.

They fell wide, but that's not to say they didn't touch our hearts. . . . We got off a few rounds, but—like the bombs—they only scared the target, and the plane was out of sight again in a matter of seconds. Of the various choice remarks passed on the incident, I will quote only one, made by a signalman on the bridge who muttered : " That's the first time I've ever seen a stick of bombs end on, and lived to be called a liar."

Another experience in fog, a bit more conclusive, came our way when we received a signal on R/T that one of the ships in convoy had been damaged in collision, and we were to find her and take her in tow.

That seemed to us to be a very easy signal to make. . . . Finding her meant abandoning our comparatively safe position on the escort screen, approaching within hailing distance of the convoy, and then feeling our way through the murk up and down the columns, calling out : " Are you the damaged merchant ship ? " to anyone we saw looming up. This seemingly reasonable question received so many odd answers that in the end we got quite self-conscious about asking it. One stentorian voice shouted back : " No, but by God I will be, if you come any closer ! " and another one, with something fairly weighty on its conscience, called out : " It wasn't me, sir," and scuttled off into the gloom again.

We found the one we were looking for in the end—
a small merchant ship holed squarely amidships and
playing a kind of drifting Blind Man's Buff among the
rest of the convoy ; but the difficulty we had in locating
her was nothing to the job of passing the tow.

This is not simple at the best of times : half a shackle
of cable, a length of eight-inch manila, sixty fathoms of
towing hawser, eighty fathoms of grass rope—all this
has to be flaked out on deck, with no kinks and no
mistakes, so that it will run out smoothly when the
towed ship heaves in. And on this occasion most of
the heaving-in had to be done by shouts and guesswork :
sending out the first line was all right, but by the time
a quarter of the tow had been passed the damaged ship
was out of sight again in the fog. We *had* to keep moving
slow ahead, to avoid getting the wire round our screw ;
and we could only guess at her position and find out,
by shouting at the blank wall astern of us, if the other
end of the tow was secure.

From the bridge nothing could be seen of the operation at all : from my position on the quarter-deck aft
I had to describe what was happening over the telephone, give an estimate of our distance apart, and judge
when we should stop engines to avoid pulling up with
a jerk and parting the tow. For if this happened, we
would have to start finding the ship all over again.
. . . In addition, there was always the likelihood of
another ship drifting in between us and getting caught
up in the wire : perhaps two ships, perhaps a buoy as
well.

It was something of an anti-climax that none of these
things happened. We were able to take the weight
pretty smoothly, thanks chiefly to some ship-handling
by the Captain which put all his previous efforts in the
shade ; and shortly afterwards the fog lifted and we
towed her out into the sunlight—a good moment, that,
like leaving a dark wood where you have been terrified
all day and finding the pleasant world again. But while

the uncertainty and the guesswork lasted, it was a formidable responsibility.

Look-out : " Aircraft bearing Green 10. Angle of sight 30. Approaching the ship."
Self (improving the occasion over the loud-speaker for the benefit of the watch on deck) : " The aircraft on the starboard bow is a Hudson belonging to Coastal Command. You can recognize it easily by the twin-fins and the thick fuselage. As it passes overhead——"
Look-out (respectfully) : " Stick of bombs coming down, sir."

Another snatch of dialogue, warranted true.
Destroyer, to German aircraft circling convoy out of effective range : " You are making me dizzy. Go round the other way."
German aircraft : " With pleasure."
And it did.

On one convoy, one very persistent straggler resisted all our efforts to make him catch up : all orders and entreaties, if they were answered at all, were met by the declaration : " I am going my utmost speed already," and he continued to lag astern till the late dusk.
Came a chance single enemy aircraft which dropped a bomb fairly close to him. That got results. Within fifteen seconds clouds of smoke started to pour from his funnel : then he increased speed till he had a bow wave as big as a destroyer's, passed like an arrow right through the convoy, and came out on the other side. Still pouring smoke, he vanished into the gloom ahead of us. . . .
Said the Captain : " There's a lot in this auto-suggestion, you know."
We once had to stand by a damaged merchant ship

all night, in filthy weather, waiting until daylight so that she could complete rough repairs and make harbour ; and I remember the occasion as being the only one, in my experience so far, when the expression " Came the dawn " has attained its full significance.

It was too rough to take her in tow, or we would have had a crack at getting her in as she was ; so while she lay at anchor, dragging slowly but managing to keep out of trouble, we went round and round a nearby buoy and made what we could of the situation—shoving our nose under whenever we headed into the wind, rolling like mad when we turned into the wave-troughs, dodging the spray and getting wet through and freezing on the bridge.

For twelve hours we went lop-sidedly round that miserable little light, which flashed feebly every twenty seconds like a drunkard opening a bleary eye, with the rest of the view as black as sin, with occasional dirty waves slopping over the bridge, and howling wind-driven rain whipping us all the time. There was really no cure for the two watches I stood that night : cocoa, chocolate, sandwiches, kapok suit, fur-lined flying-boots —they all ceased to charm long before the end. The sole relief was in passing and receiving occasional signals from the merchant ship : a contact with humanity in the wilderness which enlivened both our spirits. We took to asking each other riddles in the end : waiting for daylight in the wild darkness, we needed company,

They were very bad riddles, however. Here is a sample one, which originated in a childhood Christmas cracker and should have been long since buried by the merciful years.

Q. " Why can't a deaf and dumb man tickle nine girls ? "

A. " Because he can only gesticulate (just tickle eight)."

Their signalman took a long time to get that one.

Occasionally we are detailed for night-patrol duty—

that is, keeping a certain area under observation, guarding any shipping that may be passing through, and looking for trouble on our own account.

We like patrols, as a change from routine escorting of convoys—there is something individual, almost romantic, about them, and one has a freer hand than when one is tied by station-keeping and the speed of other ships. There are several advantages peculiar to this freedom. You can make all the noise you want to, or you can lie in wait like a cat at a mouse-hole: if you feel like going full astern, or chasing a shoal of fish for practice, you can do so, without any snarling rebukes from the Senior Officer to burn your ears off. And of course, there is always a chance that you will bump into something really juicy—aircraft on a mine-laying job, for example, or a big E-boat raid on a convoy. Those are the nights when you feel you are earning your keep, and sometimes they seem a long time coming.

Nor are they handed to you on a plate, with an invitation to wade in and have your fill: at this stage of the war, on this coast, there aren't enough battles to go round. Tantalizing occasions arise when there is obviously a party going on on a neighbouring patrol, and we try to think of a good excuse for edging into it. It is annoying in the extreme to see, as we sometimes do, star-shell going up just this side of the horizon, and tracer-bullets making neat red arcs in the sky, and to know that someone is getting beaten up and that it's none of our business. If only we could saunter over carelessly and cut ourselves a slice. . . . But we've got to play fair, if only from the efficiency point of view: if we abandon our allotted patrol and go skimming off in search of excitement, that leaves a whole section unprotected, in which anything might happen.

Poaching of this sort is not popular with anyone, and least of all with the corvette or destroyer involved, who has got his teeth into a nice piece of meat and intends to hang on to it, against all comers.

This last point was once well illustrated by signals which we exchanged with a sister corvette on returning to harbour, after a night's tantalizing inaction on the edge of what had looked like Guy Fawkes's birthday party.

They : " Any luck last night ? "

We : " No. It was on X's patrol, and they hogged it all."

They : " Did you expect them to make an R.P.C. ? "[1]

No, poaching is not at all popular : that sort of private enterprise is heavily frowned on : you may not even stand on the outskirts of the party making chirruping noises to attract attention. But the spectacle of a frustrated corvette trying to edge its way into a destroyer-*versus*-E-boat action, like a small boy crawling between people's legs at a football match, has its pathetic side, which I hope the appropriate authorities recognize.

One dark night when we were patrolling in the vicinity of a convoy, faithful and true and doing no harm to anyone, we suddenly found ourselves the centre of a blaze of light : one of the escorting destroyers had fired a star-shell directly above us, to make sure of our identity (or, more probably, simply to make us jump). I had not realized before just how powerful a star-shell is. . . . The ship sat there, brilliantly illuminated, cold and naked under scrutiny, while they looked their fill ; and on the bridge we waited for the follow-up, whatever it was to be, in some tension. It seemed possible that this was after all a serious investigation, and that they were saying : " Can't make her out for certain. Let's chance a couple of four-inch-bricks."

When the bombers go out on " 1,000-plane " nights or other big operations, some of them go over us, in an almost continuous stream which does the heart good to see and hear. At least, it does that to *my* heart. In

[1] " Request the Pleasure of your Company "—the usual abbreviation for inter-ship hospitality.

such matters as air-raids and reprisals, my "turn-the-other-cheek" Christianity turns a blind eye instead : my last ship was stuck in a dock during a seven-night blitz in 1941, and I am willing for our side to balance that account in any way they choose. And since many of this present crew come from Portsmouth and Plymouth, and have returned there in leave to find their homes razed to the ground, I don't suppose they've got much objection either.

The bombers pass over our heads in the early dusk, heading the right way : they go in line ahead, in little groups of three or four, or sometimes singly : they look enormous. At such a time they are sharply outlined against the sky : there may be the after-glow of a brilliant sunset, and across this background—pale blue and gold —moves a dark tide of aircraft seeping towards their targets. They fade out of sight and into silence, like a lovely and sinister flight of birds attending a far-off battle. When they are gone, the evening air is restored : quiet returns : there is no evidence.

Then, towards dawn, we hear them coming back ; and now the occasion and the feeling are subtly different —more informal, more relaxed. Many of the aircraft are unscathed and triumphant ; others are stumbling home, obviously damaged—there are spluttering engines, odd bits hanging down, pieces missing from wings and fuselage. Once we saw a Stirling with one of its engines on fire, limping along with a little plume of flame and a tail of smoke behind it. Looking up at it, we willed it to survive its travail and make its landing-ground. . . . But whatever the state of their aircraft may be, we know how the crews must be feeling as they come within sight of home—relieved, thankful, perhaps surprised. Where they have been, all guarantees must have lapsed for a space in their minds, leaving only nerve and brain to carry the weight from second to second.

Occasionally we get a signal that there is a plane

reported down in the sea, or a dinghy adrift with a bomber's crew in it. If they are anywhere near our sea, we double our look-outs and do our very best to find them. After such a journey into chance—to Kiel, to Hamburg, perhaps across the Alps—they deserve our utmost effort.

We took an R.A.F. bomber-pilot along with us for one trip, and he was very good company : bringing all our slang up to date and (without too intensive an effort at line-shooting) convincing us that we were in the safe service, by comparison. But it was unfortunate that the convoy chose this occasion to open up, with every available gun, at an inoffensive Lancaster which rashly appeared out of the sunset and flew rather low over our heads.

We tried to explain to our guest that this touchiness was excusable (and even praiseworthy), but he did not seem disposed to view the affair from anything but a narrow R.A.F. angle.

We see a lot more of the Air Force on this side than I used to out in the Atlantic : they are always either covering us directly, or playing leap-frog nearby with one eye on the convoy. Sometimes we see the fighters going out on a sweep, beating hell out of the wave-tops, with outriders weaving about like eels' tails in a swift stream. Within a minute or so the whole caval-cade is over the horizon, and we return to the dull domestic grind, feeling rather like Cinderella on the night of the party. But if we miss the glamour, at least we are spared the hang-over.

" You've got to hand it to them," the Gunner summed it up once. " They're not all brilliantine and gremlins."

We were detailed to escort a mine-layer while she was busy " on the job," and it wasn't the most popular assignment of the week.

The programme was, in theory, simple enough : take her out, hang about while she dropped her mines, and bring her back again. But it had strings attached to it, and they were long and curly ones, liable to catch in anything. Firstly, the navigation had to be exact to the nearest yard : we were either filling in some gaps in our own minefield or else passing through it to make a new one (I hardly cared to look at the chart), and any mistakes we made wouldn't need to be repeated. Secondly, a ship full of mines—big black juicy ones : we'd watched them being loaded up, with shadowed eyes—is always an uncomfortable neighbour ; if someone pressed the wrong button on board we might find ourselves air-borne at the same time. And lastly, the excursion was in broad daylight and would take us, to put it mildly and discreetly, farther from our own coast than usual.

There were other ships in company, of course, and we left harbour in reassuring strength : once outside, we took up our pre-determined formation, and set off. The mine-layer itself, as was only natural, had the final say in navigation, but many signals flashed to and fro before the course to steer was finally approved of, and all anxieties quietened : we didn't mind them leading us if they knew what they were doing, but there was no harm in checking up on this latter point. . . . For a long time it was simply a matter of follow-my-leader, on a course which took us (we could not help realizing) a little farther from cover with every turn of the screw; and by and by a certain wariness began to show itself on board, and ratings having no conceivable connection with look-out duties—such as coders and stewards— might be observed scanning the horizon or the sky with professional zeal.

But there was certainly no harm in a little margin of safety, and towards the end of the outward run we made the precaution official and doubled the aircraft look-outs all round the ship.

When he had given his order for this last :

"Go round gun-quarters, Number One," said the Captain; "explain the position, and tell everyone I want the best possible look-out kept. Make one of your rabble-rousing speeches, if you like, and lay it on as thick as you can—we're in the Indians' country now."

By and by we reached the assigned position, and presently the actual mine-laying began, after (one hoped) a last bout of estimating and arithmetic to put the matter beyond doubt. We had nothing to do during the final operation, except keep station and watch the regular splash of the mines as they were let go: they bobbed astern of the mine-layer for a couple of minutes, a trail of sinister black shapes, and then sank slowly beneath the surface, wallowing out of sight with hardly a ripple. No doubt they would make up for this peaceful descent on their return journey.

The jog seemed to take ages: we hung about, conscious of tension, feeling like burglars kept waiting by a finicky accomplice who insists on putting the room tidy again before leaving. Half-way through, to add point to the occasion, an aircraft made its appearance and flew round and round us in a wide slow circle: one of those unidentifiable aircraft that don't appear in the manual, with two to four engines, thick-thin fuselage, and roundish-squarish wing-tips. It really might have been anything: it seemed to be going through the motions of an air escort, but they would have done equally well for hostile reconnaissance. . . . By the time the mine-layer had brought its job to a leisurely finish, we were quite ready to go home.

Said the Captain, as we turned away and got our nose towards land:

"I suppose some people like this sort of trip. To me it seems one hundred per cent morbid."

A ship—particularly a warship—blown up by a mine can look peculiarly horrible, with an air of drunken disorder about her that is distressing in all its aspects.

When you look at her you are looking at a ruin: the decks are buckled, the bridge smashed in, the guns pointing at all angles or hanging over the side. Perhaps the worst part of it is that she looks so utterly *disorganized*: in a moment of time she has been transformed from an efficient unit into a shambles. Here was a good ship, the pride of her company: here is a deserted wreck, a section of scrap-iron, untidy and shapeless and dead.

And when you pass her even a few days later, she seems to have been dead for a hundred years already, claimed by the weed and the fish.

Swift illustration of a wrong helm-order:
" Starboard ten ! . . . Where the hell are you going to ? "

" Now this time *last* Christmas," said the Captain— and I knew that something interesting and not necessarily accurate was coming: " this time last Christmas —or it may have been the Christmas before, or even Easter, but it was a religious occasion of some sort— things were happening, and we were really in the thick of it.

" It was somewhere round here, too." He pointed towards a nearby wreck-buoy, which had just given us a lot of trouble. " In fact, I think that one is part of the hang-over. Something went wrong, anyway, and the convoy got off the channel and ran slap through a mined area. By God, there were mines going off like bubbles in soda-water ! It was more like a dream than anything else : you hardly had time to look at one ship before another one bought it.

" I remember what a horrible contrast it seemed to make—Christmas Eve, peace on earth, and ships blowing up all round us, without any warning, and we standing by, quite helpless and liable to do the same thing ourselves. Mining is a sneaking sort of trick at any time, and Christmas made it seem especially treacherous. When we saw those ships blowing up and sinking, and men swimming about in the water, it didn't seem as if peace on earth was much of a wish, or much of a weapon either."

The ship comes in for all sorts of odd jobs, and so do I: anything from boarding a doubtful character on the high seas to answering income tax queries is the First Lieutenant's assignment, and must be dealt with in short order and with equal ruthlessness.

I remember one 3 a.m. excursion to rescue the whaler which some miscalculation of the Captain's had stranded on the mud during a sailing-race earlier in the day: the salvage-operation—setting off at dead of night with waders, heaving-lines, tow-ropes, and a dozen bottles of beer—had an odd piratical flavour about it, and its successful conclusion, at dawn, seemed a memorable triumph. Another time, when we were returning from patrol, we saw a bomb floating in the sea—at least, it was shaped like a bomb, with fins and tail complete.

"I'd like to have a look at that," said the Captain. "You never know—it might be a new secret weapon. Are you interested?"

I said no, not very, but after the words "Bomb Disposal Officer" had been freely bandied about on the bridge, I was naturally involved, five minutes later, in leading the recovery-operations. I approached it gingerly in the motor-boat, while the Captain, his mind possibly elsewhere, edged the ship away from the immediate vicinity and watched through binoculars.

When I lifted it out of the water it was *exactly* bomb-shaped, the kind of thing you see in photographs being loaded on to a Flying Fortress, under the caption: "More headaches for Hitler." I held it at arm's length while we returned to the ship: as we drew near an encouraging voice from the bridge called out: "Don't look so worried, Number One. Even if it goes off, you'll never know a thing about it." The fact that it turned out to be some kind of aircraft smoke-float, pro-British and harmless, was rather an anti-climax. But (as I pointed out in the wardroom later) the heroic quality of the deed was there all the same, surely?

One has, in fact, to be ready to deal with anything, even with an apparent lack of zeal on the part of the Captain. On one occasion we chanced upon a very be-draggled corpse in the water. After looking at it closely for some moments, the Captain said:

"Number One, pick all that up, will you? I'm going aft for a bit."

It is in some way significant that I had already an-swered "Aye, aye, sir," and given the first helm-order, before the Captain interrupted in a rather hurt voice: "That was a *joke*, Number One. I'm not *really* going aft, you know."

And there was another, more elevating occasion, when by some caprice of the coding-department we received the odd signal: "Commence hostilities against Japan forthwith."

"Number One!"

"Sir?"

"Commence hostilities against Japan."

"Aye, aye, sir. . . . Starboard ten!"

Caught out, and running southward for shelter before the worst storm on this coast for many years, the convoy laboured all through the night to stay in formation and hold its course on the safe channel.

We ourselves were lucky to be stationed astern of the main body, with a certain freedom of movement; but even so it was hard to keep at a safe distance in the darkness, and harder still to control the wild motion of the ship. The following seas, short and steep, made steering tremendously difficult: standing aft on the quarter-deck one saw them hang above the stern, then lift it up and force it to one side or the other, threatening

ROLLING HAS A MADDENING RHYTHM

[*Page* 22

SHE WAS ELEGANT

[Page

to pin the ship in the trough of a wave and roll it over. Sometimes the waves jumped and broke, instead of surging underneath, and toppled over on to the after-deck with a blow like a giant aimless fist : as the spray cleared and the water poured outboard again, the ship lifted slowly like a dazed fighter recovering from a knock-down blow.

Out in the Atlantic the convoy would have played for safety long before, and turned in a body to meet the storm ; but here there was no room to turn, and no remedy save vigilant steering and an exactly-judged speed. If we went too fast, nothing would have stopped the stern swinging round and over : and too slow would mean a sluggish ship, a target for every wave that overtook us. Somewhere between the narrow margin of the two, side-slipping, rolling crazily, we dodged and fled the enemy.

It was very black all round us, and bitterly cold : occasionally a scud of snow frosted the deck, to be wiped roughly away next moment by wind or sea water. The gale tugged at the ship and at one's clothes, the stern lifted, shuddered, settled down again in a rhythm which seemed unending. The buoys we were searching for hid themselves in the murk until we were almost on top of them : there was always the danger that a straggler, unseen in the blackness, would show herself too late to avoid disaster ; and without respite, astern of us, like a vicious hue and cry, the waves smashed and snapped and chased us onwards.

It was a night of tension and waiting, twelve hours' endurance of winter's malice : dawn came up like a blessing, and showed the decks glistening, the Coxswain at the wheel (after a six-hour trick) as intent as a hanging judge, and the brave convoy still together.

There's nothing more heartening, at sea, than the turn of the year, when the nights begin to pull out of winter and dusk is delayed each evening for a few

E

minutes longer. You begin to notice the change during the dog-watches just after Christmas : gradually the first dog-watch becomes a daylight one, and when, by the middle of February, you can take over the last dog-watch (six to eight p.m.) in complete daylight, spring and hope are on the way.

It's been a long wait : ever since the previous October. But how quickly all that is forgotten.

It was odd to see the coast of France again, for the first time since 1939 ; the sight aroused the same sort of speculative attention as might a working-party of Dartmoor convicts, seen from the main road nearby. It looked extraordinarily near to us : the high ground inland showed greyish-white under the full moon, and the loom of the shore-lights, as they came up and faded out again, seemed like a secret signal from the prisoners within.

This distant prospect of the enemy was with us for about an hour. At one point a searchlight swept the sea, looking for strangers. Said a rating, as the beam came round : " There's the old bastard flashing his eyes at us." And a little later, pursuing the same train of thought : " Get the tea up, Nobby. My patience is exhausted."

The destroyer which had been torpedoed and sunk during the night was an old friend : we had heard the explosion from a long way off, and it was a relief, after the ensuing action and alarm, to be detailed to leave the convoy and look for survivors.

To us, knowing some of the men in the water on that bitterly cold night, this seemed the most important thing we could do, but it needed doing quickly if any good was to come of it : the strong tide meant that the survivors would be widely scattered, the speed of the ship's sinking made it unlikely that any boats had been launched, and the extreme cold would not let them last long in the water.

It was very dark, and the smell of fuel-oil was the first indication we had that we were near them : that, and a single dim light which was burning on an empty Carley raft. Making sure that the latter *was* empty wasted a lot of time—precious time, each minute of which might be snuffing out another life. But presently. taking a wide sweep round the oil patch, we heard distant shouting, and altered course towards it, as near as we could judge ; and after a couple of minutes one of the look-outs made out a tiny black smudge in the sea ahead. This was an old routine, with nearly three years nagging familiarity behind it. . . . As we closed the speck I looked at it through my binoculars, trying to distinguish its outline and see if it was worth salvaging.

" Two men," I said, as soon as were close enough. " And they're alive all right—waving. But I can't see a raft or anything. In fact," I hesitated, " they seem to be standing in the water."

" Stop both ! " said the Captain. The telegraphs rang down, and were answered. " I'll go right up to them," he went on. " We don't want to waste time lowering a boat if we can help it." Then he raised his binoculars again, for a long look. " You're right, Number One," he agreed, " they *are* in a funny position. They're either wearing their life-belts round their knees, or doing the Indian Rope Trick."

But there was another, surprise explanation, and it was the men themselves who gave it us, with admirable presence of mind. For while we were still thirty yards off, creeping slowly towards them with the way almost off the ship, one of them called out, in a voice strident with cold but still forceful :

" Don't come any closer, sir ! We're standing on the stern of the ship."

That seemed to me to be bravery of a very special quality. Those two men had been standing up to their waists in icy water for over two hours : they were perched on the stern of a destroyer which was balanced vertically with its bows on the bottom but which might at any moment sink altogether. They saw rescue close at hand, the promise of survival from what must have seemed a miserable and hopeless position, and yet the first thing they thought about was the danger to *us* if we came too close to them. Men such as these were worth rescuing ten times over.

We laid off to a safe distance, lowered the motor-boat, and picked them up: a signalman and a stoker, both cold to the bone, their legs nearly paralysed. They could not have lasted very much longer, even if the sunk ship had kept its position. I talked to them while they were warming through again in the galley, but they knew very little of what had happened: both had been out on the upper deck when the ship went down, had swum around in darkness for a bit, and then suddenly grounded on the miraculous haven where we found them. They had not seen anyone else for a long time, though earlier on there had been a Carley raft nearby with about twenty men on it. They did not think any boats had been lowered: there had not been time.

I left them in the warmth of the galley—their blue, pinched legs and still chattering teeth a reminder of peril —and went back on to the bridge. There had been no development during the quarter of an hour I had been away: nothing more had been sighted, though they had heard some men shouting for a bit, too weakly or too far away to gauge the direction. There had been silence now for quite a long time.

" Depressing about that," remarked the Captain suddenly : " you know so exactly the sort of men who are in the water." That was in all our minds, I think— that not very far away, but out of effective reach, a virtual duplicate of our own ship's company, with the same trustworthy hands and humorists and rogues, was perishing man by man.

It was now getting towards dawn, and we had been sweeping round the patch of oil in widening circles, as

far as we could judge them, for four hours without any
result. When daylight came we would probably see the
Carley raft, but that might be too late to save the people
on it. This was something which did not need im-
pressing on the look-outs ; probably every seaman in
the ship kept a perfect watch for the rest of that night.
But whatever their degree of concentration, it was no
use : when dawn came up we were still only two hands
to the good, not much better than failure and a wretched
answer to our hopes of earlier on.

Then at full daylight, we finally sighted the raft, and
made for it at speed. This must have been the main
direction of the tidal set, for on the way we passed
successive little groups of bodies, all lifeless, washing
about in the oily sea among oddments of wreckage.
Sometimes a lolling head jerked to the lift of the swell,
giving an illusion of life, raising hopes which died at a
second glance. This was the crew we had been looking
for, but it seemed that we had spent too long in the
search : we and they had both been defeated, by time
and the sea.

There remained the raft : an unforgettable picture as,
in the fresh sunlight of a lovely morning, we drew near
it. Upright on it sat a handful of black-faced, oil-soaked
men, surrounded by prone figures, sprawling in the lazy
attitudes of the dead. One man, who raised a feeble
arm in greeting as we came alongside, had a shipmate's
head pillowed in his lap, his hand resting on the staring
face with a cherishing touch which told the night's
story in a single gesture. Another, whose filthy face
split into a grin as we reached down for him, must have
been in agony from his shattered leg. Of the others,
some stared up at the ship as at a miracle : one might
have been singing but, heard close to, was in fact groan-
ing softly : all were in an extremity of cold.

We set to work as carefully as we could, putting into
our handling of them the overflow of compassion which
the past night and the present sight of them called forth.

All the time that we were lifting them in-board, a Spit-fire flew round and round the ship, close to the water, as guard, spectator, and mourner, all in one; and it was a moment that bit into the memory—the few up-right figures in the raft, the ungainly dead, the aircraft circling us continually, the lovely sunlight that could warm so few. We had to rig a tackle for the dead men: their bodies dangled like hung criminals as they were hoisted up, their heads fell forwards and sideways and forwards again in a cycle of supreme ugliness. The hands detailed for the job had faces of stone as they worked the tackle. These men were themselves.

We collected many bodies, all through that morning: they were laid out on the quarter-deck, their clothes smothered in oil but with the familiar badges—the leading-seaman's anchor, the signalman's crossed flags— showing here and there. It was the sight of these last, perhaps, which brought home to us with piercing clarity that they were fellow-sailors who had met their death, who were now (in that most explicit and final of phrases) marked " Discharged Dead " on the books. I remember the Chief looking down at one of them, and muttering: " Three badges—that's thirteen years in the Service, at least—and now this. . . ." It summed up the con-tinuity of the Navy, its sense of one-ness, its family pride. It was the deep feeling of a mourner who mourned, not a brother but a part of himself: the same feeling which prompts the messmates of a dead man to bid generously for all the oddments of his kit when it is disposed of. Ten shillings for a cap-ribbon, fifteen shillings for an old clasp knife—it is the measure of their comradeship, which includes his wife and family.

Since many of the destroyer's crew were still unac-counted for, and it was believed that at least two other rafts had got clear of the ship, we intended to carry on with the search. Up on the bridge I let the ship idle along at dead-slow, circling the nearest buoy, while down below in the chart-house the Captain and the Navigator pored over charts and tide-tables, trying to work out exactly where the remainder of the crew might have drifted to since their ship was sunk. Presently our signal asking permission to continue looking for survivors was answered, and we began a series of careful sweeps to cover the probable area.

That day was a memorable exercise in frustration. We crossed and recrossed the hunting-ground, we took every conceivable care and precaution, but all to no purpose : nothing was sighted save odd bits of wreckage, and not very much of that. It was maddening : the men were there, life was ebbing from them, and (it seemed) only our stupidity prevented us from rescuing them. The thought could not be put aside : we were conscious all the time of a closing gap, conscious of the race between the cold, the margin of human endurance, the hours of daylight remaining, and the square miles we had to cover. And there was one other potent item to be allowed for, in this account. The weather was growing worse with every watch ; and by evening it was getting to the point where men adrift for so long could hardly be alive. They were there still, in the rising sea and the bleak dusk ; there we would have to leave them ; and as this fact sharpened and established itself, hope foundered on it, rage grew, sadness and pity deepened.

At nightfall we turned for home. In the wardroom, off watch, I talked with the two surviving officers : it was difficult not to feel guilty at the enjoyment of warmth and shelter, and when I told them that we were giving up, and leaving the search-area, I felt a rat. What they felt, I did not care to conjecture. One of them said : " Well, you certainly did your best for us," but the remark was a cover for feeling, not an expression of it. As the revolutions mounted on the way home, the rags of satisfaction at our efforts blew away, and were left astern with the rest.

One of the survivors, talking as men talk when they would rather keep silent but cannot, said :

" I'd heard before that after you've spent a bit of time in the water, you just don't care whether you live or die. I didn't think that could ever be true in my case, as I've got a wife back home, and two children just growing up. But it is true : after a bit, you're too cold and tired to care what you're leaving behind you : all you want is to fall asleep and cut the whole thing. That's the most dangerous part about being in the drink : however much you've got to live for, if it's cold and miserable enough, you just don't want to live any longer."

We entered harbour well after dark, going dead-slow ahead, picking our way among the shipping and the buoys with deliberate precision. Lowering the whaler and hooking on to the buoy, by the light of a shaded torch, was a complicated exercise on which it was a relief to concentrate. But everyone on board was very quiet : to-day, on that particular job, we had failed.

CHAPTER IV

SWINGING ROUND THE BUOY

THE fact that, when we are in harbour, we usually lie out at a buoy, gives us an enclosed life on board, of a rather special sort. Though within sight of land, the ship's isolation is complete. We can of course regulate our contacts with the shore by running trips in, in the motor-boat ; but once you settle down to it, life in the ship can be complete and self-contained in a rather satisfying way.

She is an individual unit, running on her own re-sources ; and all the odd activities which go on, apart from normal working hours—the reading, letter-writing, card-playing, tombola, washing and mending clothes, cooking of meals, music-making—all tend to emphasize the ship's self-reliance and self-sufficiency. We feel that we can do *everything* on board, dealing not only with all emergencies but with every unlikely or frivolous impulse. Apart from fulfilling the ship's normal requirements, for such things as rope-ladders or wire-splicing, we are not taken aback by any of the following tasks : engraving a beer tankard, silver-plating a cigarette-case (by an illegal method which I will not describe) : manufacturing a complete cigarette-lighter that works : making an inlaid napkin-ring, a toy-engine, a bookcase, a pair of rope-soled shoes, or a canvas cover for a typewriter.

For a small ship, her resources seem almost limitless. Even a new balance-wheel for your wrist-watch only needs a word to the engine-room department. Or, at least, so they maintain. I'm waiting for someone else to try it out first.

With this variety of talent to draw on, together with the necessary amount of cleaning, painting, gun-drill, and harbour exercises, we need not be bored however long we swing round the buoy. And sometimes, owing to bad weather or a minor defect, we do spend quite considerable periods out there. Time flows on, tides ebb and flood and ebb again, while extraordinary rumours spread round the flotilla : that a special weed is growing on the ship's bottom, not healthy sea-green but some noxious harbour growth : that we are aground on our own empty bottles : that the cable is rusted on to the buoy, and acetylene-cutters will be necessary before we can put to sea. . . . It doesn't demoralize us in the least, but it tends to demoralize other ships. They seem to think that we are getting away with something.

There are other periods to balance this, however, when owing to " operational requirements " (as they say) or to blasted corvettes that *will* keep running into each other, we hardly ever see harbour at all : we poke our nose in, oil, and go out again, on a sort of shuttle-service that cuts sleep and recuperation down to nil.

The buoy waits for our return, surrounded by half-starved seagulls. Ashore, the girls forget us, and transfer everything to destroyers.

Example of a spoilt afternoon nap :

Signal received at 3 p.m. : " To *Dipper* from Flag-Officer-in-Charge : Away whaler, row round Nos. 6 and 10 buoys, report when whaler hoisted again."

That seemed to me, toiling to get a bung-eyed whaler's crew away in quick time, to be the naval version of an offensive sweep.

Sometimes we have an inspection, of that informal kind which necessitates everyone looking exceptionally clean and tidy, and a certain number of hands detailed to stand about in attitudes of work, complete with brooms and brass-rags. (It is a curious fact on board ship that men actually working in the most conscientious fashion always look as if they are loafing, and vice versa.) After one such occasion I had an amusing report on it from a friend of mine, Number One of a destroyer, who had been entertained by a bird's eye view of the affair through his binoculars.

He had been able to watch the procession going round the ship—Flag-Officer-in-Charge, Captain, First Lieutenant (" never seen you wearing gloves before "), four other officers, Coxswain, messenger, ship's dog, and ship's cat. " I honestly thought the head would catch up with the tail, now and then," he said : " it looked like a lot of performing elephants in a ring a bit too small for them, though when the head of the procession stopped the rest of you telescoped like a goods train. But you've certainly got some resourceful ratings on board. We watched one of them, who'd been busy painting on the starboard side when the Admiral passed him, nip across to port and start splicing a rope for the return journey. Or was that a put-up job?"

I said no, it had been strictly private enterprise, and I would look into it.

" He was taking a chance, anyway, because the Admiral spoke to him the second time. We thought he must have noticed the change-over."

It seemed to me rather likely, too. In fact it still does.

Every now and then the Gunner has a fundamental and mysterious drive on the 4-inch ammunition: emptying the entire magazine, marshalling the contents on the upper deck, and then walking round and round it with a note-book, muttering and scribbling. It is then all put back again, by ratings with expressionless faces.

Some of the shells are marked " TO HELL WITH HITLER " in block capitals, but whether they are of special calibre I do not know.

We have a decorated gun on board which usually excites comment, as well it might : its shield is marked by a pair of swastikas labelled " H.E. 111 " and " M.E. 110 " respectively, and a small drawing of an E-boat adorns the centre. Now these three items (which are official) happen to be the ship's total bag to date ; and the fact that an enterprising gun-layer has put them all on one gun, his own, which he then practically charges money to see, has been a fruitful source of argument among the Gunner's Party.

It has been agreed that, in case of doubt and to avoid an unfair distribution of the limelight, it should always be made clear that the credit-markings refer to the ship and not to the individual gun-layer ; but I have not yet seen the latter looking especially modest as he answers questions about it.   Some day I must stand out of sight, but within earshot, and listen to the sales-talk.

Quartermaster's humour :
" Hands to dinner !   C.W. ratings[1] to lunch ! "

Good example of how bad blood between two departments on board may start :
I was demonstrating a tear-gas bomb to a party of newly-joined seamen on the upper deck.   Unfortunately I had placed myself, without noticing, just under the lee of a large engine-room ventilator, and when the bomb went off a compact cloud of gas, never deviating or losing consistency, moved across towards the cowling and was sucked down in one deep breath. . . . There was a short pause—one of those pauses when you know that something's *got* to happen : then the entire engine-room personnel started to pour out of the hatchway, fighting for breath, their eyes streaming.
I might have been able to explain it away smoothly as an unfortunate accident, had not a rather intelligent-looking ordinary seaman remarked :
" That was a good example of a concentrated attack, sir.   Can we see one in the open air now ? "
A memorable footnote to this affair was given me later in the day, by an engine-room artificer who had received the full charge.
" We thought it was one of your cigars at first, sir," he said, " but we soon noticed the difference."
I felt obliged to take this as a compliment.

Challenge of nervous young gangway-sentry :
" Halt !   There he goes ! "

It's not easy for a First Lieutenant to have a book about corvettes published and circulating freely on board, and still retain an aloof disciplinary air.

[1] C.W. ratings are those recommended for commissions.

By methods which I do not inquire into (though I should like my publishers to copy them) an ex-bookseller Able Seaman sold two hundred and sixty-two copies of *H.M. Corvette* to members of the ship's company : which was fine from an author's point of view, but not so good otherwise. It altered too many things altogether. It wasn't just the fact of seeing dozens of hands all over the ship reading the darned thing, though this was sufficiently distracting : it was, somehow, that everyone had now established a claim to my favour, on a cash basis, and this had to be allowed for (or rather, *not* allowed for) in my dealings with them.

Stripped of its incidental humours, it seemed to boil down to the rhetorical question : how can you deal severely with a man who has just asked you for your autograph ? This is something which does not normally arise in a writer's life : or, if it does, he is so completely disarmed that severity melts like snow in the sun.

It happens that the only radio we have in the wardroom comes *via* loudspeaker relayed from the stokers' messdeck, and we thus have to take what they give us, or else . . . Without naming individual items, I can certainly say that during the past year I have listened to programmes I would not otherwise have heard : I had a fair idea before (and considerable appreciation) of how high the B.B.C. aimed, but this was my first glimpse of their alternative target, and their marksmanship was stunning.

If I were Director of Programmes for the B.B.C. (and I shall be looking for a job after the war), I think I should admit that a seventeen-hour day is too long to be filled with first or even second-rate material ; and I should ration the good stuff at my disposal and stay off the air for the rest of the time, instead of trying to eke it out with trash. Better to preserve an hour's silence, better (if you must have a noise) to hand over to the B.B.C. signal, rather than spread alarm and despondency by giving a free rein to the entertainment world.

The objection isn't only artistic, or even mainly so: it is directly geared to the war. If you pump this stuff out, if you fill up the minds of soldiers, for example, with thoughts of yearning and burning, and blue-birds-over-Dover, you don't get fighting men as a result: you get a lot of long-faced goons who want to go home instead of finishing the job.

These tea-time comedians and boo-hooing young women are only fill-ups, I know; but there's many a good hole in the ground that wants filling first.

Morale in the wardroom occasionally sustains a shock, too. Sales of a certain brand of gin, formerly popular, have now dropped to zero, following the receipt of a letter from the suppliers, in answer to one of ours saying that their product was becoming progressively more revolting. Part of their reply, a long apology, read:

> "You will appreciate the difficulties under which the gin-trade is working when we tell you that our supplies are now imported in galvanized-iron drums which have contained lubricating oil, paraffin, and crude petroleum."

Overheard in the wardroom:
"I believe in looking after number one—and I *don't* mean the First Lieutenant."

There is a Fighting French destroyer which comes into the Base now and then, and sometimes we are tied up alongside her: which, if only because I am very fond of *caporal* cigarettes, is satisfactory. But apart from this native bait she is an interesting ship to go aboard, being even more of a self-contained unit than we ourselves are: and she is, of course, an Idea as well as a ship—for the great majority of her company she is all that is left to them of France, taking the place of their homes and families and lost circle of friends, constituting the only world they can now depend on.

Her officers and crew are a curious mixture—some purely adventurous, drawn to the Fighting French cause by a natural taste for excitement, others more serious and determined only that their ship shall make a worthy contribution to the strength of the Allied Navies. But whatever the background, all their stories of escape from France have the same quality of desperate endeavour about them : and all of them on board are concerned with the outcome of the war in the special sense that they are fighting their way back home again. To some of them, this home-coming can only be a sad one : others are sustained in spirit by the meagre news which comes through, at agonizing intervals, telling them that their homes still stand and their families still live.

There are others who have had no news for a year, for two years. Putting ourselves in their place, we can understand their disgust at the loathsome farce that has been played on the French stage, and their impatience to set it to rights and reclaim their heritage.

It may be added, as an unimportant footnote, that at dances ashore the French ratings enjoy a formidable popularity, which is confined strictly to one sex.

Here is a snatch of dialogue, warranted true, from a Canadian corvette :

Captain (unable to remember the right command for falling-out the fo'c'sle-party on leaving harbour) : " All right—break it up, boys ! "

Resourceful Petty Officer : " On the command ' Break it up, Boys,' hands will spring smartly to attention, turn forrard, and dismiss."

There is one unvarying sentence in my night-orders which is almost part of tradition : " Call me if it comes on to blow." But sometimes it leaves the realm of tradition and is translated into fact by a determined quartermaster : which means getting up, usually in the pitch dark and pouring rain, to hoist the whaler and put out another bridle.

You spend the best part of an hour over this : stumbling about on the fo'c'sle in streaming oilskins, surrounded by hard breathing and unidentified bad language. The quartermaster has very likely left the call too late, and getting the whaler alongside and hoisted without smashing it up calls for a mixture of quickness and luck. All the time the wind howls as if it had a personal fury against you for the way you are trying to cheat it.

Then, when all is secured and the watch have gone below again, you come aft once more and stand in the wardroom lobby with the water dripping off you, cold to the bone : the clock says half-past three, the glass is still dropping, and from down below comes a chorus of snores blended into one smug undisturbed anthem.

" Angels guard you while you sleep," you think, with a far from angelic intensity. " You lucky people ! "

The ship's dance was a very superior affair—two hundred and forty empties, excluding soft drinks, and only three broken glasses. It was our chance to repay some of the widespread hospitality we had received in the neighbourhood, and the invitations covered the three main women's services, the V.A.D., the W.V.S., the marines, the local regiment, all corvettes in harbour, selected destroyer entries, and the Base Staff.

The Signal Branch had decorated the hall with every flag in the locker, and the party soon warmed up. Perhaps the greatest source of entertainment, for me, was seeing members of the ship's company in unaccustomed and unsuspected rôles : a normally quiet Able Seaman blossomed out as Master of Ceremonies, the Chief Bosun's Mate made a remarkably good bar-tender with

strong ideas on credit, the Coxswain constituted himself
a sort of combined chaperon and chucker-out, and made
a rousing success of both. Some of the crew turned out
to be expert dancers, of the kind that coil themselves
and their partners up into a sort of taut spring and then
release the whole thing suddenly, to the peril and confusion of their neighbours. Others turned out not to
be dancers at all.

The evening was further remarkable for the Midshipman's efforts to entangle me with a rather attractive
Wren officer—or " commissioned popsy," as he described her alluringly. Judging from her puzzled and
perhaps relieved air as we circled the room sedately, I
could only imagine that he had given me a romantic
build-up of the most lurid sort.

Tail-piece :
" We thought of a new nickname for you after reading
your last article in the *Telegraph*."
" Yes ? "
" Yes. ' Schermuly '."
Rather wounding, I thought. The Schermuly Pistol
is a powerful line-shooting apparatus.

CHAPTER V

NIGHT SHOOT

FROM far ahead of us, the leading destroyer made the
signal :
" E-boats now seem to be moving towards the stern
of the convoy."
That was our corner, and about time too. Starting
with a dusk torpedo-attack on the leading ships, it had
been an eventful night, in which everyone seemed to
have been involved but us ; and we hadn't suffered the

waiting gladly. Guns had flashed, star-shells burst all round the sky, tracer-bullets advertised a crowded meeting; but it had all been outside our range and we had no excuse for interfering, our job that night being to cover the rear of the convoy. Now, with a bright chance of action, the ship woke up and clocked into place as one of the party.

The change from Defence Stations to First-degree Action Stations meant that I had to leave the bridge and go aft, to take over fire-control of the smaller guns. I always find this change-over annoying: up on the bridge they know everything and see it all happening, aft on the quarter-deck news filters through in driblets or not at all, rumours fly around, guesswork reigns. Each time, before leaving the bridge, I ask them to be sure to tell me what's going on: each time they promise that they will: each time the heat of battle puts a Ministry of Information blight on the news. The ship might be ramming the *Tirpitz*, for all one can tell aft: nothing gets through. To-night was no exception, save that we had our own share of action handed to us on a plate, and weren't right out of the fun; and thus some of this account depends on the post-mortem afterwards, when the bridge-personnel, relaxing, found time to fill in some of the blanks and bring my record up to date.

It was a fine night, almost flat calm, with a glowing three-quarter moon making our camouflage nearly perfect and giving up just the visibility we wanted. But while we were waiting, a signal came through: " Believed to be four or five E-boats operating." Shortly after this there was some brisk gun-fire to starboard, and then another signal: " Two E-boats engaged and damaged." Said the Captain morosely: " There'll be none of them left by the time they get to us "—a depressing thought which for some reason they took pains to pass aft to me. . . . The whole night now seemed to be in suspense: the ship moved forward very slowly, the look-outs stared out over the water, their binoculars moving in careful regulated arcs; up near the head of the convoy another star-shell, behind a cloud, gleamed like the sunset. We could still do nothing but wait for our chance.

Then, when we were beginning to doubt whether our luck was changing after all, we heard some shouting, coming faintly down-wind towards us.

Now this was not unexpected, since a ship had been sunk a little earlier and the picking up of survivors might have been left to us. The only odd thing was the location of the sound—a good way off the track of the convoy, and in the opposite direction from where boats or men swimming would normally have drifted. That needed explaining, and the explanation (or half of it) came up pretty soon: for about a minute after the shooting was heard, an E-boat was sighted crossing the track of the moon about two miles away. And that was where the noise had been coming from.

" That's odd," said the Captain. " In fact, more than odd: almost sinister. We'll stalk that monkey and see what he's up to."

By now the E-boat, having crossed the moon-track, was invisible again, but we had a rough idea of his course and we laid ours so as to converge at an acute angle. Fore and aft, we were ready to blaze away with all we'd got; and presently we saw him again, about a mile away. This time he seemed to be stopped, waiting. We weren't going to disappoint him, either.

We turned towards him, and the distance shortened. But now, as usual, the after-part dropped back into its Cinderella rôle: our alteration of course meant that we could no longer see him from aft, and there ensued a maddening few minutes when we had no idea what was happening and had nothing to look at except a blank sea. Once again, we might have been ramming a pocket-battleship. . . . Then the bridge, relenting, came through with the news we wanted:

"First Lieutenant from Captain: He's about half a mile off, dead ahead, and still stopped. In another minute I will turn to starboard so that your guns will bear. Open fire when I do."

Nothing could be fairer than that. I crossed the quarter-deck and stood close by the gun aft, my hand touching the open-fire and check-fire gongs: at my side the gun's crew, steel-helmeted, were crouching behind their gun-shield, their fingers crooked round the laying- and training-wheels, their eyes peering out on the bearing where we *knew* the E-boat would appear. In the charged silence their breathing sounded forced and unnaturally loud: the moment had a freezing tension about it, and I felt my skin prickling as we waited, within a few seconds of action.

When the ship was about a hundred yards off, the shouting started again, and this time we could distinguish the words quite easily. They were not what we were expecting, and they were not pleasant: hoping for easy meat in the form of a rescue-ship off its guard, that E-boat's crew were calling out: " Help ! Help. We're English ! "

By my side, the gun-layer drew in his breath.

" Bastards ! " he said softly. " Sinking one ship, and then using that to trap another. . . . We'll give you some help, all right."

We began our promised turn to starboard—I felt the after-part of the ship tremble as the wheel was put hard over: she heeled slightly, and the stern swung round; and then the E-boat came into view—fifty yards away, its engines stopped, half a dozen figures roughly sil- houetted on the upper deck, and someone on board shouting in a cracked voice: " Rescue ! English sailors ! "

That last treacherous effort marked zero hour for both sides, and immediately afterwards three things happened very quickly. The gun forrard let fly with a tremendous crack, scoring a hit directly amidships on

the water-line : all the guns aft loosed off, pouring
stream after stream of tracer bullets right into the
target ; and a look-out on the blind side suddenly
yelled out above the din :

" Another E-boat to starboard ! "

I whipped round. A hundred yards away on our
beam was a second E-boat, bows on to us, in a perfect
position to run a torpedo. For continuing to cover his
proper arc instead of being drawn to the excitement of the main action, that look-out deserved a
medal.

They must have seen the newcomer from the bridge
at the same moment, for immediately the telegraph
clanged and the ship seemed to gather herself up and
leap forward as we went to Full Ahead. We passed
the E-boat we had hit, still motionless and silent :
there was no answering fire, no one trying out their
English, and she seemed to be settling by the stern.
Then a grey-white cloud of artificial smoke, made by
the second E-boat, drifted down-wind between us, and
she was quickly lost to view.

There ensued a crowded and confused three minutes,
of the sort easier to indicate by asterisks than to describe
in detail. There were at least two other E-boats in the
vicinity, and they began to make high-speed smoke-
rings round us, with considerable skill : our guns kept
blazing away, the arcs of tracer fanning out at odd
glimpses here and there or at the sound of engines :
and throughout it all, everyone on board was coughing
spluttering at the effects of the chemical smoke. Then
we came under fire ourselves : a spatter of machine-gun
bullets hit the upper works, and the repair parties aft
ducked for cover as the noise rang out and the chips
of metal began to fly. We could see the tracer coming
towards us, and we fired back on the same bearing :
the targets were hidden in the smoke, but certainly they
were there, playing a grown-up brand of tip-and-run,
with us as the ball.

It was at this point that a tracer-bullet went between my legs. I saw it coming towards me, getting bigger and bigger : I should like to say that I then turned round and watched it going away again, getting smaller and smaller. But to claim that amount of detachment wouldn't be true : I did not follow its course beyond the point where, with a business-like hum, it disappeared between my knees—a piece of calculated terrorism which discouraged further observation, as far as I was concerned.

Then suddenly we were alone, in the middle of drifting smoke, with no sound anywhere near us : the players had dispersed, without settling the score. We began a circular sweep, looking for the first E-boat, and meantime clearing up ready for the next round, if there should be one. Aft, the guns' crews were bringing up more ammunition and counting empties ; and when this had been seen to and we were ready to open up again, I looked round for signs of damage. There was very little, in spite of the noise and the activity of the past quarter of an hour. One of the bullets had gone down a ventilator cowling and (it was said) chased one of the stokers all round the engine-room ; but the only actual casualty was a steward who, having no business to be on the upper deck at all, had stuck his head out to see the fun and had been nicked on the forehead just above one eye. He was all right, though indignant in a general way.

We never found that E-boat, nor any trace of it : judging by the way she had been hit, we didn't really expect to. But she was officially credited to us, by a scrupulous Admiralty : which was the next best thing to collecting the bits ourselves. And as you know, the credit was duly endorsed on the after-gun-layer's shield, for all to see and for him to tell the tale about.

We gave a party to celebrate the kill, and at one end of the wardroom we hung a Nazi ensign, borrowed from the Signal Department. By way of adding point to the occasion, we then shot an imperial line to the assembled company, to the effect that the flag had been taken from the E-boat just before it went down.

How exactly did we get it? We passed so close to the sinking E-boat, we said, that a seaman standing in the stern of the ship had been able to reach out and tear it off. But why wasn't the flag itself torn? The halyard must have given way: the seaman was very strong. How did we happen to have a man standing ready? Well (here the Captain, in danger of flagging, nudged me), in our First-degree Action Stations there was always a man told off for this duty. He was armed with a boat-hook and grappling iron. He got three pence a day trophy-money.

And so on: Finally:

"Germany must be getting extremely short of raw materials," said the most distinguished visitor present, fingering the exhibit. "This stuff is of very poor quality—it can't compare with our own."

After that it was too late to tell the truth.

Behind it all, of course, was a more serious and more genuine feeling, of pride. The credit was to the ship: it came as a reward for months (stretching to years) of up-and-down and down-and-up, of unrelieved boredom, of bad news and bad weather. It had a score of contributing factors, including luck; but luck is something you have to be ready for, and the main core of this readiness, and of the rest, can be simplified down to this:

Being a good ship, she was four things: clean, dependable, alert, and happy. All these things, which have to be worked for, spring from people.

"Clean" inside and out: that is the Coxswain—efficient, bleak of eye, helpful—and the Chief Bosun's

Mate, whose grouchy exterior never conceals the extreme pride he takes in the ship's looks.

"Dependable," is the Chief and his engine-room and stoker branches. To put it shortly, and with suitable arrogance, things go wrong with *other* ships.

"Alert" is divided between the Gunner's Party: quick on the trigger, checking and re-checking the assembly of the guns, leaving nothing to chance; and the Signal Department, led by a Yeoman of Signals who knows all the answers to all the questions.

"Happy" is all of us. It grows out of innumerable small things. It is as potent as love. Multiplied, it explains the Royal Navy.

CHAPTER VI

WHAT SAILORS THINK AND SAY

THE great majority of the letters I received, both from home and from America, when *H.M. Corvette* was published, concerned my remarks about petrol-wasters and what sailors think about them—that is, they concerned a subject not absolutely relevant to a book of action, but not ignored or resented on that account.

That is why this section has crept into the present book: because I thought people might be interested. But it seems to me to be legitimate to include it: what sailors think and talk about affects the ship all the time, colours our corner of the war, and, matched and duplicated in the other Services, might profoundly affect the peace.

A great deal of it may seem intolerably naïve, but there is a reason for that, and a good one. Sailors, more than anyone, tend to get out of touch with things. They see newspapers at irregular intervals, and not always the ones they prefer : they may be sealed from the outside world for weeks at a time. What they read, and hear talked about, when they come back again sometimes surprises them : perhaps because they see only half or a quarter of the whole picture, and cannot tell that the emphasis presented to them is faulty or the view only a partial one.

But that doesn't stop them thinking and talking a lot : indeed, like most spectators, they talk the more for being out of the centre of activity ; there is certainly no lack of material from which to quote. Here then, simplified and no doubt " conditioned " by the eye and ear of one observer, is what they think and say.

1. *The War*. We are, of course, winning it : that has never been in doubt at any time. But it is tremendously difficult to see the war as a whole, and the amount of lee-way we have to make up—in the Far East, for example—is barely appreciated. This makes our progress seem very slow, and particularly so at such times as the New Year or the anniversary of the ship's commissioning, when the previous year's hopes are recalled. Somehow the situation always looks very much the same, the end not much nearer, and home as distant and as hazy as ever.

Events and successes at sea naturally get the most attention, and things like the *Bismarck* sinking or the Malta convoy battle are a first-rate tonic. Our big bombing raids and sweeps are rather taken for granted, though the R.A.F. is O.K. (We have entertained some of them on board, with notable cordiality on both sides.) Army successes, until the finale of the North African campaign, were always somehow mistrusted, or at least accepted with reserve : it cannot be ignored (except by sunshine students of affairs) that the Army seemed a rather backward lot till the Battle of Alamein, and only now is it beginning to be realized that they were up against a crushing superiority of equipment in the earlier days, and that the man-versus-steel excuse is, of all excuses, the most valid one.

No blame is attached to anyone for this inequality of weapons : it is how Britain has always fought her wars, and you can't recriminate against such a national characteristic as lack of foresight.

Of our Allies, the Russians make the greatest impression : they are terrific, without qualification, and the effect of this is noted later under the heading " The Peace."

One does not meet any expressed *hatred* of the Germans : atrocity stories ring no bell, and the word " Hun " is newspaper currency only. But such things as the bombing of a home town, or actual contact with some piece of treachery or ruthlessness, make for anger ; and behind it all is the determination, taken as much for granted as the water under our keel, that we must win or perish. " Roll on the peace " is a recurring and favourite catch-word, but it will have to be *our* peace : nothing sooner, and nothing less.

2. *Strikes.* I've not been able to explain to questioners why, of two men fighting the same war for the same clear stake of survival, one of them, enjoying home life, comparative security, and high-level wages, can refuse outright to work unless he is paid more : and the other, conscripted at a meagre wage and sent far from home and into danger, would be shot out of hand if he tried the same tactic.

To sailors, working like blacks under sub-human conditions for four shillings a day, war-time strikes seem a mixture of blackmail and pure treason. A country desperate for production, like a man desperate for food, is easily held to ransom : suppose the Services applied the same " bargaining weapon " in their own sphere ? " What would happen to the country and the war if we tried the same thing ? " is a frequent query ; and I have heard the idea amusingly and bitterly elaborated in the mess-decks : the ship refusing to escort a convoy the last hundred miles except for a bonus of £10 a man, or the Army in Libya demanding so much a mile for advances, with time-and-a-half for retreats, and Sundays free.

What did the Russians before Stalingrad think of such manœuvres? "I saw 'STRIKE NOW IN THE WEST' chalked up on a factory wall at home," said one Petty Officer to me when we were discussing this aspect, "and by God! that's just what the chaps inside were doing. They'd struck all right—for an extra two bob a shift. I reckon Hitler would be in Buckingham Palace right now if we all tried it on."

Illogical? A flaw somewhere? Write and point it out to me: having, politically, all the sympathy possible, I'd be glad to pass the explanation on.

3. *Food-wasters, petrol-wanglers.* This is where I have *my* say—as a sailor, of course.

We bring the stuff in, sometimes at cost to ourselves, nearly always at some sacrifice on the part of the ships we escort. Often, now and in the past, that cost has been tremendous: out in the Atlantic ship after ship has gone down, men have drowned or burned to death, survivors have gasped and shivered, the life-line has seemed as thin as thread. But there has always been one thing to balance all this, offsetting the horror and the pity: the idea that what we were bringing in was vital, that it goes straight to fill some threatening gap, that no part of it is wasted or diverted. To bring it home safely rubs out all other entries in the log. It has been worth while.

And then we read the newspapers.

The cases are fewer now, but still they come: food-wasters, black-market buyers and thieves, people wangling goods in excess of quota, people taking God knows what profit on the sale and re-sale of things they had hardly heard of in peace-time. Imagine what bloody fools we feel, knowing that a convoy of what we thought vital supplies has really gone to the comfort and profit of such people : the comfort of stupid folk who cannot visualize the price in blood of what they are wasting, the profit of assorted vermin who see, in a shipload of necessaries, only the chance of a squeeze.

I once overheard, at a restaurant table next to mine, one favoured citizen say to another :

" I'd have cleaned up another clear thousand quid if I'd held on till the end of the month."

Held on to what ? Not to a section of front-line trench, I'll bet. . . . It was almost certainly some necessary or other, delivered to his doorstep by the valour and endurance of brave men. Back from a rough convoy, it makes the food stick in your throat. Is such a man concentrating on winning the war ? Who is he trying to beat ? It doesn't sound like Hitler. And yet the game goes on—checked at one point, slopping over at another : the goods are passed from hand to hand, the margin grows, the money involved gets bigger and dirtier. If ever men should be singled out and shot for looting, these are the prime candidates.

You can understand how it looks to sailors : these men are rats, and we are the saps who keep them alive. And ten such men are not worth the right arm of a Merchant Navy survivor picked off a raft in mid-Atlantic.

Petrol-wanglers, like traitors, merit a special hell. Probably enough has been written about the hazards of bringing an oil-tanker across the Atlantic, and the fate of the ones that don't make it, to establish the background and impress it on the dullest mind. None of it has been exaggerated : tankers are dynamite, and their crews are heroes of a particular quality.

What, then, is one to make of people who licence their private cars as taxis, in order to get extra coupons : who obtain additional petrol to attend church on Sunday, and then don't go : who play golf by taxi (an isolated bit of lunacy, this): who drive hundreds of miles to a race-meeting already served by special trains: who treat petrol as if it could be got from a tap? What sort of men are they? Stupid? Incurably selfish? Traitorous? Do they feel clever when they've got their extra whack? Does it give them a sense of power to know that men, foolishly valorous, have fought and perished in hundreds, just to keep their cars ticking over sweetly? Once again, ten such are not worth the skin of the man who dies for them; and one sometimes wishes they they could be individually flayed, just to prove it in simple terms.

If there is bitterness in this last section, it is probably my own. I once saw some men failing to escape from a sinking tanker. Ever since then, that has been what I mean by "petrol coupons." Each coupon is alive—to start with.

Footnote to the above. I see that it has now been declared *legal* to put down one's place of business as "Tattersall's Ring, So-and-so Racecourse," and that a journey there (in the capacity of bookmaker) counts as work sufficiently vital to warrant an extra issue of petrol. I wish I had heard of this earlier: I am sure that many a merchant-seaman we have fished out of the water would have died the easier for knowing it.

4. *Politics*. Virtually nothing to report here: there is no time and, in effect, no occasion for political interest. The "Hostilities only" ratings have shed or put in the background whatever convictions they had previously; and among the Active Service hands, the meagre interest they took in pre-war party politics seems to have evaporated, since the main issues—low pay and slow promotion—have largely disappeared in war-time or have been over-shadowed by events.

It is perhaps worth noting, as an indication of their outlook, that a film showing Trafalgar Square speakers (mostly professional politicians) demanding a "Second Front" received a positive barrage of laughter and cat-calls when shown at the local R.N. cinema. The feeling behind the demonstration was crystal-clear: it was the expressed attitude of the people who would be at the landing-beaches towards the people who wouldn't.

They were ready for the second front at any time, but the time was to be signalled by the competent authorities only, and no others need apply.

5. *Girls*. Sailors enjoy their reputation for gallantry, but they seldom seem to exploit it beyond the limits of good order and public decorum.

In the course of three years, I have only had to deal with one affiliation case; and that one was contested with an air of such injured purity and detachment that I felt it in doubtful taste to raise the matter at all. One case, in three years, is not large-scale debauchery, or indeed debauchery of any sort. To offset the figures, you could say that luck comes into it; but these things, if they exist at all, usually show on the record, and here they certainly do not—the record is excellent.

Of course, as is natural when men are cooped up together at close quarters, the tone of conversation does not exactly reflect a humble worship at the shrine of womanhood: there is a lot of loose talk (some of it exceptionally loose) about "torpedoing" and other inelegant exploits, and a chance listener might reasonably suppose that he had to deal with a nest of old-fashioned rogues of the "Yield-or-else" type. And when several ratings are together ashore they are inclined to behave badly, chi-iking girls and generally embarrassing them. But separate one of them, and put him on his own with exactly the same girl, and he usually becomes a model of deference and attention. It is only when he is with a crowd that he lacks the courage or the initiative to treat women as normal human beings.

Incidentally, there seems to be, in the Navy, a special affection for Wrens—by which I mean that they are looked on, not as fair game but as part of the Service and thus to be protected and preserved from outsiders. And what could be nicer than that?

6. *Home.* If sailors are not the most sentimental of men, then I'd like to know who are. More than half the crew of this ship are married, but all of them, married or not, seem to have a love of home grafted deep inside them, to a degree which a cynic might not credit. It is complementary to the ship, as the inner centre of their world: it stands behind everything: when the mail, for instance, is delivered on board and distributed to the various messes, the atmosphere in the ship is a quite distinctive one, compounded of sentiment and a sort of unassailable concentration.

Furthermore, their plans for the future all seem to centre, not round jobs or a steady income, but on a house, a family, a private world which, no matter how cramped or poor it may be, will give them peace against all comers. That is what they are fighting for—the sure welcome, the bride, the old woman, the sprogs: their day-dreams are the least ambitious and the gentlest of any I know.

This is probably as vital a source of strength and endurance as could be found anywhere. Worldly success may fade out of sight or be given up as hopeless, but this inner aim is not to be quenched. Men who fight with the heart, *for* the heart, are unbeatable.

7. *The Peace.* What sailors think and say about life after the war is probably more vague and unformed than in any other service.

All the things peculiar to life afloat contribute to this: the " closed-circuit " of the ship, the absence of outside contacts, the iregularity of communications—all these put a curtain between us and the shore. It is sometimes barely possible to keep up to date with the current war news, much less with trends of opinion and " planning " generally.

To take a concrete example, singled out for ease of

illustration irrespective of its relative importance : this ship was at sea when the Beveridge Report was published in the newspapers : as a result, not one rating in ten has any idea of its scope, not one in fifty a detailed knowledge of its provisions. (It is on chances such as this that a vote and even a lifelong attitude of mind may depend.) Roughly speaking, the plan is thought to be " insurance for all "—" taking over the insurance from the big companies "—or even " instead of the dole " ; and this is all the impression it has made and all the hope it has raised.

A copy of the Report, which I later made available to anyone interested, had a minute circulation on board. Its interest, as " news," had by then vanished ; and it did not seem to arouse any *other* interest.

As well as this enforced vagueness (and in some cases, complete indifference) as regards current projects, there is a definite " Win-the-war-first " attitude which contributes to the same hiatus. All things considered, " take no thought for the morrow " is a reasonable summing-up in this section ; and the outline of opinion aboard which follows must be taken as lacking either directive force or indeed very much force of any sort.

What will it be like after the war ? It is still felt to be mostly guesswork. Perhaps things will be much the same, possibly a little better : there is sure to be un-employment and uncertainty still, but the readiness with which enormous grants for war expenditure are author-ized gives some promise that money may be found (or rather, credit furnished) for peace-time schemes to re-lieve this sort of distress. There will be more education available—" more of an equal chance for everybody." I've not talked with anyone professing fear of the future : equally one does not hear of any active *deter-mination* to make things better ; there is a simple belief that they will be so, and that we have learned from war economics enough to revitalize the peace.

It seems to be accepted that money will still be the mainspring of effort and the measure of success. When I brought back from home some of my son's christening cake for distribution to the Petty Officers' mess, one of them asked me: "What do you reckon he'll be when he grows up?" I said I hoped he'd be something like a surgeon or an architect or a musician: to which the reply was, "Plenty of money in all of them, if you get to the top." I said I also hoped that he would not feel that "plenty of money" was the answer to everything, and that he would contrive to lead a full and happy life without it. This simply did not register: nor the idea (which I probably made to sound priggish and ineffective) that my son might be content to put things into the world instead of taking them out. This Petty Officer (neither an ambitious nor a selfish man) did not visualize a world in which this would be possible without a complete sacrifice of comfort and the probable starvation of whoever practised it.

There remains this pointer towards the future, which has cropped up so often that it cannot be dismissed as worthless. The heroism and endurance of the Russians frequently provoke the remark: "They must have something really worth fighting for," and the idea, current before the war, that they were the slaves of a soulless and hated State is now dismissed as bunk. "It (Communism) wouldn't do for us, but something of the same sort might, if we could get it without a mess-up," is another remark indicating the kind of impression which the Russians' resistance and readiness to die for their country and way of life, has made. There must be something in a system which produces such extreme valour, not in isolated cases here and there, but as a national characteristic: they must feel that their country, their soil, is their very own, and that no force, either of reaction or the reverse, can betray their victory.

This is not the book, nor is it the time in our history,

F

to discuss the implications of this feeling. I am simply recording that sailors have been struck by it, as no doubt many other people have; and that, when the time comes to organize our peace-time way of life, Russia's loving and jealous defence of her own will be remembered.

CORVETTE COMMAND

FOREWORD

THE foreword of *H.M. Corvette* began with the words :
" This book is not a masterpiece : I have not had time
to write one." I honestly thought these two phrases, in
conjunction, sufficiently fatuous to escape being treated
as a serious comment : but having been solemnly taken
to task by one reviewer for (*a*) conceit, and (*b*) an over-
estimate of my own talents, I now realize that humour
is never safely recognizable as such unless confined to
a column headed " JOKES " and broken at intervals by
asterisks.

This present foreword contains no jokes : it simply
records that *Corvette Command* was written in my sea-
cabin during the course of sixty-two short convoys and
thirty-eight night patrols, and that it seems to have
some of the first-hand reality and (I am sure) *all* the
drawbacks that such an environment might be expected
to produce.

N. M.

CHAPTER I

"ON ASSUMING COMMAND . . ."

It is odd, and faintly ironic, that the crowning piece of news, for which you have been waiting ever since you joined the Navy, comes to you in a phrase of matchless insignificance. All you get—the sole spark for the tinder—is a slip of paper headed "Appointments": underneath is your name, and alongside that the single phrase "Winger in cd."

You have to look twice at that "cd." before you take in the fact that it means "Command": you have to look three times at the name before you realize that it is in truth your own. But when you have finally got the size of it, light breaks through like one of those story-book dawns. . . .

For the R.N.V.R., commands do not grow on trees—or at least, not on any tree that flourished down our way at that time. Of course, even in March, 1943, it had already been rather a long war: the supply of ready-made experts—R.N. and R.N.R.—was beginning to run out: the Admiralty were now getting down to the bottom of the bag, turning it this way and that to admit the light and see what there was to be had. Occasionally, as now, they brought up some doubtful-looking article and decided that, at a pinch, it would do. . . . But still there was a prejudice—or perhaps, more exactly, a reservation — about the R.N.V.R.: it was thought unlikely that they could successfully command His Majesty's ships of war, chiefly because there was really no reason why, as amateurs, they *should* be able to.

That was why the appointment came as a surprise, and my biggest and best so far. I was a Lieutenant with two and a half years' seniority : I had been dogsbody of my first ship, First Lieutenant of my second : now I was to command my third. As well as realizing a particular personal ambition, it was a blow for my side which I was very glad to strike.

But certainly it was a surprise. At one moment I was an old and cynical First Lieutenant, wondering why every one else had all the luck, deciding that after all it wasn't worth ordering a new suit—the present one, shiny and paint-stricken, would last out the war, since I wasn't going any higher (nor along the Mall to Buckingham Palace, either). And then suddenly came this swift change, and the absolute necessity not only of a new suit but of a new pair of gloves as well, and an expensive and theatrical cap, rather like a German general's, all peak and prestige. . . . Having been accorded this most singular honour, I wasn't going to carry it off at cut prices.

To me, it *was* most singular : I knew the vacancy was coming up, but I hadn't cast myself for the part. *Winger* was a sister ship of *Dipper*, my present one—in fact she was a replica of her in every respect : in the same flotilla, doing the same job : a twin-screw corvette, agile, elegant, a joy to handle and a triumph to own. A year ago, to this very day, I had received the appointment as *Dipper's* First Lieutenant. I remembered now my pride and pleasure when that appointment came through, and I tried to produce an adequate reaction to the fact that I now commanded her twin. That reaction was a long time coming : in fact, it was still being built up, from day to day and trip to trip, till the very end—a long honeymoon with an enduring bride.

Leaving *Dipper* would have been mortally sad if I had not been going to take over one of my own : as it was, the last day had its share of regret which no anticipation could lessen. I had a tremendous affection for her ; the year I had spent aboard her had been by far the happiest of the war. As her Number One I had had an unusually free hand under two captains, both of whom I had liked, and that had given me a feeling about her, jealously personal, which was at its most potent when I said good-bye. What sort of chap was this new First Lieutenant ? Would he keep her clean ? Was he to be trusted with the uncertain galley funnel, the temperamental motor-boat, the glory of the quarter-deck brass-work ? . . . He looked all right, it was true, and (most important of all) he looked as pleased as I had been when I first came aboard—but you never could tell for certain. He might have been an actor in peace-time.

I should be seeing her again, though, and that would take the sting out of the farewell. "I'll give you hell when we're doing manœuvres," said my late Captain, who had six months' seniority in hand. "You'll be out of station whatever you do. . . ." There was great pleasure to be had from the idea that I would be coming back to the family, to our compact flotilla wherein I had met such good comradeship, to the base whose chief amenity—the Naval Club—was so exactly what I liked. It rounded off the whole thing in the most satisfactory way possible.

In one, minor, matter connected with the change-over I had been severely stung. *Dipper* was about to proceed on her annual refit, *Winger* had just finished hers : which meant that I would now do a second year without any leave longer than the routine boiler-cleaning periods. I had been looking forward to that leave : a year of East Coast convoying, a son six months old—they both seemed to merit a rest and a break in the routine. But if it *had* to be exchanged for another year's sea-going, then my new job was giving me the best of the bargain. Command cancelled everything.

On my way down to the dockyard where *Winger* was lying, I went home for half a day—a piece of truancy which I was prepared to justify to Their Lordships on the ground that it was my total annual leave, which it was. When I told E. what they had given me :

" Oh ! " she said. " That's much better than you expected, isn't it ? How lovely." She was very pleased. Then : " Darling, I think the son and heir is starting a rash."

First things first. You know how it is.

With only one day to go before the completion of her refit, *Winger* was in the usual state of uninhibited chaos when I arrived. That air of disorganization which every ship wears after a period in dockyard hands was apparent everywhere : she was hopelessly untidy, only half-painted, blotched with red lead, lacking her whaler and motor-boat (still in the boat-sheds), and littered with every conceivable sort of spare part, packing-case, tin can, rope's end, and dockyard matey. There were the inevitable riveters letting loose their private hell on the bridge superstructure : there was a small well-organized pontoon school on the gun-platform : there were lots of people slapping paint on : there was a man up the mast, with a mallet and a rapt expression, apparently enjoying the view into the Wrens' quarters nearby. Aft, on the quarter-deck, a cluster of nodding bowler hats indicated that the superintending officials were having a last intensive session before finally chucking their hands in. I looked around me, remembering *Dipper's* polished elegance, and thought : Hell, I'll have to start all over again from zero. And then I remembered also that I wasn't the First Lieutenant any more, and wouldn't have to do anything of the sort. All I *would* have to do was complain. . . .

In contrast with the upper deck, my cabin—unlocked for me by a young steward with a wary eye—was a model of order and cleanliness : it was in fact ready for me in every respect, from the clean towel to the fresh blotting-paper. A good mark for some one ; probably the First Lieutenant. There were a few letters waiting for me, and some immediate signals ; and after dealing with these I saw all the officers in turn—First Lieutenant, Sub., Gunner, Engineer Officer, and Midshipman. That wariness which had shown itself in the steward's face was reflected, to a greater or less degree, in all of theirs : remembering my own reactions when greeting a new Captain I was not surprised. It was always a chancy and unpredictable moment. And after all, I was a new animal altogether; an R.N.V.R. captain, and a Lieutenant as well. What next, indeed ? . . .

From Number One I had a detailed account of the ship's progress during her refit, and another report— covering the engineering side, and triumphantly technical—from the Chief. The Gunner was loud (or at least fully audible) in his praise of the ship's armament : the Sub. assured me that every chart under his care was guaranteed to be absolutely on the top line. (They always are—guaranteed, that is.) So far, so good : things seemed to be in fair working order. Then the Midshipman (the Captain's Secretary) came into my cabin with what was virtually a crate full of papers, and the shadows began to fall thick and fast.

It was not his fault—nor any one's—that there was so much outstanding, so many loose ends : it was due to the fact that the previous Captain had left at short notice a fortnight earlier, and that thus I would not get a direct turn-over from him—almost an essential of a smooth start. The fatal gap—with the ship just completing an extensive refit, with stores astray, with correspondence in arrears and musters overlooked—was at least a fifty per cent additional complication to the job of taking over. Zest and enthusiasm evaporated as I waded through those cloying files : there were weeks of work here before I could be even level with the daily quota, and that would be formidable enough in any case.

I looked up and caught the Midshipman's eye. It was entirely non-committal. "I am only the humble instrument," it seemed to say. "This mess is all yours."

There was no impression to be made on it there and then, in any case. I roughed out a list of things which had to be done—hardly the same thing as doing them, but quite wearing enough . . . . Much later, considerably depressed, I went ashore to Operations, to make my number and find out the details of our programme. The man I had to see was an old friend, and the re-encounter was a pleasant one: but his congratulations hardly balanced the state of affairs on board, nor the news that we were due to come out of dock the following morning. I felt very strongly that I needed a breathing space : it seemed that I might have to take a long run at this job. After he had outlined a programme—oiling and storing, taking in ammunition, adjusting compasses, full-power trials—which would keep us busy till the end of our stay there:

"I'm damned glad you got the command," he concluded. "It's about time they tried some amateur talent. I suppose you're pretty pleased about it ? "

"Well, I *was*, about five hours ago," I said, "and somewhere in the background I still am, very. But it has a sting or two attached to it." I gave him an outline of the state of affairs on board, with some of the more exotic details by way of illustration, and finished, "I'm not exactly taking over a going concern."

He stared. "Why should you expect to ? You're meant to make it go yourself. What do you think you draw all that money for ? " He was even slightly indignant. "You've got enough jam on it already falling into a job like this, without complaining about the . . ."

"All right, all right," I interrupted. "I just thought I'd mention it."

We went and had a drink, and presently I felt better. What he had said was quite true. I had been given a first-rate job, whatever its temporary drawbacks, and nothing could alter its attraction or spoil its quality. And as for taking over a going concern—a good dinner and some better talk made such an idea seem almost boring.

Sitting in my cabin that night—the night before we were due out of dock—with a last brew of coffee and one of the wardroom cigars (an unexpected dividend) going well, I gave final thought to what I had taken on.

I felt confident about it, but somehow it was a near thing. . . . If any one had told me on the day I joined the Navy that within three years I would be entrusted with the sole charge of a ship costing many thousands of pounds, and with the lives of the eighty-eight men in her, I would not only have disbelieved him—I would have voted against it. It would have seemed too far out of my line altogether : my peace-time way of life—writing, travelling all over Europe, but living and working quite alone—had not fitted me for that sort of responsibility (though I suppose that, back in 1925, Winchester faintly had). It was not that I had been shirking the world between the wars—only a personal and political lunatic could have done that with any success : it was simply that living in a crowd, and having people dependent on me, had been counter to my choice. I felt I was better off on my own, and I had made it so. . . . I had been interested in politics, but as a study rather than a prac-tice : and my sympathies—even at their most violently radical stage—had remained sympathies and nothing much more, save for one spell of electioneering where, inevitably, the candidate of my choice had forfeited his deposit.

Presumably the Navy had taught me, and taught me quickly, that the individual, self-sufficient, self-regarding life is not commendable when it ignores strife and suffering all round it, and that responsibility, even in an alien sphere, should be welcomed as a test of personal fitness. It had, further, trained me to survive successive tests—tests of endurance, good temper, patience—and to emerge now in a position where men and equipment, both infinitely valuable, were dependent on my nerve and judgment for their survival. And more than this : the lesson, with its varied and often curious results, had been worth while from any angle, war or peace, for I had found in the Navy an opportunity for service in that exact tradition which I had thought essential between the wars, but had not really exercised with any degree of competence.

This is not the patriotic illusion that it may seem : it is a plain fact which sprang directly from my initial luck in being drafted to corvettes. The particular defensive job which my part of the Navy undertook—convoying foodstuffs, keeping people alive and healthy, collecting and caring for survivors—seemed to bear a direct relationship to my vague pre-war desire to " help," to work for more than money, to be personally effective without personal ambition. War made the task one of supreme national importance, but, even discounting that, the enduring human values on which it was based remained clear and encouraging all the time. On these lines I had been working for the best part of three years : mostly in a minor, almost anonymous capacity, but now at last with some degree of individual distinction, with a label attached.

It was impossible not to be pleased and proud about the latter development. The job itself was mundane, unspectacular without an atom of glamour : I was glad it did not mean dispensing with pride.

Here I was in the Captain's cabin, anyway : cigar, coffee, slippers, and all. . . . During the last few minutes I found I had been fingering a small rubber stamp on my desk : one of half a dozen in an imposing rack. Now I pressed it on to the inking pad, stamped down on the signal-form in front of me, and examined the result

It said, " LIEUTENANT-IN-COMMAND."

It was my favourite rubber stamp so far.

CHAPTER 11

WINGER IN COMPANY

I HAD breakfast alone in my cabin next morning : the first time I had been able to start the day in this civilized fashion since the war began. (Breakfast is something to which all ideas of human adjustment are inapplicable. It is like love : conversation impedes and spectators ruin it.) At half-past nine I saw the current signal-log, covering the previous day's activities, and then I sent for the Coxswain—mainly to discuss helm-orders and manœuvring in harbour generally. This class of corvette is fortunate in having the wheel sited on the upper bridge a few feet from the Officer-of-the-Watch, with a clear view ahead : the Coxswain can thus take the ship in and out of harbour, or alongside another ship, without any orders except a general one to begin with. But the understanding between Coxswain and Captain must be exact and crystal-clear for this kind of manœuvring in closed waters to be fool-proof : otherwise it is really no more than a dangerous attempt at saving yourself trouble—a short cut that may lead to somewhere quite different after all.

These after-breakfast interviews, incidentally, became much more elaborate later on, when I had a proper routine worked out. Zero hour, in the future, was nine o'clock : at eight forty-five I had a second cup of coffee and finished the newspaper, at eight fifty-five I put my socks on, and at nine the rush started. The Yeoman with yesterday's signals. The First Lieutenant with his arrangements for the day. Pilot with the latest local navigating information. Chief wanting to know the orders for steam. The Gunner with a piece of gun which had somehow disgraced itself. The Midshipman with a ton of mail. The rating who set the clocks right. The Steward who was going shopping ashore. The First Lieutenant again, with a new set of arrangements and a list of thirteen requestmen. . . . I sometimes felt that if they *all* started coming in again, in the same sequence, I might never notice.

This morning we were to leave the dry dock at eleven o'clock and go round, in tow, to the main basin. I put in an hour's paper-work—a determined nibble at it whenever possible seemed the best way of clearing off the arrears—and then walked round the upper deck with the First Lieutenant, for a preliminary survey. I knew these ships by heart already, but now I had a different pair of eyes. . . . Only in minor ways could she be distinguished from *Dipper*, but she had a better bridge, with a very large slice of the roof hinging back and making it almost an open one, and a Captain's chair which reminded me so strongly of the ones to be seen in film studios that I later had " SHIRLEY TEMPLE " painted on the back—to the disgust of the Signal Branch, who favoured Rita Hayworth. . . . The ship had also a most distinctive camouflage, of which I thoroughly approved : when painting was finished she would challenge *Dipper* for looks (and of course *Dipper's* looks were bound to deteriorate now). I noticed with satisfaction that the four-inch gun, now being groomed by an intent and industrious sweeper, was very well kept, and seemed to have survived the docking period unscathed. Appearance was a lot but working efficiency was all.

Already, on the pleasant sunny morning, the ship was looking much tidier—hands had turned to at seven o'clock, and clearly they had not been wasting their time. Many of them now working on the upper deck I knew by sight, from a year's visiting within the flotilla : they included one immense Able Seaman who had competed against me at putting-the-shot during the recent Corvette sports—with complete success, it may be said. The ship was now free of all but a few dockyard workers : their necessary encroachment was over, and the tide was now running strongly the other way. Stretches of the upper deck were beginning to emerge, relieved of the usual eccentricities of refitting—the derelict cups, the newspapers, the raincoats hanging on the Lewis guns. Soon it would be possible to criticize and to appraise on a normal basis.

At about half-past ten the Chief, the busiest man aboard that morning, came to me with a sheaf of papers to be signed, certifying that we were ready to be floated

off, that there were no inlets left open, and that we had
not knowingly shifted any ballast such as might disturb
our trim : and very soon after that they started to run
the water in. This was, if not an anxious moment, at
least a thoughtful one. I have never yet seen or even
heard of a ship keeling over and sinking when the
bath is filled, but that's not to say that it *couldn't* happen,
and I didn't want to be the first victim. . . . Leaning
over the guard-rail I watched the water running in,
swirling round the shores, picking up the oddments of
wood and rubbish which the weeks of refitting had
left on the bottom, lifting a thin film of coal dust and
dirt as it rose, climbing step by step up the side of the
dock. A line of men, standing by below, in waders,
to collect the shores and wedges as they floated free,
retreated gradually in a widening circle, leaving *Winger*
at last to her natural element.

Soon the water was climbing up our own side, riming
the fresh paint with successive lines of discolouration,
higher and higher : one by one the horizontal props
floated off and were retrieved, the men now reaching-
for them with boat-hooks from the dock-edge. A pause,
or rather a slowing-up, while the full area of the dock
had to be filled : then as the last shore fell free the ship
gave a tremor and a barely perceptible lurch, and was
released. I waited for bad news, but there was none :
she had taken the water just as the makers intended.

" Dry as a bone, sir," said the Chief in confirmation,
coming up suddenly out of some rare compartment
below. " We're ready to go anywhere."

Now there was a burst of activity ashore : bowler hats
sprang up from nowhere, multiple shouting set in, the
dock gates opened slowly (impelled by some very old
men straining away at a hand capstan, in the authentic
Egyptian slave manner), and we were in the hands of
God and the tug *Gripper*. The journey, though short,
took us round a lot of corners, many of them sharp,
none of them roomy : from up on the bridge I could

see the First Lieutenant harrying his fender-parties from one side to the other and back again, as the knuckles of the jetty loomed up to sabotage his paint-work. I was glad to see that he had this nervous reaction developed to a high degree, as I had myself. . . . But the towing and warping, as usual in a naval dockyard, were flawless, and by midday, with no greater mishap than the loss of one seaman's cap (neatly removed by a heaving line), we were secure alongside again in our new berth.

We were only in the basin, it was true : land-locked still : but we *were* afloat.

Good use was made of the rest of that day in every department : the painting was finished off, most of the stores embarked and oiling completed. Fresh (or fairly fresh) from a generous slice of leave, both watches turned to with a will. Down in my cabin I toiled away with the Midshipman, mustering and checking the fifty-odd confidential books, the two-hundred-and-something secret publications, the charge documents, the hush-hush letters, the special keys. We got the right answer in the end, but it was a long time coming and it cost a lot in conscientious determination : everything had to be sighted, by my own dazed eyes, from the " Notes on Oiling at Sea " to the " Handbook on Street Fighting for Junior Officers " : from " How to Invade " to " How to Repel Invasion " : from the key of the safe to the key of the Captain's private bar—both of them on one key-ring labelled, unexpectedly but quite rightly, " VITAL."

This was all what might be called the dreary side of being Captain : the finicky oddments which, totally uninteresting in themselves, were yet of paramount importance, and might trip one up (to say nothing of the wider results) as surely as would a piece of bad navigation, if anything went adrift. It happens that I have a conscience about " security " generally : the sight of, say, a secret signal left in the wardroom instead of being in its proper locked file is as good as a poke in the eye any day : I don't like pokes in the eye. The efficient custody of secret matter means endless care and trouble, often when you are tired after a hard trip : there is nothing more boring, but in many respects there is nothing more important, from any Naval angle whatsoever.

At all events we had the whole thing sewn up by the end of the day—a sizeable weight off the mind, as well as one more section of undergrowth cleared away. At this rate the arrears would be worked off much earlier than I had hoped when I first struck the balance.

Next morning we really took to the ocean. Our sailing instructions came aboard, couched in that fragrant English which so endears the Signal Branch to us : " *Winger* will unbasin at 10.00 and proceed to No. 4 Buoy under own steam." "Unbasin" . . . I ask you. . . . Punctually at five minutes to ten the Chief made his "Ready to move" report, followed by the First Lieutenant with his, and we cast off in good order. Our berthing-position made it necessary for us to go out of the dock backwards, meeting and turning against a strong steam as soon as we cleared the entrance. I had no objection to this manœuvre, provided everything functioned correctly and quick action was forthcoming from the engine-room if the need arose. But a new and untried intermediate shaft made it possible that we would have to stop engines without notice in the middle ; and as it turned out this was exactly what happened, the Chief naturally choosing the most critical moment of all to report by telephone to the bridge, in a voice almost annoyingly unemotional : "Starboard engine out of action."

As our "Not under control" signal went up to the yarn-arm, a rating on the fo'c'sle was heard to say : "My turn for leave, chum ! " . . . This was not the piece of blinding optimism it may sound : for when that message from the engine-room came through, we were in the middle of a two-knot tideway and going astern rapidly towards the opposite shore, preparatory

to turning : that is, we were caught on the hop. With
one engine out of action, we could only turn very slowly,
backing and filling a few degrees at a time : the tide
was gradually taking us down on to a line of mooring-
buoys, and two merchant ships which were coming upstream would shortly complicate the situation. What
does A. do ?—apart from dropping the pick and going
aft for a cup of tea. The chances of leave for the Port
Watch were excellent.

But I had reckoned without my friend ashore, poised
like a benign Providence for just this occasion. " Tug
coming out to us, sir ! " said the Yeoman of Signals
suddenly, and there, unflatteringly prompt, was the tug
Gripper making for us with a bow wave like the Severn
Bore. She must have been waiting behind the pier,
ready to pounce. . . . Pricked to action by this obvious
piece of nurse-maiding, I took an oath to straighten the
thing out myself, and semaphored her to lay off while
I tried it : but we were too slow in coming round,
and, as I had expected, the merchant ships did not
notice my hoist and showed no sign of giving me the
extra room I needed. In the end I had to climb down,
and it was under a firm fore-and-aft tow that *Winger*
hooked on to her first mooring-buoy. Nothing could
have been farther from my intentions than this
spoon-fed progress, and I was quite sure that my
friend in the Operations Room (which commanded
an extensive view of the harbour) extracted the
last ounce of pleasure from seeing his prudent fore-
thought thus justified.

There had been other eyes watching me, too. It was
impossible to be ignorant of the fact that all the time
upon the bridge during that manœuvre I had been under
the very closest scrutiny—by the other officers, by the
Coxswain, the signalman, the telegraph-hands, and that
down in the engine-room they had also been observing
me, trying to judge from the orders transmitted to them
how firm, or otherwise, was the hand up-top. (Those

engine-room dials can register far more than what is printed on them : they can reflect confidence, economy of movement, uncertainty, contradiction, flurry, almost as clearly as does the spoken word.) It was the first time that I had felt myself to be on public trial in that way, a trial impossible to evade, allowing no cover or subterfuge—and felt, moreover, that a cool reaction was essential, both now and for the future. I had known beforehand that it would be like that : I had known also that I would find all those observant eyes either a stimulant or a profound embarrassment, but I had not known which. The fact that they had been the former, under rather trying circumstances, was a matter for relief and a hopeful pointer for whatever lay ahead.

At all events we were now one stage farther on, slowly forging our way towards completion and the open sea.

Our ammunition was brought out to us by an old-fashioned sprit-sail barge—an odd fact, entirely appro-priate to a topsy-turvy world. Unloading and stowing it in the magazines was a job for all hands, and took most of the afternoon : both the shells and the depth-charges had to be man-handled nearly all the way—as regards up-to-date slings and derricks, the sprit-sail barge could give us points and a comfortable beating any day of the week. Then, our engine defect (a broken oil-pump) being made good, and this time guaranteed dependable, it was time to adjust compasses : a two-hour job, and a mortally boring one at that. For the benefit of the uninitiated, the operation consists of going round and round in slow circles while a mathematical wizard (in the inevitable bowler hat) takes bearings of some conspicuous object ashore and makes out a list of them. If you go too fast, he will complain or sulk : if you go too slow you yourself will probably be driven mad by the monotony. A tug stands by all the time to see fair play : in this case the inescapable *Gripper*, all readiness and knowing smile. But for once we didn't need him.

Finally, the job was completed, and that was the end of that day's work, and about time too. Dinner in the wardroom later, topped off with a glass of orange curaçao and the slight clinching formality of " The King," was a most pleasant reward and relaxation.

The next day—our last, by the schedule—was given over to the full-power trials, which might have been complicated and were actually the simplest and most straightforward operation so far. Machinery of the intricacy of a triple-expansion turbine is a closed book to me : it will always remain so, no matter how long the war continues : and though I encouraged the Chief to go into details of our past defects and current efficiency, it was with the guilty knowledge that if he told me that the thrust-block was cushioned on hard-boiled eggs I would hesitate to challenge the statement for fear of betraying my ignorance. But certainly the ship travelled well, that fine morning, bearing out his eulogy of her present condition. We went for a quick run up the coast, turned, manœuvred, went astern in a hurry—all smoothly and without fuss. She did everything that was asked of her. I took the opportunity of trying out her turning-circle under various degrees of helm, as well as her quickness to gather sternway when changing from " half ahead " to " half astern " : this latter varied so much from ship to ship that it was one of the first things I wanted to fix in my mind. The different operations furnished no surprises : a slight variation of top-weight made her more tender than *Dipper* when turning, but otherwise I was at ease, on familiar ground, from the start.

As well as showing off the ship's paces and redeeming her reputation, that day's trip was of notable significance and value for me personally. For when I brought her back at the end of it, and secured to the buoy, I felt a sudden surge of self-confidence, as if I had now made sure of something that I had doubted before. The outing had done me a power of good: I knew where I was with this ship, and with myself too—and that was the first gain on a road which would have to show me plenty more, to give me the cast-iron grip I wanted.

But it *was* a notable gain. I had been wrong in hoping to step into a ready-made job, but right in believing that the job, ready-made or not, was no tougher than the determination I could bring to it.

The trouble, of course (and it was a trouble which was to recur constantly later on) was that I had no one with whom to share this sort of self-examination and self-questioning: in fact I hardly knew if it was legal, from the Service angle, and certainly it could not be expressed or implied with the rest of the wardroom. Reassurance, courage, must be from within: I was on my own and I had to look pleased about it. It happens that to find a cure for this isolation, this occasional failure of the spirit, was one of the minor reasons why I had got married: the cure had worked—had always worked, from the beginning—but now it was out of reach, and it was the only one on which I could have called with any certainty of relief. And if this seems too personal a subject for a book on corvettes, I can certify that it is yet highly relevant to the command of one. The Navy and the course of the war make constant demands on one's patience and endurance. I happen to be quite certain where mine come from.

The morning we should have started back for home found us still at our mooring in one of the thickest fogs I have ever encountered. To be at anchor in fog is several degrees better than being loose at sea in one, but it is still a mournful and lowering occasion, not easily dispelled. This ship lay as if in a cocoon, the bridge invisible from the quarter-deck, the masthead lost in the raw grey blanket which pressed round and over us. There was still a certain amount of river-traffic on the move, as the contrasting sirens showed: our bell rang out every minute or so, beating thinly against the wall all round, trying to interpose a margin of safety between us and the menace of other ships. We were lying out of the main channel, naturally, but this carried no particular guarantee : occasionally a tug or a picket-boat nosing its way upstream from buoy to buoy, would sight us : its look-out would give a shout, the rating in charge of our bell would produce a sudden energetic solo, and the intruder would feel its way past and sheer off into nothingness again. The hands at work on deck kept looking up and staring out into the fog, unable to concentrate or take our security for granted, trying with the instinct of sailors to add their care to the sum total of watchfulness.

I had this instinct myself, and it was difficult to give attention to anything else except our present circumstances : but there was work to be done. The First Lieutenant was permanently on the upper deck, and I therefore spent most of the morning in my cabin, where the gloom rivalled the fog outside as I tackled the intricacies of the wardroom wine-books. (I am no mathematician, and a natural sucker for a dummy prospectus, but a fatherly eye had to be kept on individual wine-bills which, quite apart from the preservation of decorum, were subject to official limitations as well.) Now and again, unable to withstand the spur of a siren nearer than usual, I would climb up on deck, staying for a minute or two to peer out and sniff the thick woolly air before admitting that everything was under control, and going below again. Clearly, the time when I could delegate responsibility with an entirely quiet mind was still somewhere in the future : and as far as fog was concerned, it would probably remain there indefinitely.

The weather cleared at midday, and we started off. We had been detailed to act as additional escort for a coastal convoy as far as our base (seldom in these days does the Navy " waste " an escort ship by sending it on passage by itself) and this meant a certain amount of hanging about at the assembly point, chasing up stragglers and running errands generally. It was good to get to work again, even at this well-known routine. It happened that there was an alteration of the normal convoy route that day, which had to be passed to each ship individually by loud-hailer : there were thirty-three ships altogether, not all of them British, not all of them bright, not all of them (it seemed) even awake. The job was naturally pushed on to us in its entirety (destroyers are not angels with wings when it comes to this sort of thing), and it took a long time and a lot of shouting : each ship had to be approached, hailed and instructed : and it had to be established beyond doubt that the diversion was absolutely clear to them before another one could be tackled. Since each separate approach involved a score of orders—minor alterations of our course and revolutions— and each detailing of the route meant repeating a long signal at least twice at dictation speed, I was both tired and hoarse by the time I had finished. I was also rather cross, but (for the first time on any stage) I had full freedom to show this, which helped considerably.

Then, a few minutes before we were due to leave the convoy and proceed home independently, the fog came down again, in a rolling bank which gave us hardly any warning. As I rang " SLOW BOTH " and edged away from the nearest column of ships, I thought : " This isn't fair. I'm only a writer, really. . . ." I have always loathed fog, ever since my first ship was in collision during a thick night in the North Atlantic ; but this was the first occasion when loathing was a totally inadequate—even a harmful—reaction. Always, up till now, there had been some one to take the weight, always the Captain had been there, stepping in auto- matically and shouldering the unique responsibility of a ship moving blindly among other ships equally blind. Now (ludicrous and oppressive thought) there was no Captain—there was only me. . . .

That sudden and characteristic twinge of helplessness of being—in technical competence—unequal to a searching occasion, did not last more than a few moments: action cured it, as it always does. I took the ship from Number One, I leant over the dodger and started peering out ahead, I gave the right orders (that original " SLOW BOTH " had been over-cautious, a mistake induced by nervousness, and I returned to the former convoy-speed), I plotted in my head the sirens of the nearest ships and got a grip of the shadowy picture. But the sweating and the tenseness remained, appropriate and inescapable adjuncts to the moment. There we were, thirty-odd ships in company, trusting each other to do nothing foolish or unusual, rolling along in a close body but in touch only by uncertain sound. I was better off than the rest, being clear of the columns, but this was true only if the picture remained the same shape: if it altered, if it overlapped, if somebody broke loose, the whole fabric would be destroyed and we would in truth be running blind. Fog is always like that—a tenuous hold on safety which a single false step can shatter, and nothing can regain: there is no cure for it except to trust and to deserve the trust of others, in continuous unbroken loyalty.

In the gay and informal days of peace, when for instance I had drunk a jugful of Black Velvet in extra-ordinary surroundings, or suffered some amorous set-back in the least dignified circumstances, I would usually end by saying, " Well, that was a new experience, any-way "; and I found myself thinking it threequarters of an hour later, when we came out of the fogbank and into sunshine again. Nothing had gone wrong, and the convoy was as good as new: but the short spell of blindfold action, backed as it was by the knowledge that I had no one on whose nerve or judgment I could lean, had been like a sudden icy shower which reached new and unrealized corners of one's body. And, like a cold shower, it had been exhilarating, with a keen edge of invigoration which lasted far beyond the immediate moment. Once more, the operation had shown a profit. "That's fog, that was," I thought, and knew that I had conquered one more personal doubt. There had been an initial moment of uncertainty, and I had made one minor mistake; but if it was never worse than that, even if it went on for very much longer, I reckoned that I had it taped.

To be certain of that, where before there had been nothing but an unpleasant conviction of helplessness, was certainly a gain.

I enjoyed coming up harbour on return to our base, for a variety of reasons no doubt deeply rooted in personal vanity. But to come home with virtually a brand-new ship as my first command—what, in truth, could be better than that? We took no chances with our entrance that afternoon; the hands were in their No. 3 rig in good time, the motor-boat went down like a well-conducted lift, and our piping as we passed the many destroyers and corvettes at anchor was a model of elegance and harmony. As we went at slow speed (and rather closer than was necessary) past *Dipper*, which has the buoy next to ours, there was much stirring on her upper deck: critical eyes followed us, the Officer-of-the-Day darted out with unusual promptness, and from the porthole of the Captain's cabin an inquisitive head, intent on our progress, very nearly poked out. . . . Under such circumstances, our manœuvring up to the buoy just *had* to be good. (I noticed, incidentally, that for use on such occasions the First Lieutenant had a model phrase: "Plenty of way on, sir!"—meaning, clearly, "If you crack up to the buoy at this pace, you'll knock off the buoy-jumper.") It was the sort of lime-lit moment when some public blunder is almost certain to occur, and I waited for whatever it was to be—a swamped motor-boat, a man overboard—with fatalistic calm. But this time everything chose to go right: within two minutes the bridle was secured, and *Winger* was in company.

I signalled "Greetings" to *Dipper*, who replied, "Likewise." Strong men waste no words.

CHAPTER III

THE STEP UP

To have one's First Lieutenant salute and report: "Divisions correct, sir !" on a fine Sunday morning on the quarter-deck may seem a small thing to have waited two and a half years for. I did not find it so. Nor, as I went down the starboard side to inspect the Seamen's Division, did I feel that I was wasting my time or going through a mere rubber-stamp formality. Sunday morning is always something special on board : the ship is at her tidiest, every one is in his smartest rig, and every one (except for the few hands who cannot possibly be spared) presents himself at Divisions, gold badges and all, ready to meet the Captain's eye, and to survive and justify its scrutiny. For me, this first Sunday morning was the most special of all so far : it was impossible not to feel immense pride that my ship's company was waiting for me (as other ship's companies, all over the harbour and indeed in every quarter of the globe, were waiting for their Captains), and that I was playing this rôle in an ancient and honoured ceremony.

If pride is the deadliest of sins, it is superior in a good many other respects as well.

Very young, most of those seaman looked, as I walked slowly down their lines : young, but self-reliant and self-confident, in the manner of British seamen since the first one put to sea. Nothing has been demonstrated with more clarity in this war than that we *are* a seafaring nation, in the special sense that we breed sailors without knowing it : the sea is in the blood, and the blood proves true time and time again in countless ways. Here, for instance, were a score and more of young men, picked haphazard from thousands of others, taken from the most diverse jobs or from no jobs at all : they are set to work in a ship, almost " from cold," with a minimum of previous training ashore, and in a little while they are as much a part of that ship as her own engines, and seem just as surely designed for the job. I don't say that no other nation can do it—that would be to deny much of recent sea-history, and the staunch allies we have found there : but I *do* say that this nation does it superbly and unfailingly, as a national art that never seems to flag.

So much for *Winger's* seamen, anyway. . . . Farther ahead of them, on the same side, was the Communications and Miscellaneous Division—a rather mixed collection, but a lot smarter than it sounds. All the signalmen I knew by name already, from their work up on the bridge, and the wardroom stewards as well : the Sick Berth Attendant was another rating I had " memorized," by reason of a piece of smart salesmanship he had worked on me the previous day. I had enlisted his professional help. " This is just what you need, sir," he had said, holding out a grisly-looking bottle : " *Parafinum liquidum.*" " Good heavens ! " I said. " That's liquid paraffin." " Oh, no, sir," he answered readily. " This is much more refined." I suppose there was some sort of ambiguous truth in the answer : it was good enough to fool me, anyway.

When I had finished with this division I crossed over to the port waist, where the engine-room and stoker ratings were fallen in. For a ship of her size, *Winger* carried a large complement of these : and here again, especially among the stokers, youth was the most striking factor. War teaches quickly, of course, but it did seem almost unreasonable to expect some of these

young lads to treat machinery properly. . . . Beyond
them was a small compact body of engine-room artifi-
cers and stoker petty officers : older men, some of them
pensioners, and the very stuff of the Navy—as the
sprinkling of Long Service and Good Conduct medal-
ribbons showed. With such a strong and experienced
team to call upon, it did not seem that *Winger* need ever
stop running ; and I thought I saw in the Chief's eye
as he reported them correct, the same sort of pride as
I myself felt in the whole ship. It made an appropriate
and heartening end of Divisions.

For a variety of reasons I did not speak to the ship's
company on that first Sunday morning, although I knew
it was customary for a new Captain to take the first
opportunity of saying something to his crew, " even if,"
as some one at the club said, " it is only threats and
abuse." . . . I felt, myself, that it was too early in my
command for it to mean anything, and that whatever
I said would have more reality in it when I knew them
better, and more solid effect when they knew me. A
speech from a stranger means nothing compared with
one from some one you know and understand : and I
did not want to start off with platitudes or a stereotyped
pep-talk, for lack of material which I knew would be
forthcoming later.

" Noel Coward killed that sort of thing stone dead,
anyway," said a fellow destroyer-captain feelingly, when
I mentioned the subject later. " Nowadays the troops
expect too much glamour altogether. . . ."

In any case, I let the opportunity go, that first Sunday
morning. Instead, I read prayers, and the twenty-third
Psalm, and between us we managed a hymn, more
notable for carrying power than for harmony. And then
the First Lieutenant dismissed the ship's company, and
" Pipe down " was sounded ; and after I had inspected
and signed the small collection of nineteen books, ranging
from " Gyro Compass Log " to " Registered Letter
Book," which came up for my attention weekly and lay

solid and unescapable on my desk till they were dealt with, I myself was free to lean back and enjoy a Sunday breathing-space.

I felt I had earned it, if only by the fatiguing nature of the rounds I had gone the previous day. Captain's Rounds are what you make them—that is, anything from a negligent formality to a searching and critical examination of the whole ship : for my first occasion, I chose to make them the latter, to my own satisfaction and the surprise and exhaustion of my officers. Not only the mess-decks, but the store-rooms and magazines were all faithfully covered : it meant nearly two hours of climbing up and down ladders, squeezing through water-tight hatches, bending double to get into the cable-locker and the fore-peak : being roasted in the boiler-room, stifled in the paint-shop, dazzled by the bright-work in the Chief Petty Officers' mess : a prolonged and acrobatic session which gave me a lot of information and, incidentally, a formidable thirst. I saw much to commend—the bathrooms (always a difficult item) were exceptionally clean, and the engine-room positively fit to eat and sleep in—and one or two things I disliked: hammocks badly stowed, and an oven whose savoury smell came from layer upon layer of ingrained gravy-drippings. But I would have disliked it even more if there had been nothing for me to criticize. Perfection is no fun at all—unless it is prompted by one's own ideas or produced by one's own efforts.

That afternoon I made my way up to Operations, to lay my zeal and devotion at their disposal and (more seriously) to call formally upon the Admiral. The Senior Staff Officer Operations was out : his henchman, a friend of mine, was holding the fort (a deep armchair) with the utmost tenacity. When I entered the room :

" Local boy makes good," he said amiably. " Congratulations to you."

" Thanks," I answered.

" How's the ship ? "

" Fine."

" Have they cleared off the whole of your defect list ? "

" Yes."

" Did you have a good trip up ? "

" Not bad."

He looked at me. " You used to be more talkative."

" I used to be a First Lieutenant," I said with simple dignity.

" All right, all right. Do you want to see the Admiral to-day ? "

" If he wants to see me."

" Unfortunately he is rather at the mercy of convention. New commanding officers—*very* new commanding officers—have the *entrée*. I'll go and fix it for you." He locked all the drawers in his desk, rather ostentatiously, and then went out, while I was left to contemplate a wall-map which showed, in full colour and horrid detail, the local hazards of navigation. They were many.

Interviews with Admirals are something special and don't get into this kind of book. In any case an account of my reactions would undoubtedly make foolish reading, and especially so after the war, when very senior officers will no doubt be lumped together once more as " brass hats " and revive their public status as ignorant figures of fun. But I will record, for the honour of truth and the mockery of posterity, that I came out of that room ready to go into action with anything, under any odds.

A number of other things cheered me up, too, less authoritatively but with a pleasant sense of goodwill near at hand. There were signals from other ships, many so robustly humorous that I might have feared for the moral welfare of the younger signalmen if they had been anything but signalmen—the unshockable branch of the Navy. There were letters from stray friends ashore, some of them betraying an unfamiliarity with naval rank which always erred on the flattering side. (" Captain Monsarrat, Royal Navy," was the mode of address used by my mother—a boy's best friend, by a long way.) It became, for a space, even easier than usual to stand drinks to people at the Naval Club ashore, people whose approach seemed disinterested enough but whose congratulations could hardly be countered with a mere acknowledgment. Nor were they all entirely disinterested, it seemed. " I always said you'd get the job," said some one I had never seen before in my life. " Mine's a whisky. . . ." But this bogus phase, not without its amusing side (even at fifteen shillings a round of drinks), soon passed : normality was restored, and with it freedom to concentrate on earning the goodwill on a more official basis.

To H., a friend from my first days in the Navy, who wrote inquiring (with an eye to my peace-time interests) whether true democracy reigned on board :

" Certainly it does," I replied, " and not only democracy but fully centralized democracy at that. No decision is too small to evade official scrutiny. A select committee sits at the back of the bridge, debating my helm orders and countermanding any of them which appear to conflict with public welfare. Whether we go to sea or not is determined by popular vote, and I often have an uneasy time canvassing support before we can get under way. The younger seamen, of course, are organized into a Guild of Youth, with fully accredited fraternal delegates from all branches : their banners, boldly inscribed with such slogans as " DOWN WITH THE ANCHOR," " UP SPIRITS ! ", etc., make a brave sight, and hardly interfere at all with my own flag signals. I can assure you that my ship has a most distinctive air, and is certain to make her mark sooner or later, probably on the dock-wall."

But the job allowed, basically, no such delegation of authority, interesting though the experiment might have been : and since this is an account of a job as well as of a ship, its essentials may be worth enumerating in detail. The " step up " brought with it so many changes of habit and outlook, even within the small framework of life on board, that it was almost like entering a different branch of the service, and learning the whole thing over again.

First, and most notable, is the Captain's separation from the wardroom : this is no longer one's home and only the smallest amount of time can be spent in it. Apart from anything else, the separation is dictated by the simple demands of work : upon the Captain devolves the largest share of the ship's paper-work, in one form or another, and there are hours to be spent daily at his desk before he is free to indulge any taste for companionship he may have. Nor, once being free, *can* he indulge it as he might like : for there are other considerations even more compelling. Between a Captain and his officers there must be a gap : it is pleasant to mix freely with them without formality, on level terms, and after three years of having the wardroom as a centre of interest and activity, it is extraordinarily difficult to change one's habits : but this freedom of intercourse simply does not work. The better friends you are with your officers, the worse Captain. You may enjoy yourself, you may even seem to extend your influence, but in fact you are evading your job, which is command and nothing else.

This is a hard lesson to learn, and for some one like myself, with a personal and ingrained bias against formality and the more stifling brands of social humbug (to say nothing of a liking for parties on the heroic scale) it is a most depressing one. But learnt it must be if you are to have, when the necessity arises, absolute trust and absolute obedience. If you have bought the sort of trust which springs from being a " good fellow," if you have swapped obedience for popularity, then God help you when the time comes to cash them to the

Upper: DIPPER DIDN'T ROLL   [*Page* 105
Lower: AND CHASED US ONWARDS   [*Page* 121

TOMBOLA
[Page 129

THOSE LITTLE
ONES
[Page 91

full. You will almost certainly find yourself bankrupt, and it is a bankruptcy which only the expenditure of human life may be able to redeem.

Another, and not a minor point in this division between Captain and officers is that the wardroom is *their* home, not his, the First Lieutenant being president of the mess and the Captain only a guest there. They should be absolutely free to relax and to entertain their friends, without interference or overlooking of any sort. To cut loose under Father's eye, however benign, isn't the same thing at all. I know; I've tried it and failed consistently.

In the same way, you are now farther away from the crew and much slower to get to know them. With the exception of two or three of them—the Coxswain, the signalman of the watch—they never come under your direct orders, you are not a great deal on the upper deck in any case, and only very gradually do personalities emerge and labels stick. The fact that you no longer give orders directly is sometimes tantalizing, after being accustomed as First Lieutenant, to going into action under the slightest provocation or none at all. If you see something going or already gone wrong, it is difficult not to jump into the gap and set people working directly. But this is not now the way: a fender left hanging over the side, or a bucketful of waste carelessly tipped to windward, is not the Captain's pidgin. You have to ring for the quartermaster, who fetches the Officer-of-the-Day, who is then told to deal with it: while all the time words and phrases, exquisitely rich, gloriously appropriate, struggle for utterance on your lips. . . .

For the Captain, boredom at sea is inevitable; it goes with the job, like the hard and useless shell of a nut. As a watch-keeping officer, I always had a minimum of two watches a day—eight hours—on the bridge: now it is all short spells of piecework and (especially in summer) not much of that either. I take the ship for all the difficult bits—entering and leaving harbour,

G

manœuvring through the convoy, taking part in a club run or a shoot with destroyers or other corvettes, closing another escort for orders ; and of course I have all the time to know exactly where the ship is, and to make sure that we do our escort job properly—supervision which, at the beginning of my command, kept me on the bridge far longer than was actually necessary.

But, a routine having been established, and my initial overcarefulness dispelled by a period of complete freedom from crises, mostly it is waiting : waiting in my sea-cabin directly underneath the bridge, reading, smoking, memorizing orders or manœuvring signals, eating meals, going up on the bridge for a blitz on the station-keeping : writing letters, thinking, and waiting again.

Now and then information or signals or queries come down the voice-pipe from the bridge. It is odd to be at the other end of that voice-pipe, which for so long was the focus of my attention and to acknowledge the " Captain, sir ! " by which they call me. It was the other way about, for scores of convoys and hundreds of watches. I must have said " Captain, sir ! " a thousand times in this war, under a thousand different circumstances, and then paused, eyeing the unidentified 'plane, the torpedoed ship, the floating mine, and waited for an answer from the heart of the ship. Now I am it : on call to meet any emergency : the end-of-the-voice-pipe answer which must always be the right one.

Of course, if something happens, all this suspended activity is reversed. Waiting is finished with, and short spells on the bridge as well : a set four-hour watch becomes a picnic beside the long stretches which may then be necessary. A gale, a fog, a breakdown, an action —all these keep me up on the bridge until they are at an end, six hours, eight hours, ten hours later ; they are all, in a greater or less degree, tests of endurance as well as skill. Waiting at the end of the voice-pipe, you know that, sooner or later, whatever reserve of strength you have will be fully tried : that is the certainty which justifies your position. It is your job to have a reserve, by the way : no excuses on this point are acceptable, or, indeed, thinkable,

And when you *are* up on the bridge you have a part to play which must be nothing less than flawless. Up there, you must, to begin and end with, be a centre of absolute calm, but in such a *positive* way that the calm —automatic, inviolable, taken for granted—extends all round you. Among the dozen or so on the bridge there is silence except for the minimum exchanges—the helmsman repeating courses, the Yeoman of Signals reading a message, the Pilot answering a query, his head bent over the chart-table. Into that silence your orders, never above a conversational tone, should drop like stones : crisp, direct, final. If you show signs of excitement, the chances are that the order you give will be carried out more hurriedly than the rating concerned can properly manage ; and an order bungled for that reason is no one's fault but your own. And because mistakes like this can always be covered up and shifted to some one else, they must never be made. . . . I said at the beginning that it was a part to be played, and so it is : an elaborate masquerade which must hide almost all your normal feelings and reactions, and leave only stillness and a level voice. But it pays an incomparable dividend, this kind of restraint—for yourself as much as for the ship. Schooled down and confined to the essentials, you become, in the end, the instrument of precision that you yourself need.

Certainly you have need of the best you can get in that line, since—and here is the last aspect of command which is worth recounting—there is absolutely no one else to do your job if it seems to be growing too big for you. This is something entirely novel, and it means reversing a habit of mind which has been yours ever since you joined the Navy and went to sea. On every single occasion up to now, in any matter concerning the ships you have served in, there has always been some one to lean on : behind every decision, every development or crisis, there has always been the Captain, taking the weight and the final responsibility. The fact does not destroy initiative, but it qualifies it : whatever you do, you know you have at hand a judge and a friend—the one to satisfy, the other to turn to if need be.

All that is now ended. All trails now lead to you yourself : you are it—the focus of other people's eyes, the heart and brain of the ship. You are quite alone : you can dodge no issue, you can shelve no burden or decision of any sort. It is a moment which surprises you—it had surprised me, when we ran into fog the first day : the Navy has been training you for this moment for months and years, but only the moment itself can teach, and you are in luck if you have a comfortable space to learn it in.

For it is not something which clicks into place when the bell strikes, and thereafter stays there. It takes a little time, and now and again your instinct tries to retreat from it, and back comes the initial astonishment. That is where your self-discipline must be at hand to help you. Astonishment won't do—or it won't do on the surface at least ; somehow it must be translated into cool reaction and the usual level voice, if it is not to spread fatally to those around you. And somehow it *is* translated, and the effort itself is the cure, and presently you find that you are as fully in control as you were pretending to be, a little while ago. . . .

That is the value of the masquerade : it develops until it takes charge altogether : the character-part becomes the reality and the reality is priceless.

For once you have the central idea fixed in your brain, you know where you are, and a firm grip follows. The grip—the absolute confidence—is helped all the time by pride, in the ship and in the size of the job : probably the most sustaining thing of all.

You need something to sustain you : once again, this is it.

CHAPTER IV

EARNING IT

I TOOK over in the spring—a final blessing on the appointment. Ahead of us lay a long summer, nights shortening to nothing and fair weather : only in the far distance was the trial and turmoil of winter in view. There was also, as an additional item on the credit side, the possibility of decisive action in our particular corner of the war : " First up the Seine," was a current corvette catchword : we felt we were waiting and preparing for something, and we hoped that the flotilla wouldn't be left out of it when it came. I remember the speculation on that point at the time : on the possibility that we might actually be present at a landing on the European coast—our shallow draught and extreme manœuvrability seemed to make this a reasonable bet—or (more likely) that we would be convoying men and material on a cross-Channel shuttle service as soon as a bridgehead was fairly established. The further alternative, a grisly one, was that we would be left out of things altogether and would be kept on at our Old East Coast convoy assignment while the destroyers stole the limelight and the fun. . . . In the meantime, all through that spring and early summer, we went on with the job—in and out on patrol, up and down on convoy-escort, training, exercising, sharpening up (we hoped) for the real party which was to come. The ship looked a daisy, incidentally—though the fact is neither relevant nor strictly concerned with war.

If, at first, I found the job of taking *Winger* to sea a wearing one, it was probably my own fault. There seemed so much to remember, so many precautions to take, such a slender margin of things one could safely leave to other people. . . . I expect there *are* Captains

who don't worry at sea, who can keep off the bridge for
hours at a stretch, who are not nagged all the time by a
thousand possibilities, a thousand doubts : but I was
not one in those early days—nor am I yet, to the extent
I should like. It isn't a question of trusting one's officers,
it is a matter of balancing chances and making sure of
the right verdict : absolute responsibility needs absolute
certainty, and how can you obtain that otherwise than
by unending personal supervision ?

Something *might* go wrong, even during the simplest
operations. Number One *might* miss a buoy. Pilot *might*
get out of station. Guns *might* steer north instead of
south. Up you go on to the bridge to make quite sure.
It was a habit of mind, a nervous reaction that only
time could cure : things got better, naturally, as I came
to know each officer's capabilities and to trust his judgment in a sudden crisis : but at the beginning, for the
first few weeks, every trip was a continuous and wakeful
ordeal which left me unhappily doubtful of my own
staying power. At this pace, winter with its sixteen
hours of darkness could finish me off. Indeed, at this
pace I would never see winter at all.

In point of fact I was well served in the matter of
watch-keeping officers. *Winger's* wardroom compared
very favourably with some other ships, where the
" dilution " of war-time had left the mixture a bit weak.
The First Lieutenant had been a long time on the coast,
and had the whole thing sewn up tight : the Pilot (Sub.,
R.N.R.) was as competent as I could wish, the Gunner
(the least experienced) was conscientious and painstaking,
and the Midshipman was a valiant and independent
young man who was ready to take over my job any day
of the week and hold it down against all comers.

But I still wanted to be told every single thing that
went on. . . . One of the more helpful attributes of a
good Officer-of-the-Watch is that he knows when to call
the Captain and when to contend with a situation himself : a watch-keeper whose judgment is really trust-

worthy in this respect is an enormous asset as far as the Captain's peace of mind is concerned. It is helpful also if this ability to estimate crisis is roughly the same among all one's officers : too often it is not, and whereas one of them, over-zealous, will sing out if he as much passes a floating log, another (usually the least accomplished) will proceed with such sturdy independence that, when finally you are summoned to the bridge, the entire world seems to be compounded of ships bearing down on you from all angles, hoarse cries out of the darkness, and a line of hungry breakers just over the port rail. When, later (often much later) you ask for an explanation, you will be told that " things looked all right, but they got worse suddenly "—an account transparently and desperately true, but giving you neither satisfaction with the past nor confidence in the future.

Since there is nothing more ageing that this kind of uncertainty, I laid down in my Standing Orders a list of directions designed to cover every eventuality, as far as could be foreseen, for all our operations on this coast : the text of the relevant paragraph was as follows :

" The Officer-of-the-Watch is to call me, without fail, in the following circumstances :

(a) On sighting or hearing an aircraft not identified as friendly.

(b) On obtaining an Asdic contact.

(c) On sighting any vessel which is either (1) suspicious or (2) likely to interfere with our intended course (e.g. a destroyer on patrol or a mine-sweeper on our own side of the channel).

(d) On sighting flares or starshell at night.

(e) On a change in the weather or visibility.

(f) If a buoy or light-vessel is not sighted at the expected time.

(g) On an escort or ship in convoy leaving its proper station.

> (*h*) On any ship (escort or merchant ship) joining the convoy.
>
> (*i*) If the presence of other ships nearby seems likely to force us off the swept channel, or on the wrong side of a wreck buoy or other dangerous obstruction.
>
> (*j*) In any doubt or emergency."

It might be thought that these left no loophole for surprises : but even this list did not prevent an occasional jolt. There it was, anyway, as full as I could make it : designed to keep the ship out of trouble, and myself awake, for most of the twenty-four hours.

We started the season with a nautical oddment of the sort which, for no real reason, is a first-rate tonic for a ship and which I myself found distinctly heartening : the interception and bringing in of a couple of fishing-drifters with a number of refugees aboard.

The meeting was entirely a matter of chance. Our convoy that morning had taken us rather farther north than usual, and I was stooging about to seaward of it, wondering if the dropping of a practice depth-charge would (*a*) escape the attention of the Senior Officer, who didn't like that sort of thing round his convoys, and (*b*) stun enough fish to make it worth while lowering the whaler, when the look-out suddenly reported " Objects to starboard." Visibility was very good, and within a few moments they were identified as a pair of small drifters, south-bound, farther out than those generally are but still harmless enough. I decided to close them, nevertheless : nominally to " establish identity beyond donbt," actually to see if I could save the expense of that depth-charge. The crews of the drifters working on this coast are extraordinarily generous with their catches whenever we encounter them. . . .

There was, however, soon to be another factor : for when we were still about two miles off the signalman of the watch suddenly called out :

"I don't think they're British, sir!" He was wrinkling his eyes as he stared at them through his binoculars. "Some sort of foreign ensign—and they've got colours painted on their sides as well. Blue and red. There's some lettering, too, looks like Norwegian, sir."

That was something quite different. I increased speed, altered course to intercept them and, as a precaution, went to Action Stations. It might be any sort of a ruse, from a Q-ship to a disguised submarine, and I did not want to be caught out. As the distance lessened, and it was clear that they were both flying Norwegian ensigns, every one on the upper deck who was not manning a gun crowded to the rails to examine them : the first visitors from "over there" that we had ever seen. There was one big and one small boat, both with large flags painted on their sides, and both apparently unarmed. The people on board were staring back at us, and some of them waved energetically ; but of course it wouldn't do to be taken in by such a simple trick as that. I hoisted the International Code signal for "Stop instantly," and when this was obeyed, and I had circled them once in silence, I stopped engines and called the First Lieutenant to the bridge.

"Boarding party ready, Number One," I told him. "Yourself and four good hands. Revolvers. I'll get these chaps to come alongside one at a time : we'll take the big one first. When you get on board, see the captain, and then search the boat throughout, whatever sort of yarn he tells. The Norwegian for 'Hands up!' is . . .' I thought rapidly, without avail, ". . . is probably 'Hands up!' I don't suppose that sort of language difficulty will arise, anyway. But look out for surprises." And then, over the loud-hailer (which reached all parts of the upper deck): "Train all guns to starboard and cover those two," I said. "Make it as obvious as you can. If they start anything, open fire."

Last of all, still through the loud-hailer, "Train on the big drifter."

" Speaker trained, sir ! "

I mustered the most basic English I could think of. " Come alongside," I called out. " Slowly. One of you only. We will throw a rope."

An arm waved acknowledgment from the window of the deck-house, and obediently the larger drifter edged alongside. It was here that things got slightly out of hand. As I have indicated, we were prepared for surprises, but their next move was scarcely foreseeable. For the instant that the two ships touched, half a dozen of the drifter's crew started to shovel fish on to our upper deck from their own : enormous fish, in glistening cascades. The First Lieutenant, as he jumped across, boarded under a positive barrage of them. I thought furiously for a moment, my mind running on explosive cod. . . . Then I relaxed : after all, they *were* neutral ships, and this was a damned good visiting card—in fact, it was the best one they could have produced.

After a few moments of this, during which the piles of fish grew to huge proportions and some of the more astute mess-cooks were already staking their claims, the First Lieutenant poked his head out of the deck-house.

" It's all right, sir," he called out. " They're all friendly."

" They'd better be," I answered in a thunderous voice over the loud-hailer. Then, " Have a good look round, and then come back aboard and tell him to lay off while we take a look at the other one. And for goodness' sake stop them slinging that fish over. We've got far more than we need, and we've developed a five-degree list already."

Number One's search revealed nothing except a lot more fish below decks, and a great many talkative and happy passengers. (" Some of them kissed me," he said in the wardroom later, with no particular expression in his voice), and when the second boat had been searched he came back aboard to report. Both skippers told the same story (a slight odour which I recognized enviously as Schnapps floated round the bridge as he gave me the details). They had been ten days at sea, making for England, had lost their way (having no sextant, and only the most inadequate charts), had been bombed and gunned by German aircraft, and were now overjoyed to be free once more, after months of planning. I sent off a signal, outlining the incident and asking permission to take them in : and meanwhile I tried to circle round and round them, to keep them under general observation. (We had no means of checking their story and all the passengers might have been just so many quislings or spies, for all we knew to the contrary. But that was a shoreside worry—my job was to see that they didn't step out of line while they were afloat.) Keeping them under observation from a proper distance, however, proved almost impossible : it seemed that having found a friend they were going to hang on to him, for they attached themselves to my stern like a couple of porpoises following a whale, clinging one to each quarter as I circled. No matter what I did, they followed me as if I were towing them on a short elastic hawser. . . . It was something of a relief when my signal was approved and I could put an end to the circus parade by setting course for our destination. I didn't want to hurt their feelings : not after all that fish (already there was a most pungent odour of frying cod permeating the whole ship) : but there is a limit to what one can suffer in the cause of politeness, even under those conditions.

We were to hand them over to a trio of patrol-trawlers coming out to meet us, and when we reached the rendezvous an affectionate farewell was taken, with much cheering and waving on both sides. The leading patrol-trawler signalled (rather foolishly) : " Are they danger-ous ? " to which I replied, " Yes. Beware flying fish." In spite of interrogatives I didn't elaborate the signal for him. It would keep him up to the mark, and he'd find out, anyway, as soon as he got anywhere within throwing distance.

This was, as I have said, a chance oddment, which might have been specially planned to enliven us : the backbone of our job—patrolling and escorting—was much more mundane, with a minimum of variation and no Schnapps at all. Here, in illustration, is a sample week, of no special significance, but fairly representative of our work, elaborated from the deck-log some time during June.

No frenzied signalling preceded it : the week's work started, in fact, at the R.N. cinema on the quay, and was formally covered by the log-entry : " Leave to the Starboard Watch from 13.00 to 18.00. Canteen Cinema leave, 19.30." When the ship was under sailing orders before a patrol, leave expired four hours before sailing time—four hours being the time calculated as sufficient to dissipate the fog of love in a rating's eye or any other sort of fog anywhere else. But I usually extended this leave till the end of the performance at the quayside cinema since no one could come to any harm there, and if all liberty-men were in one definite place together they could be recalled very simply—the main consideration. Thus we generally went along in a body : the whole wardroom (except the Officer-of-the-Day) and half the ship's company. It was almost an official exercise : indeed, in the case of some films it was a collective endurance test in itself.

Surfeited on this occasion by Dorothy Lamour (if such a statement is not ungallant or actionable) we strolled along the quay towards the pontoon where the liberty-boat was waiting for us : half a ship's company, relaxed, at ease in the sunlight, enjoying a last spell of freedom preparatory to tightening up again. There was five minutes to spare before the boat left, so I called in at the mine-sweeping office to get the latest report of our patrol area, and find out if there were any special sections

to be avoided. Mines—treacherous and unpredictable
—are something I specially loathe : my friend in charge
of the M/S office seemed to have a correspondingly
tender affection for them. At any rate it was with
obvious satisfaction that he produced his sweeping chart
and pointed out the current pitfalls and queries.

" Now this," he said, tapping with his pencil an area
thick with sinister black crosses, " this is a *lovely* corner.
It's been giving us no end of trouble, and it's not finished
with yet, by a long chalk. The sweepers put up two
there, yesterday, and another one *there* this morning.
That's the lot so far, but I shouldn't be surprised if
there was another clump of them *there*."

It's me that'll be surprised, not you, I thought. But
I nodded.

" What about my actual patrol area to-night ? "

He shook his head, almost as if he were sorry to disappoint me. " It looks pretty well clear," he answered.
" Has been for weeks, in fact. But you never know, do
you ? I shouldn't go wandering off very far to the
eastward round about K Buoy, if I were you."

" I promise faithfully I won't."

" The channel itself will be swept as usual, anyway,
before you get there, and you'll pick up all the signals
if anything turns up'"

Disregarding the fact (of which he was well aware)
that the first signal about a mine is often a bang and
an enormous column of water just astern of you, I
bade him good-night and crossed the quay to the
waiting boat.

Dinner was ready when we got back on board—a
rather austere meal, as usual on such occasions, without
any alcohol before, during, or after. There is no special
rule about drinking either before sailing or when we are
actually at sea ; but my own feeling, which the wardroom shares, is that it is giving away a definite chance
to fortune if you are anything but absolutely normal and
unexhilarated when afloat. Drink always stimulates, in

a greater or less degree : a stimulated judgment is an unsound one ; and (taking the gloomy view which may always jump into reality at any moment) if the ship is sunk, and you are in the water, you are a dead duck from the start unless you can stay awake and aware indefinitely. At such times, a single shot of whisky, taken earlier on, might give you a comfortable glow, lulling you into that carelessness which is the equivalent of an obituary notice, any day of the week. So that evening, as on other evenings before sailing, we all drank water, and even contrived to give the impression of liking it.

After dinner, according to our custom, I walked up and down the length of the quarter-deck with Number One. We were not due to leave for our patrol until ten o'clock—summer had turned night-patrolling into a short operation, with an agreeably late start ; and to-night the cool air, the evening sunshine, the quiet isolation of our berth at the buoy, all made the interval an exceptionally pleasant prelude to sea-going. There were, as usual, others walking up and down in the same fashion as ourselves, in different parts of the ship : the Coxswain and the Chief E.R.A., earnestly conferring : a couple of young telegraphists up on the fo'c'sle : a lone hand with bent head, arms folded, and something weighty on his mind, who strode up and down the iron deck as if it were a deserted country lane. There were people washing out clothes at the entrance to the mess-deck passageway : there was a gramophone playing somewhere forward : there was a rating in the port waist, under the ordeal of having his hair cut by a stoker, and not pretending he was in the least satisfied with the operation. Summer evening in harbour : all of it familiar and all of it good. At such times we seemed more than a ship's company, almost a family, with the family's varied interests and closely binding ties—Number One said, suddenly : "About that pro-posed alteration to the flag-locker . . ." and I was recalled to a nearer reality. But still the surrounding peace remained with us, securely settled and comfortingly strong.

As I half-turned towards him, I noticed the quarter-master standing nearby wrinkling up his nose at a drift of my cigar-smoke, with an expression which seemed to indicate pleasure but which may have been a long way from it. Whatever it was, it vanished instantly, as if sponged off, when he became aware of my glance, and with a look of enormous concentration he bent down and began to polish the butt of his revolver. Yes, there was nothing wrong with this evening, or with this ship either.

An hour later saw us intensely active, and almost ready to go. I was down in my cabin then, first collecting and laying out the small pile of secret signal logs and Operational Orders which the Midshipman would take up to the bridge, and later changing into sea-going rig: but I could follow the exact progress of work both down below and on the upper deck, so clear and assignable were the various noises as the Chief ran through his tests and the First Lieutenant secured the ship for sea. A faint humming noise was main engines being tried, at twenty or thirty revolutions, a tremble was the wheel being put from full-over to full-over: the engine-room telegraph bells and the revolution-counter spoke for themselves, even at this distance: and the " Action Stations " bell (preceded by the pipe, " Warning : alarm gongs testing ! " so as to avoid confusion) rang through the cabin flat with the shrill and startling persistence which made it recognizable above a hundred other noises.

Earlier, there had been a far-away clanking up for-ward—the cable passing through the windlass as the bridle was changed for a slip-rope : a vile clattering just over my head had been the Mediterranean ladder coming in, a final thunder of feet was the motor-boat being hoisted. Now, with five minutes to go before sailing time, the Chief reported, " Ready to move "; the First Lieutenant, " Ready to proceed " (some subtle difference there), and the rest of it was mine.

Up on the bridge, just before slipping, the exchange of information and orders follows an automatic, almost a blindfold routine : it is like some simple tune in which a wrong note sticks out a mile, and a phrase missed out makes every one look up in surprise. Solemnly contra-puntal, it makes its way from stage to stage :

Coxswain : " Special sea-duty-men closed up, sir."

Self : " Very good."

Coxswain : " Main engines rung on, sir."

Self : " Very good."

Yeoman of Signals : " Approved to proceed, sir."

Self : " Very good."

Sub. (calling from fo'c'sle) : " Ready to slip, sir."

Self : " Where's the buoy ? "

Sub. : Close under the port bow, sir."

Self : " Right. Stand by to slip. . . . Anything moving in the harbour.

Midshipman : " Nothing, sir," or " Seventeen trawlers coming upstream," as the case may be.

Self : " Slip ! "

There is a chunk ! as the hammer knocks off the slip and we are free of the buoy.

Turning a ship in a narrow stream is not complicated when you have two screws to play with, and plenty of power in reserve : it simply needs controlling so that the ship never moves more than a few yards ahead or astern until she is heading the right way—down-stream. For students of the drama, the necessary orders go like this :

" Slow astern port."

" Slow ahead starboard."

" Hard aport."

" Half ahead starboard."

" Half astern port."

" Slow ahead starboard."

" Wheel amidships."
" Slow astern port."
" Stop port."
" Hard aport."
" Slow ahead together."
" Half ahead together."

That is an example of an absolutely straightforward
and continuous turn, with no crises and no cross-traffic
to interrupt it.   To-night we waited, after our half-
circle, with both engines stopped while a destroyer at a
lower berth who was also due on patrol went through
the same manœuvre.   There was no other traffic on
the move.   Drifting very gently downstream with the
ebb tide, I watched her carefully, on the look-out for
mistakes : but as usual she gave a perfect performance.
When she was round we fell into line astern of her,
and left harbour in company.   Since it was after sunset
we did not pipe the other ships at anchor, but slipped
out anonymously.

Once clear of the harbour, and with the destroyer
drawing ahead and away from us at a stately twenty-five
knots (I had dined with her Captain the previous evening, and to my parting signal, " No red wine to-night,"
he answered grimly, " Blood will do . . .") we went to
Action Stations as usual.   The Gunner gave his gun's
crew a quick run-through at loading and aiming (using
a startled M.L. as a target), and then we tested all our
close-range guns, firing quick bursts of tracer on a safe
bearing.   This was the time for guns to jam, if jam they
must : later wouldn't do.   There was now a certain
amount of traffic about, which kept me on the bridge till
we were well on our way : mine-sweepers coming in or
out, small independent coasters punching the tide as they
tried to get in before nightfall, a trio of motor-torpedo-
boats snarling away towards the dusk and the opposite
coast.   I flashed to their leader, " Good luck ! " to which
he replied, " Thanks.   Actually we rely on skill."   Then
presently we were clear of the approaches, with nothing

to do but plug along till we reached our patrol area,
and after checking Pilot's estimate of the speed we
wanted to make good I handed over to Number One
and went below for a smoke.

We had an official engagement that night, as it happened, and since nothing occurred to sabotage it, we
spent the early part of our patrol playing cops-and-
robbers with a flotilla of motor-gunboats—or, in the
most austere service phraseology, "taking part in the
Night Encounter Exercise with light coastal forces."
This was the first one I had done, and I enjoyed it a
lot : after a preliminary conference the gunboats with-
drew out of range, split up and then came in to attack
at various angles. We took "evasive action," plotted
their courses, and tried to work out and forestall their
tactics : and in the meantime I practised a running
commentary on the loud-hailer for the benefit of the
guns' crews.

The agreed routine was that when we spotted the gunboats, and "opened fire," we were to flash a lamp in
their direction : and when they got near enough to run
a torpedo, they were to do the same. It says something
for the vigour of the exercise that before it was completed the whole horizon was nothing but winking lights,
with our own playing a furious solo in the middle. . . .
But it was good fun, as I have said, besides being
moderately instructive ; and I was sorry when the time
came to call off the battle, tot up the score, and turn to
something a bit more serious.

Not that it was really anything of the sort : our patrol
that night was one of the patrols that don't pay for their
oil-fuel—except, I suppose, as a preventive measure. We
had one query on the way up—something which might
have been a mine-laying aircraft, but which positively
dissolved into correct recognition signals when it saw
what it was running into—and that was really all. For
the rest of the time we just ploughed up and down,
faithful and dumb as spaniels. Once, at the top of our

run, we met the destroyer who had gone out with us that evening. Equally bored with nothing to do, she challenged us fiercely, but we were ready for that one. I felt wideawake after the motor-gunboat game, and having no other work to do, I spent most of the time up on the bridge, talking to the First Lieutenant (who shared the middle watch with the Midshipman) and coming in for a noble share of the latter's recurrent brews of cocoa.

Towards dawn we had a long convoy passing through our area, during which operation we drew aside respectfully—and wisely : our camouflage was too good to get involved with fifty-odd determined merchantmen, since we looked like a vague blur at night and that was just what they preferred to open fire at. Then, when they were clear, and we were ready to sink back into boredom again, we got a signal giving us a definite job—to go and look for an R.A.F. dinghy reported adrift, with survivors, to the eastwards of our patrol. (A lot of our bombers had gone out earlier : this was presumably one of the unlucky ones.) When we reached the estimated position we went through our usual routine in such cases—a box-search of the area, in gradually widening squares ; there was a Walrus joining in the hunt, stolid and unwieldy, making slow circles round the same spot, and occasionally coming down to sea-level to inspect something which had caught its eye. Neither of us had any luck : but shortly afterwards we had a second signal to say that the dinghy had been picked up farther north by a rescue motor-launch, with all its crew safe. We were glad to get that signal : to have to leave a bomber-crew adrift somewhere on this coast, knowing (or guessing) what they endure on their own job quite apart from this sort of ordeal, is one of the least cheering things that come our way.

By now it was near daylight, a pale flush to the eastwards, a lightening of the sea from black to cold grey, a subtle and welcome change. South of us some night minesweepers came up, vague shapes, invisible and un-suspected a few moments before, each of them suddenly knitting together a patch of darkness until it thickened into the outline of a ship : they also must be glad of daylight and an end to their task.   The light, creeping over the wave-tops and spreading towards the land, seemed to answer all the night's questions with a comforting and absolute wisdom.

At sea, every dawn is a thrill : that is something which has never changed and never lessened, throughout years of sea-going, no matter how grisly the occasion. It may not be beautiful : it may indeed be actively ugly : but, by God, it is a relief ! It solves so many problems—of station-keeping, of avoiding traffic and trouble : it gives you certainty instead of guesswork : it is safety after hazard.

It was also, this time, rather cold, with a bleak wind blowing off-shore and slapping the waves roughly against our bows as we turned for home. Satisfied that there was nothing more to be done (an easy decision to arrive at, under the circumstances), I went below for the journey back, leaving Pilot, who knew this bit blind-folded, to overtake the sweepers and bring her in.

An hour's sleep was cut short by his cautious, " Rather a lot of traffic ahead, sir," down the voice-pipe : and when I climbed up to the bridge again I found that we were now close inshore, and faced by a familiar problem which turned up at the end of nine patrols out of ten. The harbour was closed, as an unchallengeable signal on the lightship proclaimed : it would not be opened till the approach-channel had been swept, at some time (beyond prediction) ahead. In front of us, as we covered the last mile was a milling collection of sweepers and coastal craft, also waiting to go in : some of them anchored, others jockeying for position in case the " Port Closed " signal came down earlier than usual. Our problem was whether to anchor or not ourselves, and it was governed by three factors : that we had to oil when we got in: that there were only two berths available at the oiler, owing to some diving operations nearby: and that just astern of us two destroyers, also coming in from patrol, were waiting to nip in front at short notice and enormous speed. If we anchored, and they didn't, we should be right out of the picture: if we turned slow circles round the lightship (it might be for an hour or more) while they lost patience and dropped their picks, we might have time to get in front of them and stake a claim.

Both of them oiling ahead of us, and keeping us hanging about in the offing, would mean a great waste of time, cutting into our very short spell in harbour. There were quite a lot of things to be seen to, and we were due to go out again, on convoy, at eleven o'clock.

This time I waited around, champing, talking to the Captain of a Dutch minesweeper (gravely introduced to me the previous night as " the originator of the Dutch treat ") and being jostled by all and sundry, until I finally got bored with it, left the main mob, and dropped anchor nearby. It was still quite early. Hardly had the riding-slip been put on, hardly had I stirred my tea, when the lightship's flag came down with a run. The assembled fleet sprang into life: the destroyers pressed the button and roared past. Unfair to corvettes, I thought, as I sped up to the bridge again and let loose a torrent of orders— to the engine-room, the cable party, the First Lieutenant. It was a waste of time, really, since whatever speed we made we couldn't catch them up, but it went some way towards relieving the feelings.

As it happened, something else relieved them too, rather more effectively. When we neared the harbour entrance the usual hoists went up aboard the destroyers (now a long way ahead of us) indicating which berth they were making for. I called to the Yeoman:

" Both going to the oiler, I suppose ? "

He shook his head. " No, sir. One's a single number. Looks like Number Three Buoy."

It *was* Number Three Buoy, which left a vacant berth for us at the oiler and saved us a lot of time. The position was retrieved: breakfast would be tolerable after all. Within a few minutes the First Lieutenant had piped the hands to their stations and the wires and fenders were ready for securing to the oiler.

I had already had, even then, plenty of practice at coming alongside, but conditions varied so much from day to day that I never felt entirely sure that a perfect manœuvre would be forthcoming. Both wind and tide dead ahead of you, of course, are the ideal conditions: they ensure that you can keep the screws turning until the very last moment, and render the ship far more manœuvrable. At the other end of the scale—with the tide under your stern and the wind blowing the ship away from the oiler or the quay—anything may happen, from loss of paint to a docking-job. On one such occasion I had first failed entirely to come alongside the oiler—our relative positions took on a closer and closer resemblance to a T-bone steak, until after three tries I had to give up altogether—and then, trying to secure up to the Senior Officer's ship, I had put the fluke of my anchor through his bow-plating, causing a neat and unmendable tear. ("I wish we could do this sort of thing to Jerry," said a rating below me, not quite quietly enough, as we backed away from the target area.)

But that had been a really bad day—the tail-end of a gale and of a very tiring convoy. Usually it is less spectacular and relatively inexpensive. And when it is neatly done (as on this present occasion it chanced to be) it has a satisfying style and finish about it. If the moment to go "Half astern both" has been properly judged the ship stops dead, exactly parallel and exactly in the right spot, with the oiler's hose overhanging the ship's fuel-pipe connection: the heaving lines fore and aft whip across together, the headrope goes to the windlass and is heaved in slowly. Between the ship and the oiler the water is imprisoned, squeezed together: it seethes with a sudden spite, and the jumbled waves slop to and fro, criss-crossing between the two ships like echoes caught in a cavern : but foot by foot it is compressed and conquered, until suddenly it vanishes altogether, the ships' sides touch and part and touch again, and the trip—good or bad—futile or satisfactory—is over.

This morning, when oiling had been completed (concurrently with a bath and shave for myself) we went the short distance up harbour to our buoy. It was still rather early, and I took care to draw attention to the fact by unnecessary (or perhaps over-scrupulous) use of the siren : nothing is more tempting when you have been out all night, than a harbour full of smug and sleeping corvettes. (Destroyers, of course, never sleep.) The boat which we had sent ashore from the oiler was already alongside with the mail and the morning papers : breakfast, backed by these, was practically civilized and certainly refreshing, even counting the fake-egg-omelette. But the breathing-space did not last long : there was just time for Number One to wash down the upper deck and for myself to answer two official letters, before our sailing-orders arrived by the signal-boat. We were to start straight away. The mail was landed in a hurry, the mess-caterers ashore at the canteen were rounded up and brought back : then once more it was " Secure for sea," " Ready to proceed," " Slip ! " and off we went again.

We were due to join up with a north-bound convoy, taking out a small parcel of ships ourselves to add to the collection—a sort of nautical bottle-party. I had a trawler to help me, nominally under my orders but by nature independent (and incidentally senior to me in rank). Rounding up our contingent, getting them in formation, and adjusting their speed so that they neither hung about at the rendezvous nor panted ten miles astern of the main body—all this devolved on me, while the trawler, belching smoke of hideous density and hue, trundled on ahead to show us how. (I might have objected to this display of individuality, but a natural reluctance to raise hell was intensified, in this case, by the conviction that I was probably better off doing the thing myself in my own way. Trawlers have a lot to commend them, but they are not exactly the greyhounds of the ocean. And—though I know there are many people who disagree—one war at a time is really enough.) At any rate we got the flock out to the interception point at the proper time, and after the usual bout of " After you, Cecil; after you, Claude," they tacked themselves on to the stern of the convoy, while I closed the Senior Officer of the escort (a destroyer) to collect the convoy papers, and any last-minute orders he might have for me.

I was rather fond of this operation, which consisted of keeping pace with the other ship on a parallel course while the papers were transferred by hand-line : it could be done in any number of ways, from creeping alongside like a sick mongrel to dashing up at speed and dropping dead on the doorstep : I usually favoured the latter method, though that was probably more than the Senior Officer did. It was generally enlivened—as now—by a cross-talk on the loud hailer, wherein a robust wit was tempered hardly at all by the knowledge that every word of what one was saying was fully audible over a range of about two miles.

Having collected the packet of papers, a rather good story about an Indian prisoner-of-war, and a compliment on my camouflage, I dropped astern between the long lines of ships to muster them and then take up my station on the escort-screen. Like everyone else serving in corvettes or destroyers, I had seen hundreds of convoys in this war ; and if they did not always impress with the same pride and the same admiration as at the beginning, that was simply because of the human inability to hold an impression, however strong or vivid, indefinitely. Certainly the sea and the ships were the same : the proof was Britain itself still fighting.

When this is all over, some one will—some one *must*

—write an adequate history of the Merchant Service in action, free from armchair heroics about "forgotten men," but not shy to dwell upon the spirit and the flame. I wouldn't be able to do it, if only because (as I have said) I took them so much for granted already : they had been for so long in the centre of the picture, a picture bound, for that reason, to lose its force— just as a photograph, even of someone deeply loved, comes in the end to mean no more than any other ornament, because of its familiarity. But the feeling did return at odd times, such as this convoy-muster, with its significance undiminished and in all its odd intensity.

In this present collection of ships, for example, which now moved past me in their slow disciplined columns as I checked names and numbers, there was probably enough of the recent history of courage to form an imperishable chronicle, if it could be faithfully transcribed. There were ships that had seen scores of long-drawn-out actions, and still came back cheerfully for more : there were men—British and Allied sailors—who dared all, not as a job for money but simply as a chosen habit, who returned to the same task and the same run after two or even three hideous ordeals as survivors, who stuck to oil-tankers as other people stick to one brand of bottled beer. Even apart from action with the enemy, the men in these ships—some of them, old friends, were waving as I passed them now—had seen their job transformed by war into something a hundred times more difficult and more hazardous : they had accepted loyally the irksome compulsion of convoys, of never moving except in crowded company—a discipline quite alien to sailors, whose foremost instinct is to beat it in the opposite direction when another ship comes over the horizon : they had accepted the necessity of wallowing along for hundreds of miles at the speed of the slowest, and of keeping close station in weather like a dirty blanket hanging all around them.

They had accepted strange companions on their journeys. In this very convoy there were new tankers moving like fortresses, powerful American freighters, coastal scuttlers rolling, their decks awash, dead-beat tramps flogging worn-out engines for the extra revs. needed to keep up even this crawling speed. (One Master, when we told him to hurry up and close a gap, shouted back : " Can't do it. The Chief will give me hell if I ask for more revs.") Under the necessity of keeping coastwise traffic moving, and of other ships reaching their rendezvous in time to join trans-ocean convoys, there was really no alternative to chucking them all together and telling them to get on with it. War conditions had made this kind of bran-tub inevitable : but the disadvantages—inequality of speed and manœuvrability, the dependable keeping station on the unpredictable—were obvious, and they could only be countered by seamanship of a high order, a blend of skill and vigilance beyond belief and beyond praise.

That these qualities had been forthcoming, in continuous and unstinting measure, since the first day of the war, was fortunate : without the valour of her merchant seamen Britain could not have survived. One could only feel proud to share a job with such men. Nominally we were in charge of them, on all their undertakings : but it was really a more complex relationship, in which admiration had its full share and a brotherly regard seasoned all the discipline we had to enforce. If an occasional blast was necessary, it was a blast delivered in the full knowledge that, were the positions reversed, we should be at the receiving-end just as often and for just the same reasons.

Men like these had died in their hundreds : I had seen them dying, had picked them up or failed to find them, had mourned their passing, wondered at their courage, and cursed their executioners. But however lonely or cruel their end, a part of them lived always, indestruct-

ible as the sea itself, to the glory of their race and calling,
and the certain doom of the enemy.

When we had said hello to another destroyer, taken
up our station astern of the convoy and dealt out one or
two hints to potential stragglers, I went below for lunch
and my afternoon nap. The convoy was progressing
slowly, butting into a head wind and a rising sea:
through the ventilator above my berth the wind whistled
on a high, discouraging note, and the patter and drift
of spray against the forward bulkhead told its story of
water freely shipped and bows buried, now and then,
under a flurry of foam and green sea. But this was an
accustomed lullaby, and, as usual, I dozed off, while the
convoy crept northwards and the Officer-of-the-Watch
kept distance and station at the tail of the columns.
Occasionally signals came down the voice-pipe—weather
forecasts, movements of other convoys in the area—but
this also was a routine chorus in the background, which
penetrated only deep enough to establish its unimport-
ance. The change of the watch, and tea-time, came
round with a good two hours' sleep stored up, in reserve for any emergency later on.

Then there was a more definite interruption, delivered
by the Sub-Lieutenant *via* the voice-pipe:

" Captain, sir ! "

I rolled over. " What is it ? "

" Signal from the leading destroyer, sir : ' Are there
any stragglers ? ' "

" Are there ? "

" One starting to drop back a bit, sir. The small one
with the funnel aft."

" What revs' are we doing ? "

He told me.

" Slow enough. . . . All right, I'll come up."

I put on my sea-boots and stepped out into the wind
and the spray, and up to the bridge. The convoy was
now spread out over several miles, and though visibility
was still good we were only just in signalling-touch with

the leading destroyer. Tailing on to the starboard
column, a good mile astern of it, was the first straggler,
whom I had actually marked down as a possibility as
soon as we joined up : a very small, very old-fashioned
packet liberally daubed with red lead, the after-part
hung with cleanish washing which had little chance of
emerging as such from the billows of smoke pouring
out of her funnel. She was making heavy weather of
it, stubbing her nose into every second wave, shaking
herself free of water in a listless fashion, as if she knew
she was doing the wrong thing and did not greatly
care either way. After watching her for a few minutes
I called to the signalman :

"Signal to the leader : 'One dumb chum. I will
turn on the heat.' All right, Pilot—put her alongside,
and we'll do some talking."

We increased speed and closed to within comfortable
hailing distance. As we drew near our quarry an old
man wearing, of all things, a bowler hat, walked to the
side of the bridge and peered over the rail, prepared to
give battle. That was probably all he was going to
give : he knew what I had come for, well enough,
and looked quite ready to swear he hadn't got it in
stock.

I began mildly. "Can you do anything about this
gap in front of you ?"

He waved his hand in a gesture which might have
conveyed any one of half a dozen different meanings :
despair, indifference, promise, leave-me-alone-blast-you.
. . . But he said nothing.

"Can you go any faster ?"

Faintly across the water came the answer, through a
megaphone :

"Doing the best I can."

"Well, you want to close this gap somehow, or I'll
have to send you in."

The megaphone was shaken furiously heavenwards.
"The commodore's going too fast."

" He's going very slowly. Now what about a few extra revs. to make up."

" I can't do it, I tell you. Chief's sitting on the bloody safety-valve as it is."

I made an appropriate comment, which was well received, Then : " Well, do your best for the next hour, and we'll see what happens."

Another wave of the megaphone, less energetic, told me that the message had got through. We sheered off and regained our station, while from the straggler's funnel a slight thickening of the smoke gave promise of an extra effort. I called to the signalman again.

" Make to the leader : ' Straggler is doing his best to close one mile gap. Will report in an hour's time.' Let me know what happens, Pilot. If he drops back any more he'll have to go in."

" Aye, aye, sir."

At the end of an hour the position was much the same : he was no farther astern, but the gap was still there. (That extra cloud of smoke had probably been the cook disposing of the tea-leaves.) I signalled : " Straggler is holding his own, but cannot close gap at present convoy speed," to which the reply presently came back : " Don't want to reduce speed. Remain with him and report position at dusk." After another bout of prompting over the loud-hailer, during which the old man remained obstinately dumb, acknowledging my remarks by a subtle variety of megaphone waves, we settled down astern to await the outcome.

At dusk the gap was still there, and it was now slowly increasing. In the old days it would have mattered rather a lot ; we would probably have been bombed already or, more likely still, the gap in the escort-screen astern would have been noticed by reconnaissance aircraft, and the ships ahead attacked while we were still a mile beyond effective range. But now, with enemy air activity against shipping reduced virtually to nothing and with almost continuous air-cover provided by the

R.A.F., the straggler was more of a nuisance than a danger. It was too rough for E-boats to come over— the only thing that could have menaced the position. Of course we were wasted where we were, toiling along astern with this funny little crate : but as it happened we weren't likely to be needed anywhere else, and could afford to play nursemaid to the problem child in the bowler hat.

The provision of air-cover over these East Coast convoys had simplified our job, during the past year or so, to a very great degree, and we were always glad to see the R.A.F. around, whether they were Spitfires wave-hopping at speed, Walruses hovering like mid-Victorian buzzards, or some unidentifiable American machine using his own—his very own—recognition-signals. Out in the Atlantic they were proving invaluable as U-boat spotters and strikers : here they were a steel umbrella over our heads and a most effective deterrent to hit-and-run raids on coastwise shipping.

In short, we wanted their help, we were glad to get it, and we were not ashamed to say so. Need any one else have been ashamed on our behalf? The question occurs because the fact that the Navy had to have air-cover at many points had latterly been used to promote inter-Service *rivalry*, highly partisan, often ill-natured, and indeed (in some quarters) not rising above the "I-told-you-so" of the triumphant schoolboy. The wrangle did not affect the men on the job, it was true : it started (and finished) ashore, among people with no better occupation than that of scoring off each other in the correspondence columns of *The Times :* but if it was really the fact that there were in the background persons *of influence* dissipating their energies in such struggles, then the sailors who sailed and the airmen who flew might well feel alarmed and despondent.

When I had made my dusk report the Senior Officer had answered : " Not worth sending straggler in now. Not an E-boat night, anyway. Stay with him and report position in the morning, by R/T if necessary. Good night." I had a last interview with the culprit, who was now about two miles astern but not (it seemed) correspondingly repentant, and then settled down to the probable boredom of the dark hours. It turned out a depressing sort of night : the wind and the sea eased off, but rain made the visibility very poor, and it was difficult to keep in proper touch with this exceptionally sluggish companion. We made our way north yard by yard : the buoys seemed to crawl past, the rain flogged the bridge windows continuously, the straggler yawed and loitered and occasionally went off on some inexplicable course of his own choosing, from which he had to be retrieved, straightened up and started off again. At about midnight there was a short-lived scare : somewhere to seaward of us a trawler opened up at a low-flying aircraft, and the tracer-bullets, passing across our bows not far ahead, were a stimulating reminder of the real thing. Later still a patrol destroyer, cruising southwards rather fast, came close enough to cause two minutes' slightly hectic activity on the bridge. I imagine that, having passed the main body of the convoy ahead of us, they thought the channel would be clear of shipping and had relaxed their look-out somewhat : at any rate the switching on of our navigation-lights resulted in their turning sharply with an impressive wash, and sliding between us and our charge. In full daylight it would have made a pretty picture— " Destroyer manœuvring at speed " : in a rain-squall on a dark night it failed to charm.

(At such a moment, thoughts of a deplorable irrelevance present themselves. Though aware, at the critical point, that she would have to alter course within the next five seconds to avoid cutting us in half, I found myself recalling that I had not answered an invitation from this destroyer's Captain to attend a " select party, with actresses " on the following Saturday night. I decided that I would do, if spared: and would certainly balance the present scare by stinging them for an extra gin—or actress.)

But soon it was daylight again : another dawn, another letting up of tension, as good as ever. When full light came, the last ships of the convoy could only just be seen, hull down ahead of us ; and having reported this on R/T I was told to route the straggler independently and then rejoin the convoy as soon as possible. It seemed slightly fatuous to tell my charge to " proceed independently " when he had been doing little else for the past twenty-four hours, and when I closed him and passed the formal order by loud-hailer it was received with a most expressive smile, and a lifting of the bowler hat which I think demonstrated the victorious rather than the courteous spirit. But at least we had discharged our responsibility and were quit of a trying job : nursing a straggler can never be anything else, whether you are left alone or not.

After taking the most dignified farewell I could muster under the circumstances, and tendering some good advice which probably had as much effect as a blast on the bagpipes, we cracked on speed and presently caught up the convoy : and until the late afternoon we made good progress northward, the weather moderating all the time. There was little to do except maintain station and apply the whip occasionally, so as to keep the tail of the convoy neatly tucked in, and I spent most of the day sleeping or working on the monthly returns which would be due as soon as we got back to harbour. Then ships were reported ahead of us, and identified as the south-bound convoy which we were to take in : and having got permission to leave we crossed over to make the change.

It was, for once, a very small convoy. (" Too many for bridge, not enough for tombola," I signalled to the Senior Officer of the escort, who considered the remark in silence before replying, " Take up your correct station.") Once more we steamed down the middle, collecting names and numbers; once more we exchanged greetings with another escort: then we fell in astern, as before, to complete the screen and seal off the rear of the convoy from without and from within.

When we turned south, to start our homeward journey, we had a light wind astern of us and the sun hot on our faces: the sort of perfect cruising weather which, ironically, war seemed to bring far more often than peace. There was, on that lovely afternoon, a sensual pleasure in sea-going, in being afloat on a dark blue-green sea which was now our ally: the ship seemed, for that short spell, to lose its warlike character and to be concerned only with giving us a gentle and effortless passage. I lay at ease on the roof of the bridge, the iron plates hot under my hand when I stretched out my arms: I watched in turn the water slipping past below, the clean line of our bow wave, spreading in infinite creamy ripples, the slow-moving ships ahead, the pale sky which the mast was lazily probing. The sun warmed my whole body through and through, the following breeze took all thrusting out of our forward movement: only an occasional gentle roll, only the ship deep beneath me stirring and lifting to the swell, confirmed that we were held in balance on free and friendly water.

All afternoon and evening we progressed thus, burnished by the sun, blessed by a cool sea, lulled to an absolute security. Nothing obtruded, though sometimes stray movements from inside the dream would touch the surface for a moment—a helm-order louder than usual, a sea-gull enclosed, as if by enchantment, in a triangle of mast, shroud and yard-arm, a look-out's call: then the sun would flow over everything again and the woven peace would be restored. Hours slid by, with a smooth sameness like the water sliding past our keel: the watch was relieved; down below in the waist the hands sunbathed till the light declined, and it was time to darken ship and return to the war again. The bosun's pipe which finally broke the stillness seemed, as it

H

cut the air, to be the first insistent sound within the memory.

Night came like any other night, with its last per-persuasive hints to the slow movers, its dimmed exchange of signals between escort and escort, its final bedding-down. The head of the convoy faded gradually to nothing, and our view was bounded by a circle of black water, a green-flashing wreck-buoy, and five dark smudges in the gloom ahead. To these we clung, as they clung to each other : straining the eye to preserve an exact distance, watching for the fading-in of a too sharp outline or the fading-out of everything : altering course as the main body altered, but keeping a separate check on our navigation, in case some one ahead slipped up. (A whole convoy had been led astray before now, through playing follow-my-leader with an inexperienced Commodore—five ships aground in half an hour, and the rest backing away like rabbits from the wrong hole. It took a lot of explaining : for all I know it is still being explained.)

By now it was intensely cold. Going up on the bridge at midnight, I was glad of my duffle-coat and of the brew of cocoa which I had been counting on as the watch changed. But already, after no more than two hours of darkness, the night had brought a query.

"No. 25 Buoy should be in sight by now," said the Gunner, as he prepared to go off watch. "In fact we really ought to be up to it already. But perhaps it's not working. I don't think the convoy can have missed it ; their course has been O.K. That's the position, anyway," he added, with the cheerfulness of the man to whom the position will, in thirty seconds' time, mean less than nothing.

"The ship may be anywhere, in fact," said the First Lieutenant, who was taking over the watch. "Fry's cocoa, and all's to hell. I suppose you'll be turning in quite comfortably just the same ? "

"Yes," said the Gunner. "Good night."

" Good night, Quisling."

Listening in the darkness, on one wing of the bridge, I smiled to myself. That end-of-the-watch feeling was familiar, and unalterable.

The Gunner tramped off below, to his camp-bed under the wardroom table : the First Lieutenant received and acknowledged the routine report from the Petty Officer of the watch—" Guns' crews and look-outs correct : galley fire burning low." The Midshipman, his head under the chart-table screen, answered my questions about our course and the tidal set affecting it. Time passed, and No. 25 Buoy still did not appear. Since, in this particular corner, we would have to go a long way before we ran into serious trouble, I was not worried— yet : but I was curious to know what had happened and how we had come to miss the buoy, as I believed we had. Visibility was inclined to be patchy, but not as patchy as all that, and if the light were extinguished (which seemed the most likely explanation), I should have to report it to the shore authority.

Presently : " I thought I saw it a moment ago," said the First Lieutenant. " But it's gone again. Probably a ship showing a light by mistake. This is just about the time they make up the galley fire."

The signalman joined in suddenly. " Flashing light ahead, sir . . . right among the port column. It seems to be irregular, though."

" We'll see in a minute. It may have been damaged earlier on."

But we didn't see in a minute. Fifteen of them passed, and still we were not up to the light nor, apparently, any nearer to it. Now and then I thought I saw it, now and then the sighting was confirmed by someone else on the bridge : but uncannily, we didn't seem to be catching it up. Then, very slowly, a ship ahead of us drew out of its column and turned to port, crossing our bows. She looked as if she were in trouble of some sort, and she appeared to be signalling to us :

single flashes, curiously low down, came in our direction, though they didn't make any sense—they were simply spaced at regular ten-second intervals. It was the Midshipman who, when we were about five cables off and still wondering, jumped to the right conclusion.

"That's the buoy flashing, sir!" he exclaimed suddenly. "It's caught up amidships—you can see the shape of it against the hull. They must have been pulling it along with them all the time."

This was the correct answer, as the ship herself confirmed when we got within hailing distance. It had just been one of those things. . . . Miscalculating the strength of the tide at one turn of the channel, she had got foul of the buoy and for the past hour had been towing it down the fairway, flashing industriously all the time. Number 25 Buoy had been taken for a ride.

When I asked the ship why she had not stopped immediately the buoy became attached, instead of plugging away until she was firmly tethered, back came the reply, "I thought I could shake it off if I steamed hard enough"—an answer which seemed to contain, deep within it, some of the elements of a nightmare. Now, however, she was stopped, a few yards from us. Her dark grey shape overtopped our bridge, and the flashing light alongside advertised her indifferent navigation every ten seconds, with what must have been mortifying persistence. An unwise but habitual flippancy made me call out to her: "Well, you're certainly right on the swept channel now." This uproarious sally was coldly received and shortly afterwards a man climbed down and tied a sack over the lamp. I felt tacitly rebuked by this manœuvre—as was no doubt the intention when the order was given.

Meanwhile the convoy felt its way slowly past us, while I got in touch with the leading destroyer and explained the situation. I suggested that the ship be taken in tow then and there (part of the buoy-cable had now become entangled with her rudder) and presently I received an answering signal : " Instruct the tug to take her in tow, and remain as close escort yourself." Finding the tug (which had wandered off, as usual, to a safe night-position well clear of the convoy), passing the order, guiding her to the derelict, standing by while the tow was passed, and leading them both back to the channel and the next buoy—all this took time : we must have been a good ten miles astern of the main body, when we finally made our start in the right direction and the speed of towing, with a ship of this size, was very slow. After a session in the chart-house, I had just made the mournful calculation that we were unlikely to get home by the following night, even if the tow held until the end, when we had an unexpected respite in the form of another signal from the leader : " Make contact with the trawler, tell her to take over escort, and rejoin the convoy."

Why the Senior Officer had changed his mind I didn't know, though certainly we were better occupied escorting the convoy than looking after a single ship, and the trawler could more easily be spared. At any rate it was good news, once the complications were accepted. These were the normal ones attending this sort of manœuvre at night, but they meant a certain amount of extra care : the time was now two a.m., the night at its blackest, and to catch up the convoy, overtake half of it, and find the trawler (which might or might not be in its assigned position) was less easy than a lot of other things. But we cracked on speed with a will—anything was better than seeping along at nought knots at the tail of a towing-party—and set out to chase the main body.

It took us a hard-running hour to catch them, and in the end they came up with startling suddenness—an untidy cluster of ships, no more than blurred smudges, ahead of us, where a second before had been a blank horizon and safe sea-room. I stared at them through my glasses, trying to determine which column was which and to work out the angle I was approaching at; but there was really no satisfactory answer to be had—they had lost their strict daytime formation, and to overtake at speed we would have to dodge and trust to luck. At the moment they almost seemed to be coming towards us, darkening outlines on a pale sea. I swung wide to starboard, to give them a safe clearance, and straight away another one came up dead ahead, a low-built straggler (of the type we called a " flat-iron," almost impossible to see in the dark) nowhere near his proper column and steering no particular course either. It seemed a good moment to reduce speed: clearly the ships at the tail of the convoy were jogging along independently, safe from father's eye, and their various positions were quite unpredictable. We eased down to two or three knots more than the convoy speed, and then began to feel our way past, ship by ship, looking for the trawler.

We found her in the end, though I don't really know why. On a dark night a trawler looks like any other ship until you are close up to her, and we must have sighted and examined a dozen likely candidates—approaching them gently so as not to alarm them into ramming tactics, keeping careful watch for other ships nearby, extricating ourselves again when the current choice turned out to be something quite different—before we finally got the right one. But when we *did* find her, her indignation at being disturbed, and her clamorous disbelief of the orders which would send her back at least fifteen miles and keep her at sea for an extra night, almost made up for our trouble. At one point I thought she would crack the diaphragm of her loud-hailer. But she sheered off in the end, turning round very slowly like a child doing something it dislikes but doesn't dare to refuse; and soon afterwards it was dawn again, and time to whip in the stragglers, before a fine sunrise brought some warmth to the bridge and made breakfast sound good and taste better. It had been a long night, but taking it altogether we had got off lightly, from a situation which might well have become the extreme of boredom.

We carried a strong tide with us all that morning, and by late afternoon we were near enough to our base for me to ask permission to leave the convoy and go home independently. There were no ships to be taken in, and (this time) no tug or trawler to accompany us, which made it very different from the usual end-of-convoy manœuvre. For generally there was a merchant-ship or two due to break off with us, which of course had to be escorted the whole way in; and for this purpose the tug and the trawler came under my orders. It was here that the fun would start.

In theory the three of us should emerge as a separate flotilla, whose constituent units I could move about like pawns on a chess-board, and which would respond to my touch like a restive horse; but it was never as straightforward as that, and " restive " remained the only operative word. It was their natural ambition, when we were nearing home, to slip away at speed and leave me holding the baby; and to this end every artifice was employed, with a diligence which, used against the enemy, might well have shortened the war. Since early morning they would have been hiding themselves behind other ships, dodging my signals, and generally playing stupid in the hope that I would give up and do the job myself. But it was nearer home, when we were actually preparing to leave, that the more active and less scrupulous part of the operation would begin, and close supervision became vital.

Possibly I might go below for a few minutes, for a cup of tea and a change into harbour rig. Without fail, when I returned to the bridge, the trawler would be edging away towards home, and the tug increasing speed as discreetly as its vast billows of smoke allowed. After a sharp word to the tug, designed to discourage any such initiative, we would call up the trawler, intending to signal: "Take up your proper station and remain with our portion of convoy." Visibility, at this point, unaccountably deteriorated. For a long time no answer would be forthcoming: then they would start giving us a succession of "W's" (code-letter for "Train your light properly"); and then, our signal being spelt out with immense care and precision by a hard-breathing Yeoman, they would begin to read it very slowly—missing words, asking for them to be repeated, sprinkling "W's" here and there like coarse interjections. All the time, of course, they were slowly fading out of sight, contriving to lay a smoke-screen between the two ships which further complicated the signalling. Finally we would crack on speed, and come too close for them not to acknowledge the signal and to act on it: then, cursing all individualists, we would turn about and go back to the merchant-ships. And then we would start looking round for the tug.

Occasionally, in the street, one sees a harassed-looking woman trying to take half a dozen dogs, of assorted breeds and sizes, for a walk in a given direction. It is a grim and discouraging spectacle: often she will age ten years between two lamp-posts.

Getting four merchant-ships, a trawler and a tug to go the way you want them to, at a level speed, was sometimes rather like that.

This time, however, we had no one but ourselves to think about, and there were no complications to delay us. Increasing to the maximum permissible speed, we darted off homewards, cutting corners, whipping round buoys, passing everything on the road. An hour later we were tied up to the oiler, and looking forward to all-night leave; in the wardroom the mail was being distributed, in the rough proportion of the more junior the officer the greater the number of his letters. I myself had a couple of bills, and the Midshipman, as usual, a positive mound of assorted envelopes, all to himself. Then the quartermaster knocked on the door, looking for the Officer-of-the-Day.

"Signal boat coming alongside, sir."

I opened the sealed envelope when it was handed to me and then looked round a wardroom which had suddenly become attentive.

"Not so bad," I said, when I had glanced over the pink slip. "We've got to-night in, anyway. All-night leave to-night, convoy again to-morrow morning. We'll have to start about ten o'clock."

"It's like going to the office every morning," said the First Lieutenant, after a pause. "Backwards and forwards. One of these days I'm going to put in for a bowler hat and a season ticket."

That was one routine convoy trip, with nothing special to it. It could be (and was) multiplied *ad infinitum* with only the smallest variations. Obviously, as Number One implied, the job had an element of boredom in it: you could be interested the first twenty times or so, but after that. . . . If any one, reading this far, has not already asked, "But where is the enemy?" he may ask it now, as we ourselves did every time we came back from a featureless trip. Broadly speaking, it could be said that the enemy simply was not there. The East Coast used to be a hot assignment, earning all its reputation and most of its lurid nicknames, but that was quite a long time ago: for the past year or more it had been extraordinarily quiet, and the very occasional air-raids, E-boat sorties, and attempts at mine-laying only served to show up the general flatness of the whole. Of course that did not alter the sea-going part of it, which demanded the same care and the same endurance whatever was or was not going on besides; but it was a let-up as far as one kind of tension was concerned, and from my point of view it cut, by half, the worry and strain that necessarily went with the job.

There *were* occasional variations, however. Certain things claimed the attention and stayed in the memory, adding subtlety or shadow or some fresh and vivid significance to the old picture. There was the dark night when some enemy aircraft overhead started looking for the convoy, dropping flares with a leisurely Teutonic thoroughness which, it seemed, *must* be successful. The flares started quite far out to sea : they crossed ahead of us, they went step by step round the stern, and then out to seawards again, but they never quite landed in the middle, and the convoy slipped by anonymously after all. Up on the bridge, aware—in myself and in the people close round me—of the constraint and tension of Action Stations, aware of the Coxswain craning his neck for a quick look skywards when he had the ship steady on her course, I had found myself privately betting against that piece of good fortune.

For the crews of the merchant-ships on our beam it was a test of nerve which one could feel going on all the time. Up and down those long lines there must have been scores of fingers ready on the trigger, scores of minds speculating as to whether it wouldn't be better to open up now instead of waiting for the aircraft methodically crossing and weaving overhead to start their bombing. One urge of impatience or of fear, one single tracer-bullet loosed off for luck, would have given us all away. Afterwards, it seemed natural that no single gunner in forty-odd ships had failed in the test or had played his own hand : at the time, the temptation and the likelihood had seemed inhumanly strong.

There were occasional bouts of vile weather, that spring and summer, as unpleasant (if not as long-lasting) as anything I had met in the Atlantic. There were many times when, from a convoy labouring hours late against wind and tide, we would come driving in for home, rolling, side-slipping, the glistening decks shaking themselves free of water and then falling away again for another sluicing plunge. There was, especially, one very heavy gale in a harbour crowded with ships : normally the shelter was perfect, but this was not normal,

and things started to go wrong. A destroyer broke
adrift, and crowded down on top of another : the tug
sent to extricate her was crushed between the two of
them, and put completely out of action : the second
destroyer began to drag her own moorings and menaced
a third which only just managed, by superb seamanship,
to slip out before it was too late, and to keep clear of
the *crescendo* of trouble which was developing.

It was distressing to watch the gradual deterioration
of this scene, from order to disorder, until at the height
of the gale, the harbour seemed to be verging on ir-
reparable chaos : the three destroyers in a perilous
tangle, the wrecked tug caught in between, two other
tugs cruising up and down trying to get to grips with
the situation, a ship's whaler adrift and battered to pieces
against the pier, a cluster of small craft which had nosed
upstream into a creek for shelter : and all the time this
incredible screaming wind which seemed to be scooping
up whole sheets of the surface of the water and tossing
them bodily against the quay.

Out at a midstream buoy, in the very centre of the
fury, we were ready for anything—steam up, Coxswain
at the wheel, myself on the bridge waiting for the cable
to part or the buoy to break adrift from its moorings.
For more than an hour—the worst hour—we steamed
slow ahead against the weight and thrust of the wind,
taking the strain off the buoy which, barely visible in
the spray-filled air, was tugged and battered without a
moment's respite. Both the moorings and our own
cable held : towards evening the wind veered and
dropped, and the harbour returned to normal again, in
an almost shame-faced way. But the afternoon remained
in the memory, a reminder that ships, no matter how
securely berthed, are never quite beyond the reach of
the sea.

There were other occasional crises : unfair strokes of
fortune, things that went wrong for ourselves or for
other people. There was the time that the gyro-compass

went haywire, not suddenly but by a treacherous creeping action which deceived the Quartermaster and the Officer-of-the-Watch into steering, in the end, not less than sixty degrees off our proper course. Only the unexpected appearance of a very rare buoy, which I myself had never seen before and indeed had only heard about vaguely, gave us a clue as to where the ship had wandered in the meantime. There was the night the steering-gear broke down, and we kept our course and station for several hours by the tiresome operation known as " steering by main engines "—that is, keeping one screw turning at a fixed rate and adjusting the speed of the other so as to control the swing of the ship. It was interesting to begin with—like threading needle after needle for someone you love. But in the end . . .

I remember, too, once surveying the violent aftermath of a collision between a corvette and a destroyer, and being shown over the corvette's damage in detail—the mess-deck cut in half, the torn plates, the wires hanging like entrails. She really was a horrifying sight : the destroyer's bows had gone deep into her, and almost out the other side. Only the presence of mind of the Officer-of-the-Watch, who had pressed the alarm-bell half a minute before the crash, had prevented a startling loss of life. The mess-desk had been crammed with sleeping men when that alarm bell went. Easy to remember, also, was the dejected face of her Captain, as he told me how it happened. He was blameless : it was just one of those things : but that was the least important part of it. I touched wood when I saw that corvette : having one of my own to lose, equally vulnerable and equally loved.

One thing didn't change in this corner of the war or in any other : perhaps it is worth remarking on it in passing and letting it go at that. Now and then, up and down the coast, ships were sunk and survivors had to be collected. It was hard to find any variety here, at this stage of the war, and, as I have said, it need not be enlarged on in detail : but here and there some superb or pitiful act, some exceptional ugliness or some odd warping of the horror, would strike a new note and prove that the theme was not yet exhausted.

There were plenty of things on the tonic side, too. A clutch of E-boats getting thoroughly beaten up, or a succession of really big convoys coming in, as good as when they left the other side, crammed with food or war materials. There was an occasional glorious circus of a night-action, with mine-sweepers, patrol-trawlers, corvettes, destroyers, M.L.'s, and motor-gunboats, all having a smack at the same wilting bunch of E-boats, while an R.A.F. rescue launch, somewhere on the outer fringe, tried to squeeze between people's legs and sneak the prey for their own branch.

One very satisfying (and more orthodox) show which the R.A.F. laid on for us, one afternoon, was the shooting down of a high-flying reconnaissance 'plane almost over the convoy. It had come in from seaward, so high as to be almost invisible, but betrayed by a lengthening streak of vapour astern of it. As it crossed the coast another pair of streaks—British fighters—came hurtling in from the westward to intercept. The enemy 'plane turned sharply, the fighters set a course to cut him off, their trails thickening as they increased speed : the three streaks converged, and blended into one, and then there was a sudden burst of orange flame from the very tip of the vapour-trail, and the enemy 'plane fell, twisting and turning, growing larger, taking on the hard outlines of the Dornier, until it finally dropped into the sea ahead of us and became smoke and vapour once more.

There were a few other departures from the normal, which served to give the job a saving degree of variation. Sometimes, when nothing special promised, we would take passengers on a trip with us—R.A.F. officers, for instance, whose nearly incomprehensible slang would gain currency in the wardroom, so that for a few days we would all talk freely of " blacks " and " binds " and " pranging." (The Midshipman, handing over the watch, was once heard to say, " Just keep on stooging around at nought feet." I did not really object to this, but his later use of the expression " Glamour-pants " to describe an attractive young woman of my acquaintance was *not* approved.) Possibly, for further variety, our guests would be officers from the Intelligence Division, whom we christened " Warrant Spies," and filled up with careless and colourful information which they would have no difficulty in proving false as soon as they returned home. But whoever they were, we enjoyed having them : a new face and voice was always a welcome diversion, in the cramped and limited world on board.

Occasionally, we were given a short holiday between trips, at a rarely visited Northern port : a five-day respite which we would fill in by painting ship throughout, polishing every conceivable metal surface or object, and emerging at the end like a newly hatched butterfly, to dazzle the flotilla and provoke jealous signals when we came up harbour again. At other times, when there was nothing " operational " to do, we would go out on a shoot with the destroyers—a humble rôle, this, consisting of following in their wake like a well-trained terrier and getting in an occasional shot at a half-demolished target. More fun were our own flotilla manœuvres, when five or six corvettes would proceed to sea in company and perform prodigies of evolution, some of them in the Fleet Signal Book, others (as the Yeoman would patiently explain) not, and never likely to be either. But at least it was a family affair, and the signal " *Winger* astern of station," which the Senior Officer appeared to keep bent on to the halyard, ready for immediate use, was no more than a paternal scolding administered in sorrow rather than in anger, and received by every one on the bridge in the same spirit.

Lastly, among the things designed to keep us on our

toes and out of the nuthouse, there were such unclassifiable oddments as the bomb that near-missed us, one dark night in the middle watch. It happened without any warning. There was a loud metallic clang, a golden rain of sparks, a lot of dirty water, and finally the First Lieutenant's brooding voice as he wrote in the deck-log: "Near-missed by medium-weight bomb, thirty yards off starboard bow." But whose bomb? The sky was full of friendly aircraft at the time, and when the convoy, incensed, opened fire in a vaguely vertical direction, it became full of correct recognition-flares as well, with hardly a second's delay. Suspicious? I suppose it *might* have been an enemy intruder-'plane mixing in with our out-going bombers, but somehow I doubt it—a doubt shared by the ship's company, who seemed to be convinced that it was one of ours jettisoning its bombs (or, as one able-seaman put it tersely: "Too bloody lazy to fly to Berlin.") But we were none the worse for it, since there were no casualties and no damage— "if" (in the words of my report) "a slight and temporary cooling of inter-Service relations be excepted."

It was not, by the way, a very big bomb—to start with. But (defying the laws of perspective) it tended to grow bigger the farther away it got. About a fortnight later some one at the Naval Club said to me: "I hear you were near-missed by an eight-thousand pounder."

It is never easy to scotch that kind of rumour: in fact, hardly worth trying.

I returned an evasive answer. It was not too evasive either way, however.[1]

But mostly, as I have said, the job was purely a routine one, without variations even as mild as the foregoing: a series of blank patrols and uneventful coastal convoys which, for me, boiled down to taking the ship out,

---

[1] Further example of a baseless rumour: "I hear that unless your requestmen can produce a copy of *East Coast Corvette* you won't even see them at the table."

bringing the ship in, waiting for something to happen and keeping out of trouble in the meantime.

None of us could really complain : we had volunteered for boredom as well as for action, and as far as I was concerned the actual *sea-going* part of it was an incomparable way of passing the war. I am not warlike, though if chance had placed me, for example, in my younger brother's job—Royal Artillery, till his death in North Africa—I would no doubt have made some kind of a soldier, though not as good a one as he. But luck put me in the Navy : the rest followed : and it was impossible to deny that there were some parts of my job I should be sorry to lose, when it was all over. If, for instance, our peace-time way of life promoted half the comradeship, laughter, and self-respecting pride of endeavour which going to sea in corvettes had done, I should be very lucky—and so would Great Britain. This feeling and this experience (however widespread they may be) of course do not go an inch of the way towards " justifying " war—i.e. making it worth while for its own sake ; but they certainly affect, in a vital degree, the day-to-day business of hanging on until the war is won.

I loathe war and all its works, with my whole heart : it is wasteful, confused, lying, and often futile ; but the Naval side of it was none of these things, and since the war has to be got through somehow, this was by far the best way of getting through it.

It seemed, also, to be one of the fastest. At this job, the time flew by so fast that when one tried to recall a certain month, even in the recent past, it might have been missed out altogether, so swiftly had it vanished from the memory. I had taken over the ship in the early spring : a few times up and down the coast, a few spells of leave, a fully established confidence, and winter was round again—the fifth of the war, my fourth at sea, and a most familiar testing-time for ships and for men.

But as a final sweetener before it started, I was promoted to Lieutenant-Commander. Since I had the job and the ship I wanted, I had not been worrying overmuch about my slow progress up the scale ; but it was pleasant to leave, at last, the ranks of the Dead End Kids (there are an awful lot of Lieutenants, R.N.V.R., in the Navy) and to get once more within striking distance of my friends, all of whom seemed to be either Wing-Commanders or Colonels.

CHAPTER V

PEOPLE

To start with a very small person.

I saw my son at intervals just long enough for him to record a perceptible change on each occasion. Leave—in short and fleeting spells—came fairly regularly, and each time I was home was marked by another stage in his progress : sleeping, rolling over, sitting up, crawling, steaming round on all fours, standing unaided, walking, sucking his teeth like a disgruntled A.B. Other people's children are always boring, and there is no reason why mine should be an exception, so I will not enlarge further on the details of the growing-up process, and not at all on what I felt about him. But I found him absorbing to watch, apart from anything else. He was yet another reason why it was, each time, good to come home and sad to leave it.

It sometimes seems that this whole war is nothing but saying good-bye, usually in grisly circumstances—on black winter mornings, at railway stations, outside dock gates in the rain : circumstances rendered more grisly still by one's knowledge of what waits close ahead—the cold, the exhaustion, the boredom. But it is easy to forget all these things during leave, if you are helped.

Women are remarkable in this respect—in their bravery, their disguise of emotion, their studious ignoring of time; they can fashion a centre of warmth and peace, giving it their whole care although they know it can be enjoyed only for a little space, and this they maintain secure, under the very shadow of dispersal. They spend themselves to the utmost limit when one is there, knowing that zero hour—the end of one's leave—means a kind of bankrupt solitude, a total loneliness, for themselves.

Or is this only one woman? I hope not.

Indeed I hope not. I was married four days after war broke out: a war which (particularly when I was on long Atlantic convoys) I do not think I could have supported without a personal background of an exceptional quality. Innumerable other people must find, at home, the same source of strength, and must be sustained in the same way by a security and a happiness they can count on in every conceivable circumstance. What really beats me is how anyone, in this bloody war, can do without it. It is, of course, a matter of individual capacity and inclination. Some people, naturally self-sufficient, seem to prefer a leave-period consisting of a few days' full-calibre racketing followed by a recuperative trip to sea—and indeed, thirty years ago (or ten, anyway) it might even have suited me: but now it would be quite inadequate, from any point of view whatsoever. As far as I am concerned, war can be made tolerable by a background of love and sanity: anything else would bring the machine to a dead stop.

I have said that I hope other people, who may need this sort of help, are able to count on it in their home life. This is probably true for the majority, though from personal knowledge I know it is not the universal rule. Now and again I have to see someone " privately "— that is, a rating requests an interview alone with me, free from witnesses and the formality of the quarter-deck, and almost always it is something gone wrong with a marriage which prompts the request. The unfaithful wife, the bastard child, sexual maladjustment, the wife who "turns funny" after a child is born—these are all sad variants of the same theme. Much of the trouble is due to sheer ignorance, much more to lack of imagination. But war-time separation is itself a potent factor, working (as it were) against our side, and sailors, determinedly sentimental about women, are sometimes let down.

"When I went home last time, sir," said a young rating who had asked me about a legal separation, "I found the wife sitting about in one of those hotel lounges, drinking port with some chaps she'd never seen before." I saw the whole woman in that single phrase—blast her.

"Blast her," because so much depended on her—as on all women at home. Individual morale falls to nothing if there is a doubt of that kind nagging away all the time, and for me to answer such a story by saying that there is "probably nothing in it" is a foolish evasion. From the only important angle—the *instinct* (as against the physical fact) of faithfulness—there is everything in it.

Morale is made up of odd things, some of them trivial to a degree, some of them paradoxical in the way they manifest themselves. The *general* level of morale in the Navy is so high that it is something no one worries about; but—here is the paradox—it is high because the average sailor is often more of an individual than a member of a unit, however happy and efficient that unit may be : he keeps intact his prejudices, his humours, his stubborn self-respect, and he makes it blessedly clear that when he does his best he expects due recognition of the fact, and a parallel effort, from his superiors.

Here is a very short snatch of dialogue which I think illustrates this high individual morale perfectly—though it is only fair to say that so far every one I have told it to says that it illustrates gross insubordination and nothing else at all.

The scene is the bridge on a very unpleasant night, with the spray washing over and every one, from the Officer-of-the-Watch down to bridge-messenger, inclined to be rather sick of the sea.

> *Look-out* (reporting some lights seen with extreme difficulty through the scud) : " Ship on the port beam, sir ! "
>
> *Bad-tempered Officer-of-the-Watch* (very crossly) : " How do you know it's a ship ? "
>
> *Look-out* (fed up at last) : " Too near to be a horse and cart, sir."

Does anyone else agree that this classic back-answer indicates an admirable spirit of independence ? I may be on the wrong lines entirely, but that is what it demonstrates to me. The man knew that he would be punished for it—that is the whole point : but he had established the fact that when he was doing his job under trying circumstances (it was a *very* black and dirty night), he wasn't going to be mucked about by a harassed officer looking for someone on whom to work off his bad temper. To establish that personal integrity, to prove himself a man and not a spiritless and unresisting block of wood, was judged to be worth the punishment, whatever it was : and I am prepared to bet that that seaman would be a better man to have at one's side in a tight corner than any yes-man accustomed to turn away wrath by producing a smile and a soft answer on every single occasion.

(*Note*. These are unorthodox views, I know, and I may well be the only officer in the Navy to hold them ; but there it is. It may be added that they do not indicate the general level of discipline on board H.M.S. *Winger*, which was not the ship it happened in. Nor, incidentally, should they be taken as a reliable guide for the future behaviour of look-outs, in any ship under my command.)

Here is another short exchange, funny in itself, and demonstrating the same sort of independence on a less provocative plane :

> *Captain* (to defaulter) : " The evidence is that you got drunk when ashore, went to the local Y.M.C.A., got into bed while still smoking a cigarette, fell asleep, and set your bed on fire. What have you to say ? "
> *Defaulter* : " It's a lie, sir ! The bed was on fire when I got into it."

It seems to me that enshrined in that answer is the same refusal to accept defeat, against all the odds, as has stood this country in such very good stead for three-quarters of the war so far. I think it is a native product. For instance, I cannot imagine a German soldier or sailor thinking up an excuse like that, or not being practically crucified for producing it. That may sound like patriotism of a provincial sort, but I believe it to be true. In any case, as long as we have that kind of humorous self-reliance to draw upon in case of need, we can leave most aspects of morale to take care of themselves. They will not suffer.

The Royal Navy produces " types," as does every other walk of life : it also produces remarkable *men*, who, while conforming to these types bring along their own special brand of loyalty and devotion to illuminate and adorn their respective jobs. They are not machines : they are complete individuals, reliable to an infinite degree, and often prompted by loyalty to the Navy, and love of the ship they are serving in, to work and fight and endure beyond all reasonable expect-ation. Much of it is training, of course, but there must always be something else—a spark, a continuous thread of inspiration ; and it seems that there always is.

One can appraise and admire the types as well as the men, knowing that one is reasonably certain of meeting them in any ship one serves in. Take, for example, the Coxswain of a small ship, a corvette or a destroyer. A good Coxswain is a jewel : most of them *are* jewels : they have been rigorously trained as such, and they have undertaken to play the part themselves as well. The Coxswain can make all the difference on board. As the senior rating in the ship, responsible for much of its discipline and administration, he has a profound effect in producing a happy and efficient ship's company. Usually he is a " character," to use an overworked but explicit word : that is, a strong personality who would make himself felt in any surroundings, and who is, in his present world, a man of exceptional weight and influence. He keeps an eye on everything, from the rum issue to the cleanliness of hammocks, from the chocolate ration to the length of the side-whiskers of the second-class stokers. It is his duty to find things out, however obscure or camouflaged they may be—a case of bullying, a case of smuggled beer, a case of " mechanized dandruff " in the seamen's mess— and either set them right or else report them forthwith to a higher authority. In the majority of cases, as might be expected, he is fully competent to set them right himself, and can be trusted to do so.

He is the friend of every one on board, and a good friend too—if they want him to be, and if they deserve it : failing that, he makes a very bad enemy. He knows the regulations off by heart : he knows when to cite them, and when to turn the page quickly. He is, above all, a jealous guardian—of Naval tradition, of the ship's good name, of the Captain's reputation and his peace of mind as well.

He is always an unmistakable figure on board: a purely Naval product, and one of its very best.

Somewhere at the other end of the scale—in one sense —you have that legendary character, the Three Badge A.B. "Three Badge" because he has three good-conduct badges, denoting at least thirteen years in the Navy: and " A.B." because—well, either he hasn't the brain and energy to pass for Leading Seaman or he doesn't welcome responsibility, or he " likes it where he is," or for any other reason which can keep a man an Able Seaman and nothing more till the end of his days in the Service. He may sound dull and stupid, but he is rarely that; more often than not he knows it all, like the Coxswain—but from a different angle.

The " angle " is something between laziness, lack of ambition and a self-respect inseparable from long service and patiently acquired seamanship. Give him a job and he will work his way through it: not with any flash display of energy, like one of those jumped-up young Petty Officers, but at a careful and steady pace, which escapes both commendation and criticism. He can go on all day like that: he often has to, thanks to the First Lieutenant, so why should he break his heart trying? And (assuming that time doesn't matter) you will be able to rely on the job when it is finished. If it is a bit of painting it will be smooth and economical, if it is a wire splice it will hold till Domesday. That's because, lagging astern or not, he is still a seaman, with the seaman's contempt for a botched job. No length of service, disfigured conduct-sheet or lack of promotion can alter that.

As might be expected, he " knows it all " in the other sense too, habitually steering within an inch of the Law with the straightest of faces and an absolute confidence that, one way or another, he will always get away with it. He can return on board time after time, not strictly sober but not drunk enough to attract attention. He knows his rights, and the way to get them : at the table (i.e. when appearing as a requestman or defaulter) he can extract the utmost advantage from every stage of the proceedings, and if the reporting officer makes any sort of a slip he will give him hell—in a respectfully injured way, of course, but hell all the same. In that sense he needs careful watching, though that is not really a drawback. It is, in fact, the reverse : by rendering necessary a strict attention to procedure and the letter of the Law, he keeps every one up to the mark. He is, in his own way, a guardian of Naval tradition just as much as a senior rating, safeguarding the proprieties from mixed motives, but safeguarding them none the less.

He is certainly an engaging type, but of course there *are* others, just as engaging, who don't need watching like a hawk the whole time. If you want an example of alert intelligence in the Navy, a young signalman, interested in his job and keen to get ahead, is probably the best specimen. From the very nature of his work, he knows more about the ship and her movements than any other rating ; and he has the opportunity of learning much more besides. He sees almost every signal that comes in, on a very wide variety of subjects ranging from the First Lord's anniversary greetings to the provision of tropical underwear for Wrens. He spends long hours up on the bridge, in the centre of things, where he has the best opportunity of talking to his officers and of picking up fresh ideas. He learns flotilla routines, the types and names and movements of other ships. The job of signalling itself enlarges his vocabulary—he deals in words, and they are the currency of intelligence. He can often acquire, too, a formidable knowledge of navigation : the charts are always there for him to study, and if, as is usual, he has an inquiring mind, he makes good use of the chance, aided by an officer who is probably only too glad to find someone interested—someone, moreover, who can often be most helpful in supplying information quickly and accurately at an awkward moment.

Watch-keeping is a boring job. Signalmen are usually talkative, retailing (among other things) the cream of the crop of rumours put out by the galley-wireless : their talk makes the time pass a bit quicker, and that, God knows, is something on the credit side at sea. When I was in a corvette doing Atlantic escort duty, burdened with a standing middle watch for nearly eighteen months on end, their companionship often made all the difference between a spell of rank boredom and a tolerable watch. I have had something of an affection for the Signal Branch ever since.

If I have singled out these—Coxswain, Able Seaman, and Signalman—for special mention, let no one think that they are first and the rest are nowhere. This is no place for a catalogue or a List of Complement, but certainly a lot of people go to the running of a ship : not least the engine-room ratings and stokers, who attract less attention but whose vigilance is essential and who can take as much pride in their work as any seaman. It leaves out, too, the Telegraphist and Coding branches : unobtrusive, also, working out of sight at a job largely routine and often intolerably boring, but vital to the efficient working of the ship, both in action and otherwise. And when reckoning up these " out-of-sight." ratings and their value to a smooth-running whole, the contribution of the wardroom stewards should not be left out of account : a good steward can make or mar a wardroom and, consequently, the life on board of any officer, whose exacting job does need a certain minimum of comfort and service if he is to be free to concentrate on his own specialized duty to the ship.

I have met people who are ready to argue this latter point, on " privileged-class," " life-of-luxury " lines : but I think it can fairly be said that an officer who has the immense responsibility of a ship on his hands for eight hours a day should be relieved of *all* other worries, as far as is humanly possible.

Speaking from the personal angle, I certainly found it essential in my own case, and I was very lucky in this respect. My servant made an enormous difference to my comfort and well-being at sea—always on hand at the right moment, producing cups of tea or extra scarves when they were most needed, fashioning by his personal care and loyalty something like a separate home for me, where I could be at ease whenever I wanted. His efforts, in harbour, even included an embarrassed search for a special brand of infants' food, at a time of local shortage at home : which, since he was a bachelor and a rather shy sort of man in any case, was devotion of a high order.

If anyone thinks that to be a naval steward is not a man's job, let him think again. Better still, let him come to sea and try serving a hot meal to six officers in the middle of a gale of wind, struggling against his own sea-sickness in a rolling, tossing, over-heated pantry, and still finding the strength to administer to their needs and to make them comfortable on and off watch. It needs a man to do all that : stewards take it in their stride.

These are some of the men who go to sea in corvettes They are all sailors : they and the Merchant Navy are the same breed. In this war they have done work not to be measured in terms of earning money or medals : they have done their utmost, and left it at that.

When the war is over the vast majority of them will be returning to civil life. Of the Royal Navy " regulars," also, some are certain to be axed from the Service and will have to fit into the same framework. They have deserved a lot in this war ; they will be entitled to present the bill at the end of it. Are they going to get a fair settlement, or are they going on the scrap-heap again?

Let us start by forgetting fairness and straight-dealing, and reducing the question to its lowest level, in terms of pure national self-interest. These men may one day be needed again; but whether they are needed or not, their continued loyalty and love of country is a national asset, to be prized above very many other things. It is worth keeping that loyalty: that is to say, a fair deal will pay a dividend which one day we may want to cash, and it will be as well to make sure that we have it at our disposal.

If we default, if we cheat, if we just forget and turn our backs, we may be caught short when the wheel comes round again.

We are learning that now, to our cost and embarrassment. Strikes—in the coal-mines, the engineering shops, among the dockers—are part of that cost: absenteeism and slacking are others. I abhor war-time strikes: it is, to me, ridiculous that the strike-weapon should be taken away from one section of the community—the Services—and left for free use in the hands of the rest; but, by God, you can understand how strikes come about! The dictum " As ye sow, so shall ye reap," covers them exactly, and it is idle to look beyond that. Many of these men who strike now were treated like dirt for years before the war: almost literally like dirt—they were tipped and shovelled out of the way and on to a sort of slag-heap of unemployed and unemployables. They didn't learn love of country from that. . . .

Now they have power, almost paramount power, and they use it to square up the account. It isn't patriotism, certainly (the system which pauperized them wasn't patriotism either): it is not in the end even common sense; but it is assuredly human nature. The argument seems, to them, crystal clear: why should they listen to appeals to their better feelings now, when they wore their hearts sick *making* those appeals—futile and neglected ones—in the lean and seedy years between the wars ?

Why indeed should they *have* any better feelings ? They are working at the same jobs as in peace-time, jobs which present no challenge to their courage, no real incentive to selfless endurance : naturally they fall back on peace-time tactics whenever a chance of " improvement " comes their way.

Incidentally, it is the merchant seamen especially who have risen above the peace-time grudge they might well bear, and have glorified their calling by an unmerited generosity. Their valour and spirit have heaped coals of fire : no class in Britain was treated worse, or was more brutally disregarded, than merchant seamen in the early nineteen-thirties, and no class forgot it more quickly and completely when the call to action came.

Are we going to do better this time ? Are we going to improve on that sort of world, where competing forces, individual and national, snap and snarl at each other like so many hyenas, enforcing a cut-throat competition in which the real loser is the common man : where human values are disdained : where the weakest goes to the wall—and even there is charged a luxury price for standing-room ? There are signs of hope, I know, but there are other signs too : indeed, one current pointer indicates that we are *not* going to improve on it at all, except to make the competition fiercer and the fate of the losers more permanently miserable.

The pointer is, shortly, that there are still people, of consequence (or at least of financial standing) whom the war has not affected at all, except that it has served to enrich them at a prodigious rate. They are not contributing to the national effort : they are playing a lone hand, with some very familiar cards in it. Sailors have to fight and endure for *them*, as well as for their true countrymen. . . . After the war, clearly, these people expect Britain to pick up exactly where she left off :

and the fact that this means the dying and futile nineteen-thirties again, with their masses of dying and futile victims, doesn't seem to have penetrated at all, except as a clarion call to plunder.

For instance : anyone with an eye for detail and a retentive memory can give you the names of half a dozen firms who are doing nothing in this war except buying and storing second-hand motor-cars, in the certainty of making enormous profits out of them during the first scarce days of peace. Often, with loathsome effrontery, the operation is covered up by some such phrase as, " Sell your car and help the war effort "—which, to put it at its most polite, is all eyewash and hot swill. The firms involved are *not* helping the war effort in the remotest degree : they are simply buying for a rise, creating scarcity under privileged conditions with an eye to a future squeeze, when the gallant lads in the Forces (God bless 'em) have finished the job and cleared the ground.

Now these people may be high-class rodents, but they are rats for all that. Nor are they alone : there are others playing a similar game with other classes of goods which are certain to be in short supply at the end of the war—second-hand furniture is one example : and there have been some fragrant deals in building-plots and " bomb sites," deals which will stultify any intelligent town-planning except at enormous cost, deals which tell the same story of predatory ambition in its most selfish and cynical form.

Is this the sort of world we are coming back to ? Is this the noble future ? We might as well chuck in here and now if it is.

We might as well chuck in because it means that all the jokes we make in the wardroom about life after the war—about match-selling, about hawking trays of carbon-paper and india-rubbers, about buying chicken-farms and selling vacuum-cleaners—all those grim fancies, products of a sense of insecurity, aren't going to be jokes at all. They are going to come true : there *will* be millions of unemployed, medals pawned, Welsh miners in the gutters of London : there *will* be barrel-organs again, with men as the flea-bitten monkeys in attendance.

Unless we improve on that grisly progress, we can all forecast its exact course and its gross and pitiful details. A blue-print of misery exists already—the one we used last time. Some people are acting as if we are going to use it again : as if, indeed, there was no other sort to be had, and no real need for a different one either.

There *is* a different one : there must be : and of course we *won't* chuck in because we are hopeful—and, it may be said, determined. Perhaps only some of us, perhaps only a few, but enough for the spark—for such ideas spread easily, backed by the stimulus to co-operation which war furnishes, and the plain *success* of comradeship which it demonstrates.

We are going to improve on last time, because we clearly have the collective will, spread all through the Forces—the young men. An army does not fight the breadth of Africa and then allow itself to be sold down the river when it gets home : sailors develop qualities of determination which are useful in any sphere : the "few to whom the many owe so much" can easily decide to collect their debt.

It need not demand money as the mainspring, this new world, but it will certainly require generosity and understanding, and continued service, too. It will need, most important of all, a social conscience working con-tinuously all through the social scale. With a few blind spots, the war has produced evidence of all these things, in abundance. If we can carry them over to peace-time, we have high hopes of the future.

CHAPTER VI

PERHAPS NEXT TIME

I HAD intended this chapter to record the past winter in *Winger*, with (I had hoped) a certain amount of action and some really phenomenal line-shooting as regards the weather. But in this intention I was forestalled by the Admiralty, who in the early autumn took *Winger* away from me and gave me a frigate instead.

It was a surprise, after only seven months in command, and a bigger job and ship than I had ever hoped to get : and it brought my time in corvettes to an end, after three and a quarter years. They had been full and varied years, and I had grown to love the ships and admire the men who served in them : but I could not help looking forward to the North Atlantic again, and to a ship bigger, faster and more powerful than any I had yet sailed in.

The book, therefore, remains as it stands now, with an almost total lack of incident ; recounting only the privilege and the test of command, and the dead-level of convoy-escort : the record of a ship plugging away at a routine job but engaging the enemy more remotely every day. I must acknowledge that this lack of explosions, screaming Stukas, and Indians biting the iron-deck is a serious flaw ; as someone reading the first draft for me said, " Don't you think the cheese is grated a bit fine this time ? " But I'm prepared to take a chance on it, in the hope that perhaps next time (if there *is* a next time) I will be able to reach the required standard of violence. Command of a frigate in the North Atlantic might well provide an adequate background.

But whatever the future, I won't forget *Winger*—my first command, and a very happy one. The small model

of her which the ship's company gave me on leaving
(at a presentation ceremony which left me quite speech-
less with embarrassment, shyness and pride) will recall
a grand ship and a first-rate crew.

As I wrote in a letter to the Coxswain, over the first
drink of my leave in the only hotel in London :

"This place is a lot more comfortable than *Winger's*
bridge on a wet night, but I don't like the people half
as much."

Even after the last drink, I still thought that.